"Christ-centered preaching often means telling it like it is. Telling it like the text says it and telling it so we can be transformed and conformed to God and his calling for us. Eric Mason's volume on 2 Corinthians leads us through Paul's call to bring the Corinthians into maturity. What they needed, we also need, and this exposition takes us there. Read it, reflect on it, and grow closer to God."

Darrell L. Bock, executive director for cultural engagement, Howard G. Hendricks Center for Christian Leadership and Cultural Engagement, and senior research professor of New Testament Studies, Dallas Theological Seminary

"In this wonderful commentary on 2 Corinthians, my dear friend Eric Mason unpacks the truths on the Apostle Paul's heart with compelling clarity. The insights are anchored in and arise from a supreme confidence that every word of the text is the inspired Word of God. As you read through this volume, not only will you gain greater understanding of 2 Corinthians but you will also experience the challenge, relevance, and warmth of the truth found in this book. Thank you, Eric, for this gift."

Dr. Crawford W. Loritts Jr., author, speaker, radio host; founder and president of Beyond Our Generation

AUTHOR **Eric Mason**

SERIES EDITORS **David Platt, Daniel L. Akin, and Tony Merida**

CHRIST-CENTERED

Exposition

EXALTING JESUS IN

2 CORINTHIANS

REFERENCE

NASHVILLE, TENNESSEE

Christ-Centered Exposition Commentary: Exalting Jesus in 2 Corinthians
© Copyright 2024 by Eric Mason

B&H Publishing Group
Nashville, Tennessee
All rights reserved.

ISBN: 978-0-8054-9651-2

Dewey Decimal Classification: 220.7
Subject Heading: BIBLE. N.T. 2 CORINTHIANS—
COMMENTARIES\JESUS CHRIST

Printed in the United States of America
1 2 3 4 5 6 7 8 9 10 • 30 29 28 27 26 25 24

SERIES DEDICATION

Dedicated to Adrian Rogers and John Piper. They have taught us to love the gospel of Jesus Christ, to preach the Bible as the inerrant Word of God, to pastor the church for which our Savior died, and to have a passion to see all nations gladly worship the Lamb.

—David Platt, Tony Merida, and Danny Akin
March 2013

AUTHOR'S DEDICATION

I dedicate this book to Dr. Crawford Loritts. Your influence on my life, family, ministry, and me personally, only eternity knows. You and sister Karen have been a blessing to Yvette and me. You know I love your kids a ton and feel like an adopted member of your clan. Much love to you and yours. Your legacy has many, many miles on it! I'm eternally grateful for your life and ministry.

TABLE OF CONTENTS

ACKNOWLEDGMENTS

God is great that through Christ he took a young man with a learning disability and gave him the opportunity to be published. This work is a testament to the fact that there is no obstacle that will prevail against God's calling on any of us.

To my dear wife. You are a gem. Giving me the space for writing, creating, and visioneering is a blessing. Your testimony of suffering is a blessing and helped shape a lot of what is in this work. To Immanuel, Nehemiah, Ephraim, and Amalyah, each of you is my legacy, and I love that you like that I have books. Your enthusiasm about it brings me great joy.

My beloved Epiphany, thanks for being the breeding ground for my musings. I hope this serves you and others well.

Thanks, Andrew, for helping work through this resource to get it done. Thanks to Dr. Cristen Campbell and Michelle Alston, my mother-in-law, for helping me bring this resource together. Dave Stabnow, thanks to you and the Lifeway Bible and Reference team for helping work out all the kinks in this in order to help shape it into a helpful resource for the body of Christ. J C Jones, thanks for all your administrative coordination on this. Lisa Hobbs and Jana Henry, you all are a dynamic duo.

SERIES INTRODUCTION

Augustine said, "Where Scripture speaks, God speaks." The editors of the Christ-Centered Exposition Commentary series believe that where God speaks, the pastor must speak. God speaks through His written Word. We must speak from that Word. We believe the Bible is God breathed, authoritative, inerrant, sufficient, understandable, necessary, and timeless. We also affirm that the Bible is a Christ-centered book; that is, it contains a unified story of redemptive history of which Jesus is the hero. Because of this Christ-centered trajectory that runs from Genesis 1 through Revelation 22, we believe the Bible has a corresponding global-missions thrust. From beginning to end, we see God's mission as one of making worshipers of Christ from every tribe and tongue worked out through this redemptive drama in Scripture. To that end we must preach the Word.

In addition to these distinct convictions, the Christ-Centered Exposition Commentary series has some distinguishing characteristics. First, this series seeks to display exegetical accuracy. What the Bible says is what we want to say. While not every volume in the series will be a verse-by-verse commentary, we nevertheless desire to handle the text carefully and explain it rightly. Those who teach and preach bear the heavy responsibility of saying what God has said in His Word and declaring what God has done in Christ. We desire to handle God's Word faithfully, knowing that we must give an account for how we have fulfilled this holy calling (Jas 3:1).

Second, the Christ-Centered Exposition Commentary series has pastors in view. While we hope others will read this series, such as parents, teachers, small-group leaders, and student ministers, we desire to provide a commentary busy pastors will use for weekly preparation of biblically faithful and gospel-saturated sermons. This series is not academic in nature. Our aim is to present a readable and pastoral style of commentaries. We believe this aim will serve the church of the Lord Jesus Christ.

Third, we want the Christ-Centered Exposition Commentary series to be known for the inclusion of helpful illustrations and theologically driven applications. Many commentaries offer no help in illustrations, and few offer any kind of help in application. Often those that do offer illustrative material and application unfortunately give little serious attention to the text. While giving ourselves primarily to explanation, we also hope to serve readers by providing inspiring and illuminating illustrations coupled with timely and timeless application.

Finally, as the name suggests, the editors seek to exalt Jesus from every book of the Bible. In saying this, we are not commending wild allegory or fanciful typology. We certainly believe we must be constrained to the meaning intended by the divine Author Himself, the Holy Spirit of God. However, we also believe the Bible has a messianic focus, and our hope is that the individual authors will exalt Christ from particular texts. Luke 24:25-27,44-47 and John 5:39,46 inform both our hermeneutics and our homiletics. Not every author will do this the same way or have the same degree of Christ-centered emphasis. That is fine with us. We believe faithful exposition that is Christ centered is not monolithic. We do believe, however, that we must read the whole Bible as Christian Scripture. Therefore, our aim is both to honor the historical particularity of each biblical passage and to highlight its intrinsic connection to the Redeemer.

The editors are indebted to the contributors of each volume. The reader will detect a unique style from each writer, and we celebrate these unique gifts and traits. While distinctive in their approaches, the authors share a common characteristic in that they are pastoral theologians. They love the church, and they regularly preach and teach God's Word to God's people. Further, many of these contributors are younger voices. We think these new, fresh voices can serve the church well, especially among a rising generation that has the task of proclaiming the Word of Christ and the Christ of the Word to the lost world.

We hope and pray this series will serve the body of Christ well in these ways until our Savior returns in glory. If it does, we will have succeeded in our assignment.

David Platt
Daniel L. Akin
Tony Merida
Series Editors
February 2013

2 Corinthians

More Than You Can Bear

2 CORINTHIANS 1:1-11

Main Idea: God does allow on you more than you can bear so that you can learn that you need him.

I.   **We Are Blessed in Christ (1:3).**
II. **We Receive Mercy and Comfort (1:3).**
    A. God is the Father of mercies.
    B. God is the God of all comfort.
III. **We Comfort Others (1:4).**
IV. **God Holds on to Us (1:4-7).**
V.   **We Are Overwhelmed (1:8).**
VI. **We Learn that We Need Him (1:9-11).**

My parents' generation was a different generation in how they raised children. Parents and children had distinct roles. Parents didn't cater to children's feelings or be buddies with them. Their goal was to raise children. And in my family, if you hated them in the process, they accepted that as long as you became what God wanted you to become.

Their discipline was tough and left an impression. I was never merely punished. I don't remember them saying something like "You're not doing such-and-such for a while." I just knew that I was restricted from what I was able to do for a season until the temperature of the house changed. I knew everything was okay, but the discipline was harsh, and there was no one to report it to in those days. It was just a different day and age. My oldest sibling is about seventy years old, and all of us remember living under our parents' strict leadership.

As much as we would like to exalt the glory days, although good parents, our mother and father could have used some compassion pills when correcting us. One deficiency was how they dealt with family issues. In my late thirties and early forties I began learning stuff about my family that I never knew because in that generation, parents didn't communicate with their children. My parents didn't deal with issues. You wouldn't know your dad had cancer everywhere in his body until you found out at the funeral. They withheld intimate communication.

3

And we viewed our elders as strong because they wouldn't tell anyone anything. They wouldn't talk to you. They weren't emotional. They were emotionally unavailable most of the time, and that created relational distance between parents and children.

Respectability was maintained, but intimacy was absent in those relationships. There can be no deep relationship without intimacy. There can be no deep relationship without sharing our brokenness. If people think we're okay all the time, it's a problem. I can't be around someone who is lying about how he is doing all the time. I can't be around someone who doesn't ever go through difficulty. I can't be around someone who can't say, "I'm having a bad day." I can't, because to be human is to wrestle and to struggle at times. We must recognize this; if we're not wrestling, it's a problem.

In fact, as we look at 2 Corinthians, we find a letter teaching believers in Christ to "keep it 100"—to be truthful and authentic—in every single area of life. Yet many of us aren't experiencing the freedom and the enjoyment found in Christ because we don't engage our brokenness.

Many of us aren't experiencing freedom because we try to medicate ourselves into believing that our brokenness doesn't exist. But Paul, being an apostle of the Lord, writes one of the most heart-wrenching letters in the Bible. Other letters, like Romans, reveal his theological astuteness, the might of his pen and his mind. But we see Paul's heart in 2 Corinthians. We hear a shepherd being honest about his brokenness. We hear a shepherd being transparent for the sake of the sheep. We discover that Paul needed counseling, and he went through counseling. We encounter Paul as he goes through numerous trials. Indeed, sometimes he felt like dying. But he doesn't leave us in those desolate places. He wants to shepherd us and help us see that being honest about our own struggles opens the door for God to help us.

If we can't be honest with what we need, we can't receive what we need. We may be determined to act strong and self-sufficient, but Scripture invites us to see our weakness and to be people who know that if it had not been for the goodness of God, we would be lost. Paul in 2 Corinthians offers us the freedom to be truthful people who can say, "I'm tired, I'm sick, and I'm tired of being sick and tired." Scripture encourages me to admit, "I want to look at my life and deal with the issues. I want to deal with the mess. I want to deal with my past. I want to deal with my pain. I want to deal with my disappointments. I want to deal with my medication. I want to deal with myself. I want to deal with my family. I want to deal with my children. I want to deal with all of that."

We can examine everything because whom the Son sets free is free indeed. "You shall know the truth," says Jesus (John 8:32 NKJV), and the truth isn't just the information that's in the Bible. It's our telling the truth about what's going on with us so that the truth can set us free. So we come to a passage where Paul is direct and transparent. I only have one main point: **God does allow on you more than you can bear.**

We Are Blessed in Christ
2 CORINTHIANS 1:3

Paul speaks straightforwardly in this passage. In verse 3, he says, "Blessed be the God and Father of our Lord Jesus Christ." Notice *blessed*. The word here is not a verb. Paul is not asking us to bless God. *Blessed* is an adjective. Now, if we understand the adjective, we'll respond with the verb.

In other words, *blessed* describes God as being inherently self-sufficient: God doesn't need anyone. So God looks to himself for what he needs, but he doesn't need because he's always supplying to himself. He never experiences how to do without because he has everything. *Blessed* means one who is inherently filled with everything he needs for himself. Paul is describing God as being in a constant state of sufficiency. Can you imagine that—never needing because you *are*? That's God. That's why we're not God: because we feel the need for need, but he never feels the need for need. That's what makes *him* God and not *you or me.*

Paul says, "Blessed be the God and Father of our Lord Jesus Christ." He establishes it relationally. We're in a relationship with Jesus Christ, which connects us to him being blessed. Because he's blessed inherently, we can't be around him and not experience the blessed One. It's impossible to be in God's vicinity for real and not experience what he's releasing. We need to be open to recognizing that he's inherently self-sufficient and doesn't need anyone. Grandmama used to say, "He's God all by himself, and he don't need nobody else." She could have written a doctrine manual because she recognized the self-sufficiency of the almighty God and said it in a way that could be understood.

We Receive Mercy and Comfort

2 CORINTHIANS 1:3

God Is the Father of Mercies

Paul calls God two things in this verse. He's "the Father of mercies and the God of all comfort." When he calls him the Father of mercies, he's talking about his relational activity with us as a father. Some of you can't relate to him being father because you've experienced heartache with your father. But don't transfer your heartache to God the Father. God the Father is the only real one. He's not a deadbeat dad. He doesn't miss a payment. As a matter of fact, he doesn't have to make a payment because he supplies all we need. So we don't have to get with anyone to set up a way to give us what we need. God just releases it on his own as the Father of mercies. So he fathers us, he shepherds us, he's relationally related to us. Additionally, Paul put "mercy" in plural—"mercies." Now, perhaps you will understand why it's not just "mercy." God is the Father of "mercies" because we who are messed up, who know we're messed up, know that we can't have only one dose of mercy.

If you really know how messed up and broken you are, then you know you're in need. One time my grandmother showed me a counter with probably fifty medicines on it. I said, "Grandmama, what's all that for?"

She said, "Baby, this is my heart medicine. This is my high blood pressure medicine. This is my foot medicine."

And I said, "Why do you have all that?"

"I have all these medicines because each medicine is necessary for me to take in order for me to deal with what I'm going through so that I can feel better."

Mercy is a multivitamin pill of God for everything we need. God has a mercy for our hurt. God has a mercy for our frustration. God has a mercy for our loss. God has a mercy for our grief. God has a mercy for our depression. God has a mercy for every single thing in our life. I'm so glad and I'm so excited that I have a God who has enough for me because he's enough. The progressive walk of life with God leads to realizing that he is not only constantly giving us what we need but also *not* giving us what we deserve: that's mercy. Sometimes mercy is God not giving us something.

God Is the God of All Comfort

Next, he's the "God of all comfort." The word *comfort* means coming alongside someone and holding her up when she's going through a trial. It assumes we're going through something. The Bible even uses a form of this word to talk about the Holy Spirit, the *paraclete*, the one who comes alongside and gives help in the midst of brokenness and struggle.

So we see that our God is the God of every mercy, and he's the God of all comfort. This word here for "comfort" reminds me of a word or idea in *Star Wars*. *Comfort* means to give someone resilience for sapping energy. In the battle of the Jedi against the Sith, sometimes Jedi troopers are beaten down. Their resilience and emotional strength are waning because the battle is raging against them. However, the Jedi have a force capability that they keep secret. It's called "battle meditation."

Battle meditation allows them to fight alongside their troopers and use the Force to boost morale and turn the tables against the enemy. Similarly, in the midst of loss, God's comfort is battle meditation for you on this earth when you're going through hardships, when you're in brokenness, and when you're in a battle. God can send strength through his comfort for all that you're undergoing.

God does sometimes provide relief in the midst of the stress. Scripture says we have a God who "comforts us in all our affliction, so that we may be able to comfort those who are in any kind of affliction" (v. 4). I remember when I was weightlifting and trying to build up to 350 pounds on the bench press. I was on the bench with 275 pounds on, and I was lifting.

My arms became like spaghetti and every muscle just said, "Eric, it's over; stop it." But someone was standing over me as I was holding the weight.

He said, "I think you've got one more in you."

I said, "I don't have one more."

He said, "You've got one more." He didn't fully take the weight off of me, but he tapped it to encourage me that I had a little bit more push. He wanted me to extend my muscles just a little bit more. Suddenly, I found strength from somewhere that I didn't know I had because someone was standing over me and encouraging me. I'm trying to communicate that the God of all comfort will comfort you and me in our distress.

Notice, too, that he comforts us *in it*, not from without. That means that when we go through difficulty, he's in there with us; he's there with us in our distress. God is present in the distress with us. So no matter what we're going through, we're never alone in our distress. That's why he's called the God of all comfort. That means he comprehensively knows how to give us resilience in our brokenness. But look at what the text says: God does this so that we can comfort others.

We Comfort Others
2 CORINTHIANS 1:4

God trains believers in their suffering to comfort others by the comfort that he gives them. He is with you, but you may go through points in your trial where you don't think God is there with you. Scripture says "in any kind of affliction." That means you don't have to go through the same thing someone else went through to comfort them because affliction is affliction. In other words, all affliction makes an emotional impact. We'll see later in chapter 4 that affliction points to being surrounded by crowds.

God is training you and strengthening you—not just for your own sake. You thought you just wanted relief for yourself, but the goodness of God, who's the God of all comfort, has enough comfort for you that can overflow to someone else. My wife is my hero in this because you can look at her and not know she has an illness. She has ulcerative colitis: there are open sores inside her body. Yet if you saw her, you wouldn't know this.

I remember when my wife started going to a support group. She said, "Babe, I went through all this, and I want to go to support group because I need to be encouraged. But I also think that somebody else can hear what God did for me." She said, "When I look back over our marriage, I see many times God was my comfort. Early on, our son Manny went into the ICU. At one point I couldn't walk. Later I needed a liver transplant, and I got a liver transplant in my twenties. Then I went from the liver transplant to having cancer twice—then the third time when we were starting a ministry. And then, all of a sudden, I get rejection and infection. And I've been to the emergency room two hundred times in our marriage. I've spent six months of our marriage hospitalized." So she goes into the support group and starts telling her story, and the members respond, "You should be a little more bitter than you are. You should be angrier than you are."

God Holds on to Us

2 CORINTHIANS 1:4-7

What happens in her support groups? Sometimes I've gone, and I've seen when people who were complaining hear her story and stop complaining. What can you say to a person who's been to hell and back? When God takes you somewhere and brings you back from it, it's not for you to brag about that. You made it; it's not about your bragging that you survived. It's about your bragging about the God who held on to you because, if truth be told, you didn't hold on to him.

There were some days when you wanted to curse out everyone. There were some days when you wanted to shoot someone. There were some days when you wanted to hurt someone. There were some days when you wanted to hurt yourself. If you think about what God brought you from, and if you can be honest about where he brought you to, the testimony is God's holding on to you, not that you're holding on to him. You are not that strong. I am not that strong. The testimony of our lives is the strength of Christ.

When we share abundantly in Christ's suffering, God has a comfort level that meets our pain levels. I remember when my wife had her second C-section. She went into surgery, and she was in pain. They gave her anesthesia, but she started feeling pain again. I said to the nurse, "You're going to put some more in her, right?" So he gets the supervisor, and he gave her some more. When we got back to her room, they gave her a cord with a red button and said, "Whenever you feel pain, Mrs. Mason, just press the button." When she went home, she was beginning to heal but was told to take Tylenol for her pain. At every level of her pain, the medical team had medication for her.

For every level of your pain, every level of your brokenness, God has an "anesthetic." He has something that can give you and me comfort, but we have to push the red button. Christ can comfort us.

Paul next said, "If we are afflicted, it is for your comfort and salvation" (v. 6). How interesting that he speaks so much of suffering. We don't hear it as much today. We hear, "It's your season," and "Your breakthrough is coming." I share that perspective as a pastor every now and then, but the overshadowing reality is pain. We're either going into a trial, we're in a trial, or we're coming out of a trial. Now, if you haven't been in one yet, it's coming. Another one's coming because your life is filled with the cycle of brokenness to help you know God more deeply. If you and I did not know affliction, we would not know the Lord.

Paul goes on to say, "Our hope for you is firm" (v. 7) He's saying, "We know that as you share in our sufferings, you will also share in our comfort."

We Are Overwhelmed
2 CORINTHIANS 1:8

Paul is confident in God. He's confident that God will cover the Corinthians in the midst of their brokenness. Look at verse 8. He says, "We don't want you to be unaware." He explains, "We were completely overwhelmed—beyond our strength—so that we even despaired of life itself." Now what type of preacher tells people, "I had more on me than I could bear"? I imagine you've heard it said, "God doesn't put on you more than you can bear." But 1 Corinthians 10:13 is speaking of temptations that we choose. The verse says, "No temptation has come upon you." The context refers to acting like a fool in the world and God loving us enough to not let us continue in our folly. So he won't allow on us more temptation that will destroy us completely.

We like to think God won't put or allow on us more than we can bear because we like to be viewed as strong. But in order to be strong, we have to be viewed as weak. Paul said, "We were completely overwhelmed." We were so overwhelmed that "we even despaired of life." In other words, he said, "We wanted to die."

Notice he didn't say, "Right now, in the name of Jesus, I tell you, despair, go away!" Yes, Paul healed people. Paul raised the dead and cast out demons! Nevertheless, his life became so painful that he wanted to die. Yet interestingly we, as believers, can't admit our burdens: "I want to die. I was suicidal. I'm sick of what's going on in my life." Let us begin to recognize that God is using our suffering to bring us to the end of ourselves.

We Learn that We Need Him
2 CORINTHIANS 1:9-11

But listen to the reason Paul shares his brokenness. He says, "Indeed, we felt that we had received the sentence of death" (v. 9). He said, we felt like it was over, but that was to make us rely not on ourselves but on

"God who raises the dead" (v. 9). So God allows on you more than you can bear so that you can know you need him. Theologically, we'll say, "I need the Lord." But practically we function like we don't need the Lord. Indeed, no matter how mature we become, God has to remind us that we need him. So he will allow something bad to happen to us.

Why? Because when everything's okay—when money's in the bank, you have a significant relationship, you can go on a date without breaking the bank, you can go shopping and buy a bunch of stuff, your bills are paid, it's warm in the house during the winter, it's chilly in the house during the summer, everything's all right for you—God says, "See, that's why you're not praying anymore." Then he takes some of that hedge of protection off of you and lets some stuff happen to you. All of a sudden, a little bit of hell comes into your house. Then you start praying again, "Father God, I need you today! God help me!"

The problem is, you needed him just as much on the day when you had everything as on the day when hell broke loose. God has to remind you that you need him—when you become too self-sufficient, when you become too self-reliant, when you are a boss and run it all. Yes, "you running you" puts all kinds of things on the table. You have deals on the table, but God is going to make some deals not come through. He's going to make you lean. He's going to let you get sick. He won't let some good stuff happen to you so you can cry. He's more concerned with your being close to him with nothing than to have everything and not have him.

God does put on you more than you can bear, so that you can know that you can't bear it. My son Manny once didn't fear anything. He didn't fear heights, and he wasn't afraid of water when he was about three years old. I said, "Boy, you can't just dive into the pool. You can't swim."

He said, "No, I want to jump into the water."

"Okay," I thought, "I'm going to get into the water this time. I'm going to let him jump into the water." I got into the water, and I strategically placed myself. Then he jumped into the water, went under, and I said, "One, two, three, four, five." Then I went and got him. All his McDonald's shot across the pool. People started getting up out of the pool. I looked at him. I said, "What lesson did you learn? Can you swim? No. No." I said, "One day, you're going to learn how to swim, but you can't just dive in there. Okay?"

"Yes, sir." And guess what? He learned that day that he needed me. Sometimes God will let you begin to drown. He'll let you take in some water. Then he'll grab you like a cat grabs its kittens and hold you up and look you in the face. "What lesson did you learn today?" And do you know what you need to say? "God, I need you." That's your life's purpose statement. God is pushing your life in a direction so that you consistently know your need for him. Everything you go through is for you to be reminded of that reality. Never forget it.

And the moral of this story is, "What do I do about this?" Just get ready for another challenge. When you forget that you need the Lord, learn to need the Lord. When you don't think you need the Lord, learn to thank him. When everything's full, learn to lift him up. When nothing's going wrong, learn to know that everything you have in the good season is because of him, not because of your hard work.

There are many people working hard, and they still don't receive anything in return. The harvest you receive could not come if it had not been for God. The glory of this life is that Jesus Christ came, and he got on the cross and experienced the feeling of abandonment; he experienced the brokenness of the pain and the loss of his life, so that as we follow in his example, we wouldn't say, "My God, my God, why did you forsake me?" In other words, he experienced the feeling of forsakenness so that you and I wouldn't ever feel that way. And God raised him up on the third day so that we can know this hope: that trouble doesn't last always.

Until you learn the reality that trouble doesn't last always, you need to learn that he's a mind fixer. You need to learn that he's a heart regulator. You need to know that he's a healer. You need to know that he's a bridge over troubled water. You need to know all those things, but you don't learn those in the daylight. You learn those things in the midnight.

Reflect and Discuss

1. What kind of parent would you like to be? How much would you like to communicate your feelings to your children?
2. What kind of father do you think God is? Has your image of what kind of father he is changed? How so?
3. When someone asks how you are doing, do you always say, "Fine"? Are there some people you would answer truthfully? Why?
4. How do you feel blessed through your relationship with Christ?

5. What mercies have you received from God?
6. How has your past helped you comfort other people?
7. Do you believe God never gives us more than we can handle? Why?
8. When have you thought you did not need God? Does that thought tend to come when you are feeling comfortable or when you are succeeding through difficulties by your own strength?
9. How has God showed you that you need him?
10. How has your relationship with Christ provided mercies, comfort, and assurance?

The Decisive Disciple

2 CORINTHIANS 1:12-24

Main Idea: God calls us to be decisive disciples in every area of our lives, so others may be joyful.

I. **Decisiveness Involves the Removal of Unnecessary Complexities (1:12-14).**
   A. Purity and godly sincerity are key to removing clutter in our lives (1:12).
   B. God's wisdom leads to good decisions (1:12-14).
II. **Decisiveness Involves a Commitment to God's Promises in Spite of Criticism (1:15-22).**
   A. Decisive disciples will face criticism (1:17).
   B. Jesus is our example of decisiveness even in opposition (1:19-21).
   C. God gives us everything we need to be decisive (1:22).
III. **Decisive Christians Work toward the Joy of Others instead of Themselves (1:23-24).**

In Garry Friesen's book *Decision Making and the Will of God*, we learn that most of our decision-making we want help with is based on Gideon's fleece instead of Spirit-filled guidance based on God's Word. Many of us make poor decisions and think it was God who led us in that particular direction. As we look dazed and confused, however, the Bible calls for us to discern and be decisive. Friesen's book helps us recognize the ability to be a decisive believer who makes decisions based on biblical maturity and discernment.

Many of us ask what the will of God is while waiting for a mystical guiding act to help us know what God's will is. Many of us say, "God, if you want me to go this direction, let the wind blow east, west, and then north, and then have somebody come up to me and ask me for a cup of water. Then I'll know that you want me to go that direction." Or people say something like "Lord God, I have three beautiful women in front of me. I don't know which one is to be my wife, Lord. Help! The one who lifts her hands the highest in worship—help me to know that she's supposed to be my wife." Or, "God, the first man that comes up to me and tells me what job he has—and it's above sixty or seventy thousand a year—God, in the mighty name of Jesus, I ask you to let me know that he is supposed to be my husband."

We have all types of mystical examples of trying to find out the will of God. Usually in the Old Testament, those mechanisms were used when there wasn't much Word available. Now, by the Spirit of God, we receive the ability to make godly decisions based on raw data of Scripture and God's promises. If you notice, Romans 12:2 says, "Be transformed by the renewing of your mind, so that you may discern what is the good, pleasing, and perfect will of God." God gives clarity. That doesn't mean we don't take time to pray or to find focus. That doesn't mean we won't feel stalemated. But the Bible reveals that discernment of clarity based on God's Word is what helps us make good decisions.

We make good decisions based on the amount of Word we have available to us. The less Word we have in us means that our immaturity quotient is up and we're going to have a more difficult time navigating life. So we need to be filled with the Word. That's what the Bible says in Colossians 3:16: "Let the word of Christ dwell richly among you." That means not only is it present, but it's like some chocolate cake—real rich. You almost can't take it. That's what it's supposed to be like when you are a decisive believer.

Paul is challenging the Corinthian church because they are viewing him as a flighty apostle. They are viewing him as flighty and with a chip on his shoulder, yet throughout the book he doesn't put them on blast—he doesn't publicly denounce them—overtly. He does it covertly. He does it by exposing the immaturity, not overtly communicating the immaturity, but asserting his role as loving them to help them go from spiritual infancy to spiritual maturity.

In this passage he shares why he couldn't come to them. They have some issues with Paul not coming to them. They thought he was scared. They thought he was a fool. They thought he was delinquent because he didn't come to them, but he wanted them to grow up and understand how things really were. They had a warped view of the will of God. When you have a warped view of the will of God, you view things that fail to happen based on immaturity versus understanding the broad scope of the missionary work of God in your life.

Decisiveness Involves the Removal of Unnecessary Complexities
2 CORINTHIANS 1:12-14

Paul says, "Indeed, this is our boast" (v. 12). I like that he gives some things we can boast about in the Lord, and he's boasting about something God has provided for him in his apostolic ministry toward the Corinthian church. He says, "The testimony of our conscience is that we have conducted ourselves in the world, and especially toward you, with godly sincerity and purity" (v. 12). Let's pause here and consider the phrase "the testimony of our conscience." What a rich and potent reality Paul invites us to!

God has given every human being a conscience. Conscience is the alarm system God has placed in everyone; it involves our values and mindset. So when we go against our conscience or move in tandem with it, our conscience signals that something's wrong or sends a thumbs-up. Think about a relationship or friendship with someone that went awry. God is sending you in a different direction, but you don't have closure. You know there's something there that you need to work through with that person because you sense inside of you that something isn't complete. That's God using your conscience as a mechanism to communicate to you about that situation. The relationship feels unsettling, so you are stirred to address the unfinished business. But your conscience also affirms when there's nothing unresolved in the relationship and you're in the clear.

However, if you're not a believer in Christ, your conscience is seared. That means even though you are born in the image of God, it's defaced but not erased. Therefore, you have some elements of the image of God, but you don't have Christ and the Spirit and the Word to help navigate a conscience that can steer you wrong. When you don't have Christ and his Word, there can be navigational tendencies that can misdirect you. When you trust Christ, your conscience has to be subservient to Jesus.

It's subservient to Jesus because he lets you know, according to Hebrews, that your conscience can try to condemn you for things God has already freed you from. That's when he tells you that your conscience has become deficient—when it tries to override the work of Christ in your life. But when your conscience is under the authority of the Spirit, under the authority of the Scriptures, and under the authority of Jesus

Christ, it can help you know where you are with other people. Paul says here, our boast is this: the testimony of our conscience. In other words, our conscience has been talking to us sensibly, and we behave in the world with sincerity and purity.

This is a powerful statement for us to parenthetically park on to get some principles. The idea of the word *world* here is not just the physical, celestial ball we sit on. *World* in the New Testament usually points to the reality of a system of satanic existence. The word *cosmos* is where we get the word for "world." But *cosmos* literally means "organized arrangement." Now with Satan in it, it's an organized arrangement of chaos. So Paul is saying that in the organized chaos of the messiness of this world, you have a messed-up body that is fleshly and wants what it wants.

We live in a world where the prince of the power of the air (cf. Eph 2:2) is at work through the demonic forces in the unseen world. We live in a world with a lot of messed-up people who don't know Jesus Christ as Savior. And even we Christians have fleshly thoughts. That's the residue of the old nature that needs further modification. So when you look at all the things that are organized against us, the "world" is what the devil uses to organize his ministry of demonic attack against God's people. *World* is an organized effort to push against the glory of God and to exalt the kingdom of the enemy. When Paul says, "We have conducted ourselves in the world," he is communicating that we are able to do right when we want to do wrong. When we're able to behave when everything we want is before us, that's powerful.

Purity and Godly Sincerity Are Key to Removing Clutter in Our Lives (1:12)

Every one of us wants to rebel against the Lord, whether on Monday morning or Saturday night. However, God offers us forgiveness. Now Paul says they behaved amid the organized arrangement of the worldly attack against the glory of God. How did they do it? "With godly sincerity and purity." "Sincerity" points to a word that means holiness. But "purity" means to declutter. Purity means to remove unnecessary things from your life that would cause you not to serve the Lord. For many of us, the reason we're not able to serve the Lord is because we have too much. Some of you have some complex lives because you're "bougie."

You know your life is not simple if you say you need stuff that isn't a need. The Bible says we maybe need six things: the Lord, the Word, his people, food, covering, and clothing. Everything else is a greed, not a need. What can happen, though, is we become so worldly that we stack up around us needs.

I'm a coffee snob. I don't like Starbucks. I call it charred bucks, but I like the Clover machine. They have this $13,000 Clover machine, and it is magnificent. They have pressed coffee. They put it in a vacuum, press it out, and you can just layer the notes. I like to go to La Colombe, and they do pour-overs. I'm just telling you my bougie tendencies. I don't go to Wawa, and I can't do Dunkin' Donuts, but what if the Lord leaned things? He can say, "You can have coffee, but you can't have bougie coffee. Matter of fact, you don't have to have coffee at all, but I'm going to be gracious enough to let you have some. Can you handle me downgrading the clutter of your commitments to what you say you need in order to follow me more effectively?"

All of you have some people in your life. Many of you have some stuff in your life. There's just clutter. You've been dating seven years. There's no direction, no commitment, no visionary picture from God in your life.

We were supporting some missionaries, and the people couldn't go to the mission field. They were ready and had their theological education. They were godly, but they couldn't go because they had too much debt. The missionary organization said, "You can't go to the mission field until you get out of debt because we don't want you on the mission field making a decision to stay because you have debt."

Some of us need to let go of some things that we've made the central will for our life to experience the central will of God for our life. Because the more cluttered your life is, the more stuff you must have in your life and the less potent your ability to be used by God.

I'm talking about the stuff you decided to put yourself in that's gotten in the way of your ability to be used. Some of you need to come out of school for a while. Get out of the debt you're already in because you're going to be in three-quarters of a million dollars of debt by the time you're done with school. You're not going to be able to enjoy it fully because you have $750,000 worth of debt. When you are putting cars and apartments and restaurants on your student loans and your life is encumbered because of what you say you need, that's really a greed.

Some of us want to start businesses, but we don't want the lean season of the first few years of a start-up because we can't get rid of some stuff we say are necessities. Everybody wants to be the boss, but they don't want to pay the cost. Purity actually helps you to be happier. Some some of us—but I'm talking about myself—need to just say, "God, what in my life is working against me being fully mobile?"

God is in the business of making his people more user-friendly. Who wants to go back to the flip phone? Who wants to go back to the rotary phone? Who wants to go back to the phone booth and having quarters in your pocket? Nobody does! God is out to make us mobile. He wants to be able to use you at a moment's notice. He wants to be able to use you and for you to be at a point where you're not being pulled by inclinations of what you make into a need, because he wants to use you for his divine glory to strip it because then you'll be decisive. You're always going to be indecisive if you have needs that you've created that aren't biblical needs because you always have to think through how much clutter you have to get through to get to what you truly need.

Paul says in the positive, "I don't fool with a whole bunch of attachments." That doesn't mean God doesn't want you to enjoy yourself. But it means that many of us have to pray, "God, I want you to help me make my life as maximized for your glory, purity, and honor, for your name's sake, as possible."

Paul not only speaks about purity but also about behavior in the world with godly "sincerity." Sincerity has to do with your mindset, meaning an unmixed and unwavering disposition. But if your life is cluttered, you can't have sincerity. There are some seasons when God just wants you to be mobile. He wants you to be out. I'm not just talking about full-time ministry. I'm talking about lifestyle ministry, so purity is for everyone.

Next, he says, "Not by human wisdom" (v. 12). Human wisdom is finite thinking. It means to think only in a natural way and not to think spiritually about things. It's the antithesis to purity. God is speaking through Paul of a conscious plan. What gave him a clear conscience were his sincerity and purity that weren't influenced by mere human wisdom—earthly wisdom of philosophies that are alternative to the Word of God.

God's Wisdom Leads to Good Decisions (1:12-14)

When you don't have purity and sincerity in your heart because you're so worldly connected, your life begins to unravel. You must make decisions based on a nonbiblical standard. But God's grace brings God's wisdom, and God's wisdom leads to good decisions. When I first trusted Christ, I knew myself. So there were some things I just missed out on. I missed out on the Biggie rap era. I missed out on the whole thing by choice. I'm not saying everyone has to do this, but I got rid of a lot of music I couldn't handle at the time. I had to get rid of Big Daddy Kane for a while. I had to get rid of EPMD. That's my favorite hip-hop group of all time. I had to not watch the *Martin* show because in that season there was some stuff in it. And I had to get rid of my R & B because in that season of my life, it was just too sexy for me.

See, if you're going to be keeping 100, you have to keep it 100 with you.

I had to turn off my New Edition. I had to turn off my Bobby Brown. I had to turn off my Father MC. I had to turn off Mary J. Blige because the sexiness of that made me cluttered. So now I'm always thinking about my wife. In that season, I didn't need to think about a wife. I needed to be devoted to graduating.

When you decide that the long term is better than the short-term sacrifices, you'll get ahead better. And you'll be able to enjoy more because you starved yourself of what you thought was a must. People are always asking me, "Pastor, how do I discover my spouse?" I say, "Well, if you're called to a mission field, and that person feels like they should do art in Southern California, you're not supposed to be together. Don't try to force what God is releasing you from."

So this is the way you can make some good decisions—whether you're overwhelmed because you have to do it on your own or you're overwhelmed because you're not trusting the Lord. A mature believer knows the difference. If you're overwhelmed because you're trusting in yourself, but God is clear that he wants you to go this other direction, you have to follow God. But if you're just overwhelmed because of what you have to do, you need to be a mature child of God and let go of the clutter. We do this by the grace of God. Paul said that his conscience was clean. He was walking in purity and in sincerity, he said, in the world and toward the Corinthians, by the grace of God. He said it was a grace for him to deal with them. He said, "You need a whole lot of grace." See, he's putting them on blast a little bit.

He continues, "We are writing nothing to you other than what you can read and also understand. I hope you will understand completely." What is Paul saying? "What you see and what I'm saying are what you get." He's communicating that there's going to come a point when they will celebrate God, the mutual benefit of his apostolic relationship with them, and their sheep relationship with him—how they blessed him and how he blessed them. It all goes to the glory of God and will be based on their commitment to being mutually decisive about how God has called them together to do ministry.

Decisiveness Involves a Commitment to God's Promises in Spite of Criticism

2 CORINTHIANS 1:15-22

Paul says, "Because of this confidence, I planned to come to you first, so that you could have a second benefit" (v. 15). He wanted to come share with the Corinthians. He wanted to come minister to them. Then he says that he planned "to visit you on my way to Macedonia, and then come to you again from Macedonia" (v. 16).

He's saying, "I plan on going to Macedonia, but I'm going through you. And I was going to pass back through Corinth on my way from Macedonia. I want to connect with you two more times. We connected once before; I want to connect with you two more times." This was not vacillating. When Paul wanted to do this, he said, "Do I plan in a purely human way so that I say 'Yes, yes' and 'No, no' at the same time? As God is faithful, our message to you is not 'Yes and no'" (vv. 17-18). So what is happening here? They're getting on Paul's nerves because they're saying, if he was a real apostle, he should have known ahead of time by the Spirit when he was coming.

He's saying, "I'm trusting that God is going to navigate my journey." As a decisive believer, you make plans. You move in that direction. Sometimes as you're moving in that direction, God turns it or closes a door. So you won't go in that direction, but you don't change your commitment and decisiveness about what God wants you to do because God closed the door. That is, you don't walk away from the Lord because God didn't do something you may have wanted.

Decisive Disciples Will Face Criticism (1:17)

Paul is saying, "Why are you talking to me like this because I wanted to come to you and I wanted to serve you? God didn't allow this to happen now, yet you're pushing me away, saying, 'You're not even an apostle.'" So as he worked through this and he challenged the Corinthians with their criticism, with this idea of his decisiveness, he was trying to help them formulate their understanding of the will of God and how to connect to the promises of God. He continues, "For the Son of God, Jesus Christ, whom we proclaimed among you" (v. 19). He says, remember we came and shared the gospel with you. When it comes to us, it's always a yes. Do we want to spend time with you? You get on our nerves, but we still want to be around you.

Jesus Is Our Example of Decisiveness Even in Opposition (1:19-21)

Then he adds, "For every one of God's promises is 'Yes' in him," in Jesus (v. 20). That is why it is through him. What are the promises of God? "Yes" in Jesus Christ because Jesus is the most decisive of all time. So because he's the most decisive of all time, the promises of God are "Yes" in him because his death unlocks all the promises of God. That's why he's called the key of David (Rev 3:7; see Isa 22:22). The key of David points to the fact that everything that was promised but didn't come to pass back then gets unlocked through the Lord Jesus Christ. So he's saying that the death and resurrection of Christ commit us to being decisive believers. Why? Because Jesus was the most decisive. How was Jesus the most decisive? Jesus was the most decisive because he got a whip on his back and didn't let it stop him from being decisive about dying on the cross.

Can you be that decisive? He had the purity of a simple life. Foxes have holes, birds have nests, but he wasn't thinking about a house; he didn't have one. He wasn't thinking about the money; Judas had stolen it all. He wasn't thinking about anything extraneous. The only things he thought about were the cross and his sheep. He shed his blood for our sins, and he said, "I'm done." Christ is so committed to decisiveness that he is the model for what it looks like to be decisive. So Paul says, "Because Jesus is the model of decisiveness, we should draw from him strength in being decisive. If he can be decisive in getting torn up, why can't we be decisive in things that don't even really matter that much?" All the promises find a "Yes" in him because he accomplished it through his decisiveness.

That's powerful to me. I'm so glad he stayed there, and we also say amen to the glory of God. The Bible says, "A person's heart plans his way, but the LORD determines his steps" (Prov 16:9). The steps of a good man or woman are ordered by the Lord. These are promises. That means that in our life, when we make plans, sometimes in making those plans, God says no permanently. Or he says yes, probably. And sometimes he says no with a future. Yes in the future, but right now it's no. But that means God is working out his promises, even in the navigation of your life. Sometimes God gives you choices—multiple choices. Some of us get overspiritual and say, "Which one, God? Which one do you want me to pick?" And God has said, "I'm giving you multiple choices, so enjoy whichever one you decide."

Paul also helps us understand our commitment to Jesus. He says, "Now it is God who strengthens us together with you in Christ" (v. 21). He roots it in Jesus over and over again to help us recognize that our connection to one another as believers in Christ is based on Christ working in us together. Then he says that he "has anointed us" (v. 21). He rarely uses *anointed*, but he had to use a word the charismatic Christians in Corinth would understand. You know what I'm saying? So he said, "You like the two-cent word *anointed*, so I'm going to use *anointed*. He anointed us. He anointed us for the purpose of serving you. And we are committed to that."

God Gives Us Everything We Need to Be Decisive (1:22)

That's a promise God has given in Paul's ministry to help him know he's supposed to serve them. That's the will of God for him. If God says no at that time, that means not then. But look what he says, what he continues to say, which is amazing. He further affirms this idea of decisiveness by theologically rooting it, not just in the gospel but in the results of the gospel. He says, "He has also put his seal on us and given us the Spirit in our hearts as a down payment" (v. 22). What is he saying here? The down payment communicates the investor is serious about his investment being fully paid. God's giving us his Spirit is also a metaphor to let us know how serious God is about redeeming our lives.

The work of his giving us the Spirit is to show us how to be decisive. God empowers us to be decisive because of the Spirit's presence in our lives. Because Christ is going to come back and fully redeem us, we can decisively look eschatologically at what God is going to do and be empowered to be decisive in the present sense of our lives.

When you buy a house, you must put up what's called earnest money. That lets the person you're buying the house from know that you're so serious about this house that you're willing to lose that amount of money if the plan doesn't go through.

The Spirit of God communicates to us he is serious about empowering us to be decisive. The Spirit is in us to empower the clarity of our decisiveness so that we know that what God began in us he'll finish. God must accomplish it because it cannot be left up to you and me to accomplish it.

God cannot just trust your heart—and you cannot just trust your own heart—to make the right decisions. The Bible says, "The heart is more deceitful than anything else, and incurable—who can understand it?" (Jer 17:9). So God doesn't make decisions for your life based on your heart. If he did, we'd be in trouble. He makes decisions based on his heart. He knew that in order for us to be decisive, he can't trust us to be decisive. He must put everything in our life to empower us. He had to give us the blood of Jesus—his cross, resurrection, and return.

Decisive Christians Work toward the Joy of Others instead of Themselves
2 CORINTHIANS 1:23-24

This is mature Christian theology here. Paul says, "I call on God as a witness, on my life" (v. 23). Who can say that? Who can be so decisive to know that he is going in the right direction with the Lord? Paul's saying, "Let the Lord witness against me. May something happen to me if I don't have a clear conscience in how I'm dealing with you." Can you go to someone who feels hurt by you and frustrated by you and say, "May the Lord God witness against me. If I've ever done anything to hurt you, I'm not conscious of it. It's so clear that I invoked the Holy Spirit power, the might of heaven, to come into this situation to deal with what's going on."

You must have a clear conscience to speak that way, but it points to a trust: God has decisively given you strength to receive clarity. God did not anoint you to be unclear. As a believer, God did not appoint you to be all over the place, running over here by every wind of doctrine. Christ died; the Spirit came to you. You are supposed to be decisive. Some of us don't know where we're going.

He said, "I do not mean that we lord it over your faith." That's good leadership, that's good parenting, and that's good pastoring. "Lord it over" leadership seeks to control people. "Lord it over" leadership controls people because they don't trust the Lord. Let me give you this for free: if any leader in a church tries to control every decision you make in your life, they are wrong. You don't prepare grownups by doing everything for them. "Lord it over" leadership wants to control people and outcomes for their own purposes, but a decisive disciple maker gives you room to fail. Paul refused to lord it over them.

Parents, we have to learn this. When I send my son to the corner store by himself, I'm scared to death. I say things like "Make sure when you cross the road, look both ways. Make sure you cross on the green light. If somebody tries to attack you, just punch him."

Some of you need to let some people go. Some of you are holding and trying to control people, and you're codependent. Some of you need to let children go. Let some parents go. Let some friendships go. Your need to be needed is your clutter keeping your life from becoming simple because you've made yourself God in someone else's life. Some of us have built our lives around being needed in a way that's not for the benefit of the other person, but it's really about our self-esteem. Our self-worth is rooted in that person needing us. We communicate, "As long as I'm in the know of your life, you're okay. If you do everything I say, and if you do everything I want you to, then I'm okay."

But Paul says, "We are workers with you for your joy." Now, what does that mean? Joy is simple, unending satisfaction with God. We work for you to have satisfaction with God.

Are you going to be decisive? You have to let some folks go and let them hurt themselves. You have to let them not listen to you. You have to let them get in debt. You have to let them break. You have to let them get it. And they're going to get pregnant. You can't control the results of anyone's life. If they are grown up, you can't control them. Some of you will sleep better if you just open your hand and let it go. It isn't spiritual for you to lose sleep worrying about people you need to let go of.

Some of you are going to have to put someone out of the house. Some of you have had people sleeping on your couch for a long time. And you're in the shower, fussing about, and you think, "Oh my God, why is he in my house? I'm sick of him eating up all my food." But see, you could have been in your shower, chilling, talking to the Lord about your day and your future, but you're so codependent and you need to help everyone. Let him go. Paul is okay with the Corinthians being mad at him for letting them go. You have to be okay with people being mad at you so that you don't continue to handicap their growth.

Then he says, "Because you stand firm in your faith" (v. 24). Now you have to understand, they don't. He is believing that for them. He says, "I worked for your joy. I want your joy. And I refuse to stand in the way. But I will not allow your indecisiveness to impact me. So I love you enough to tell you the truth. I've told you what I need to tell you."

Reflect and Discuss

1. How do you typically discern God's will and make decisions?
2. What role should the Word of God play in shaping your decision-making?
3. Would you consider yourself to be decisive in every area of your life?
4. What are some things you need to remove from your life to simplify it? What are some things that really aren't needs in your life?
5. Have you ever been criticized for making a tough but necessary decision? Why?
6. How does Jesus's decisiveness in the midst of opposition encourage you?
7. What has God given you to help you be more decisive? How can you maximize all that God has given you to be more decisive?
8. Do you lord it over people in your relationships? Do you seek to control people?
9. How can you die to self and work toward the joy of others?
10. How will that in turn bring you true joy and fulfillment?

How to Love People Who Are Hard to Love

2 CORINTHIANS 2:1-11

Main Idea: We must love people who are hard to love because God loved us while we were unlovely.

I. **Be Willing to Face the Barriers in Your Relationships (2:1-4).**
   A. Deal with people's sin issues to produce change and joy (2:1-3).
   B. Confront people in love even when it's painful (2:4).

II. **Be Willing to Accept Authentic Repentance (2:5-11).**
   A. Don't pass blame (2:5).
   B. Understand the evidence of authentic repentance (2:6-7).
   C. Reconcile with people who repent, and reaffirm your love for them (2:8-9).
   D. Don't fall for Satan's designs by continuing in division (2:10-11).

Many of us can testify of someone we know who is hard to love. As a matter of fact, we often arrange our lives to avoid being around the person who is hard to love. Some of us can only endure being with that person (or certain people) once a year. Whether an eccentric uncle or a difficult neighbor, we hope to avoid these people because they're hard to love. Some of us may even have had an abusive family member—perhaps an abusive father or a controlling mother—who is difficult to love.

Yet one of the things I have discovered about people who are difficult to love is that they don't know they're difficult to love. They're oblivious, which makes it more difficult to deal with them. Indeed, the more unaware they are, the more they seem to pour out the thing that pushes your buttons to remind you that they are difficult to love. But the reason we have a hard time loving on people who are difficult to love is that we don't realize that all of us are difficult to love.

All of us have something about us that is difficult to love. But God in Christ made clear that, no matter how messed-up we were, he was willing to roll up his eternal sleeves, take on an additional nature, and come after us to love the unlovable. In the eyes of God, all of us are equally unlovable. I know we have levels for how bad people are in our world, and there are varying consequences for sin, but equally before a Holy God, all of us have issues we need God's love poured out on us for. I'm wondering whether we have dealt with the hardship of our brokenness and its consequences. Yet God makes it look easy for him to love us. The Bible says that while we were yet sinners, in Christ, God demonstrated his love.

He demonstrated his love. Notice it didn't declare how he felt about us. I mention the feeling because, if God had based his love for us on how he felt about our sin, we'd all be in hell, washing our underarms with the heat of the flames of the fire. However, God demonstrates his own love for us in that, while we were jacked up, while we were not thinking about him, while we thought we were thinking about him while we were trying to give him our attitude, while we were creating a list of why he should love us and it was damnable before his sight, at that moment, Christ died for us. That's powerful to me. So we come to this passage where Paul is keeping it 100 with the Corinthian church and challenging them.

He's being blunt and honest with everything that he's working through and addressing. He transitions from chapter 1 into chapter 2 and examines a challenging issue that has developed in their congregation: the forgiveness, restoration, and reconciliation of a repentant person who is holistically repentant. Paul discusses not only this situation but also the broader circumstances in the Corinthian church so that they may recognize their need for a wider view of love. He's essentially exegeting an application of 1 Corinthians 13 again by taking the practical implications of that chapter and infusing it into this chapter. As we unpack this text, I have two points on how to love people who are hard to love.

Be Willing to Face the Barriers in Your Relationships
2 CORINTHIANS 2:1-4

If we're going to love people who are hard to love, we must face barriers. Paul admits, "In fact, I made up my mind about this: I would not come to you on another painful visit" (v. 1). Paul's admission is interesting because he was in anguish about the state of the Corinthian church. He was frustrated with their spiritual immaturity and brokenness as well as their love for the world rather than for the heart of God. Paul implies,

"As a matter of fact, it wasn't merely God who stopped me from coming to you. I didn't want to come to you because I was not optimistic, based on the reports, that you had repented. So coming back to engage you about the same thing would have been painful all over again." Paul wasn't willing to reexamine the Corinthians' immaturity, pride, and lack of teachability.

Have you tired of repeatedly engaging someone about what's causing your broken relationship? You have an unsettling feeling because you don't think the situation has been resolved, but the other person has moved on in his mind without any growth. You're not nitpicking his flaws. Rather, this flaw is systemic and corroding everyone and everything around him to the point that, in order to be in relationship and fellowship with this person, you must deal with the issues.

To be a Christian and avoid confrontation is impossible. I'm not speaking of being a jerk. However, you have to be confrontive at times. This passage is rich with love; Paul is not just someone who is angry. "I want to get something off my chest. You know, I've been wanting to say this for a long time. You know, I want to get this off." I'm not speaking about feeling better because you got rid of something that was weighing on you. Or sometimes you don't want to deal with the person; you just want to speak your mind so you can feel better. That's an emotional purge. That's not reconciliation.

Paul's disposition toward the Corinthians suggests he had made a visit before. He had led them to Jesus and also endured their confrontation. This experience was painful because of their immaturity, warped thinking, and lack of responsiveness to his team's investment in them. It almost seems Paul is speaking of Christianity itself here and not just of Corinth. Have you ever invested in someone and expected more in return out of him than he gave? You believe God wanted more for him than he wanted for himself. You invest in someone's life with your time, talents, money, and moving some stuff out of the way just for them. And then the person is not only ungrateful but also unchanged!

Paul is effectively stating, "I don't want to come if it's going to be this." In other words, "I'm not going to go back and forth until I see something break." Paul is challenging them. He is thinking that the previous visit was painful enough; the reports had shown little progress, so he is pessimistic about any fruitful resolve. In verse 2 he observes, "If I cause you pain." The word here means "sorrow, grief, or disappointment." *Pain* and *sorrow* are synonymous in the emotional impact it has on a person who is wanting something for someone. So now he's speaking to a specific issue in the church.

Deal with People's Sin Issues to Produce Change and Joy (2:1-3)

We don't know what the issue is. We don't know if it involved the man in 1 Corinthians 5 who had his father's wife. He was committing a form of illegal and spiritual incest with his stepmother. Perhaps a person is being divisive in the church against the spiritual leadership of Paul, and Paul is coming there to communicate face-to-face to that person and reduce the person. It could be both. At the end of the day, the issue is a disciplinary action that had to be taken by Paul and the church to engage someone because of constant, unrepentant sin. But then the whole church had lived in a sense of comprehensive brokenness. So Paul was hard on the Corinthians because they allowed carnality. He confronted not only their sin but also their disposition toward its presence in the church. A church has to deal with sin issues.

Often people say, "None of us is perfect." Perhaps, but when your children need correction, you don't just say, "None of us is perfect." So in the midst of your brokenness, even though you're broken, God has given you a role to play in the lives of others when it comes to correction. Not to play that role with humility—to fail to deal with their issues while God is dealing with your issues—would be bad stewardship. Thus, Paul suggests, "I know you are a mess, but you still have to deal with the hypermess that's in your midst. If you don't deal with mess in the local community, it festers and grows."

People can deal with people who have issues and admit they have issues. Even the world can deal with that. They call that keeping it real. But no one can deal with someone who acts like he doesn't have issues.

As we consider correction, a lack of commitment to the holiness of God also confronts us. We seldom stand in awe of God anymore with fear and trembling. The process of restoration and discipline is rooted in the holy love of God and is not about being better than others but rather about making them better.

A sense of cognizant fear should stir all of us as we take a closer look at ourselves. So Paul is troubled that the Corinthians are not dealing with their sin. He asks, "Who will cheer me other than the one being hurt by me?" (v. 2). The holistic plan of the Spirit and the work of God is for that particular person to feel the pain and be offended for the right reasons, not the wrong reasons. Conversely, an unrepentant person takes what you confronted him about and makes it about you. That person is not repentant if he blames you. If he passes the blame, he's not repenting or owning up to his offense.

A person is repentant when she can separate what you said from you, receive it as godly, and respond and turn toward repentance so that she can develop, grow, and be better. That's the way of a Christian. You must be willing to be rebuked and be better. Christian community isn't just about getting together and hanging out. Every now and then, if we're going to be real with one another, we have to get in one another's faces. Most of us want to come to church with our Bible up under our arm, look pleasant, and then go back to things as they were and say, "That was a nice word. I had good time at worship." But nothing's different.

Church being the church is about being confronted about being confronted. If you declare, "I don't want anyone in my business," Scripture counters that you gave that up when you became a believer. We know some things are off limits, but for the most part, somebody should be able to talk to you. A lot of us are so nonconfrontational that we run from opportunities to grow. When that happens, you won't grow, and it will follow you. One of the hardest parts of shepherding people is when you challenge someone lovingly, yet instead of receiving pastoral care, he runs and creates another story of what happened. Then people find out the truth way later and realize that person never dealt with the issues. When a person wants to create a story about someone else in order not to deal with his issues, he's going to go deeper into his brokenness because he's looking for someone to coddle him in the stuff that he doesn't want to change.

Paul is challenging them in a loving way. He says, "Cheer me up." Or, "What will bring me cheer is not rebuking you. What brings me great cheer is your transformation." His reflexive question, "Who will cheer me other than the one being hurt by me?," reminds me of what Christ does. In John 15:11 Jesus says, "I have told you these things so that my joy may be in you and your joy may be complete." In other words, you should want for yourself what I want for you; it's good for you.

Earlier in John 15 Jesus declares that God "prunes every branch that produces fruit so that it will produce more fruit" (v. 2). Sometimes challenge and discipline are painful, but actually God is using his people to cut off mess that shouldn't be there. When the mess is cut off and you

submit under the cutting, new growth can take place out of the brokenness of what was removed. If you don't submit, you won't grow healthy.
God has to prune you. And sometimes God uses people's mouths to cut
at you as you grow and develop in Christ.

But sometimes I fail to listen; I don't like to be challenged. I remember one of my boys said something to me, and I literally could have put
my fist through his mouth. I thought I was saved from that kind of tem-
per. I'm not talking about something years ago; this happened this year.
God is still working on me. He said something to me, and I knew he was
right, but I reacted. Being challenged is painful, but everyone needs it.

Paul said he wanted them to give him joy. Likewise, our desire is not
to tell people off; our desire is for change. So, because of that desire for
change, we should rejoice when change happens.

He said, "I wrote this very thing so that when I came I wouldn't have
pain [or sorrow] from those who ought to give me joy, because I am
confident about all of you that my joy will also be yours" (v. 3). Paul is
helping the Corinthians through their difficult situation.

He says, "What I'm desiring to do should be something we should
hold in common and what everyone should want to be a part of. All of us
should want to live joyfully." What does it mean? Joy means—remember
our definition based on the Scriptures—having unending satisfaction
with God no matter what. So sometimes joy involves pain. Joy and pain
are like two sides of the same coin. Paul says, "I wrote the way I did in
order that this may happen" He declares that his joy would be the joy of
everyone in the ministry.

This is not a person confronting vindictively. Vindictive confrontation and redemptive confrontation are different matters. Paul is not
telling them off. He has purpose behind his direct words.

Confront People in Love Even When It's Painful (2:4)

Paul acknowledges, "For I wrote to you with many tears out of an
extremely troubled and anguished heart." In other words, his emotions
were crowded with all types of thoughts. He was weighed down and in
anguish of heart, which means to be in constricting distress. Paul is
admitting it's hard to approach the subject, and he's having a hard time.
He says, "With many tears." Can you imagine Paul writing this letter and
crying because he's broken down? Have you ever wanted something so
bad for someone and you just cried, even as you move into confronting

her because of her lack of commitment to change? Paul observes, "I didn't do this to cause you sorrow but to let you 'know the abundant love that I have for you.'"

That's the goal: unconditional love. You know someone loves you when he tells you about yourself. That's a simple principle. If you have people in your life who don't ever confront you, they don't love you. You don't need people in your life to just talk about you, talk around you, or put something on social media. You need people willing to confront you and talk. It can be over a meal or cup of coffee if that's helpful. Now, there are times when it's so tough and someone has been so bad that you don't need a meal in the middle of you. You need to cut to the chase because you don't want him to feel a certain way to run from it so he can hide behind the food. Some people are so hard of heart that you just have to remove the obstacles. We can remove the sweetness of the ice cream so you can feel the bitterness of soul that happens when you don't respond properly to confrontation.

So Paul sheds "many tears," yet he has "abundant love" for them. Have you ever felt that way? The conflicting affliction of pain and anguish but deep love for someone, and you want more for him than he wants himself. Then when you confront him, you are trying to figure out a way to communicate the pain you feel when you're having to be honest with him. You start praying to God, "Lord, I don't know what to do. But I know we have to deal with this because 'Faithful are the wounds of a friend; but the kisses of an enemy are deceitful'" (Prov 27:6 NKJV). So God, I have to deal with this issue, but I want this to somehow be surrounded in love."

And sometimes you have to start with good stuff, the way Paul had to find some good stuff about the Corinthians, as hard as that was. You could begin, "I love you. And you dress nice. You can cook." Find ways to show people love and let them know that you care for them.

In the Bible, before God confronts his people, he always says something like "I saved you from Egypt with a mighty right hand and held up Moses in the wilderness." He reiterates his faithfulness and care. Then he says, "Now let's take out the Bible." God never harshly rebukes his people first. He's always speaking of his abundant love and kindness for them. And then he'll get right in there and love on them by communicating to them. Likewise, Paul does the same, and this points to the fact that he is willing to deal with some difficult subjects. Love involves hard conversations. Chronic avoidance is a sign of hate, not love.

Be Willing to Accept Authentic Repentance
2 CORINTHIANS 2:5-11

You have to be willing to confront, but don't be like Jonah, saying, "I told you, God, that you are abundant in loving-kindness and full of love. And I knew that if they repented, you were going to start that forgiveness stuff and restoration stuff that you do. I didn't want them to repent. I want you to destroy Nineveh." That's not what we're discussing here. Consider the sons of thunder, James and John, who said, "Lord, do you want us to call down fire from heaven to consume them?" (Luke 9:54). Jesus suggested in response, "You don't know what kind of spirit you're of when you wish bad for a person God is calling to repentance. You have to check yourself because now you need restoration."

Don't Pass Blame (2:5)

Paul observes, "If anyone has caused pain, he has caused pain not so much to me but to some degree—not to exaggerate—to all of you." So Paul is facing an issue in the church where a person has done something heinous and grievous. The person who was under church discipline is repenting of his sin, and Paul is challenging the Corinthian church on their lack of acceptance. But instead of looking at themselves and their lack of acceptance, they point at Paul as the one who caused all the problems. It's as if they were declaring, "Paul, we wouldn't have been in this predicament if you hadn't call on us to do what the Bible says."

Have you ever felt like the truth of the Bible got you into worse trouble? You knew it was the right thing to do, but you kind of wish it wasn't because you really wanted to avoid it. God wouldn't let you avoid it because he loves you enough to help you deal with it in the first place. Paul suggests, "The person who caused you trouble is you."

My mom always said, "Eric, if you ever get locked up, don't call me."

"What do you mean, Mama? You're not going to bail me out?"

She said, "No, I'm going to leave you in there."

Then I started thinking, "Do you really love me? So you would let me stay in jail as a fourteen-, fifteen-, sixteen-year-old to prove something?" I didn't utter this out loud. I'm saying it to my mind because I know not to get slapped into another time zone. But then I just asked her, "Mommy, why wouldn't you bail me out?"

She said, "Because, baby, your problem is if you got locked up and you think me not getting you out is my fault, then that's your problem." And she wanted me to know that the consequences of my sin are the consequences of my sin. But at the end of the day, she was saying, "It's not my fault that you get kept in a situation you put yourself in." Paul is taking the onus off of him; he's not letting people blame him for their condition.

You have some people in your life who are constantly blaming you for their condition based on their choices. They make a bad choice, but they want you to feel bad while they feel good. That's confusing and frustrating. When they don't want to change, they're going to just make you angrier and more frustrated and anguished as they try to blame you for it. In reality, some of us need to stop getting in the way of God's discipline. When you get in the way of God's discipline, you get hit. One of the rules in my house when somebody is getting a spanking is don't get in the middle. There's no switching between people. The person who did wrong gets disciplined. That's what the Corinthian church failed to understand.

Understand the Evidence of Authentic Repentance (2:6-7)

When you look at Paul's disposition, he means, "I don't want to put it too severely or put a psychological burden on you." He says, "This punishment by the majority is sufficient for that person" (v. 6). This person had been removed from the church because of his sin. And he was holistically, comprehensively repentant. We don't know if it was the man mentioned in 1 Corinthians 5 or someone else, but it's clear that this person had come to repentance to the point where he was begging for return with a repentant heart. He wasn't just asking for replacement. He was asking for reconciliation and restoration without any strings attached to it. Paul will later talk about this idea of repentance and what authentic repentance looks like.

If people are broken, they're not demanding anything. If someone tells you she wants reconciliation but gives you a list of demands, then she is not repentant. If she's arguing the particulars of the sin that was committed to give you an accurate view of what she wasn't guilty of, then she's not repentant because the repentant person just says, "All the things I did, I repent of." When you sin, there are unforeseen things that you've done and impacted that are even beyond the actual sin you first committed. So a repentant person realizes, "I don't want anything, and I don't have to argue with anyone. I just want to be right with you and right with God." When someone admits that, we can rejoice and affirm, "That's a good place to be in because that's true repentance."

The last evidence of true repentance is to avoid causing division among God's people. Avoiding division is the challenge—the church has to be bold enough to face it. I wish I could say that over the twenty years of ministry I've never had to be involved in church discipline. I would love to say that nothing ever got to that point. Most of the discipline cases we've dealt with never go public—about 99.9 percent—because the person who is addressed behind closed doors repents, and it's resolved. I don't believe in sitting down people unnecessarily.

Let me take it further. Saying "sit down" just means you sit punitively so that you're not doing any ministry, but there's no counseling. There's no service. There's no ministry. There's no building up. Sitting down just means punishment. That's like going to a corner. But restorative discipline means care for the person who's repentant. When a person's repentant, that means he's open. He's not just jumping through hoops. He wants to be made right. That's what biblical discipline looks like— the willingness to confess, "I'll do whatever it takes."

The person who is repentant is forgiven, but it takes time for trust to be restored. That's biblical. You don't entrust a person immediately if there's a breached confidence in any way. If someone stole money, you don't make him the treasurer and say, "We're restoring you." Restoration means we're not going to hold your sin against you for fellowship. But trust must be regained based on the severity of the sin. Don't confuse forgiveness and trust. Forgiveness and trust are two different things because some of us withhold forgiveness because we don't trust. We wrongly merge trust and forgiveness in that situation. And yet, some things God has forgiven me of he won't let me do ever again because he doesn't trust me with them anymore.

Paul spoke about the punishment by the majority, which means everyone didn't agree with him about it. It was a majority; it wasn't unanimous how the issue should be handled.

Look at verse 7. He says, "As a result, you should instead forgive and comfort him." "Comfort" here in the context of 2 Corinthians means you've been comforted because of the same brokenness. Therefore, you have the ability to turn and comfort that person with the comfort that you received from God yourself. He may be overwhelmed with excessive sorrow, which would be deep church hurt. Overwhelming sorrow points to despair, hopelessness, and depression when a person is pushed away, never to be engaged as a repentant person.

Reconcile with People Who Repent, and Reaffirm Your Love for Them (2:8-9)

Paul implores, "Therefore I urge you to reaffirm your love to him" (v. 8). That is, "I want you to love that person. I want you to love him unconditionally. I want you to reaffirm. I want you to ratify. I want you to vindicate your love for him." In other words, the love you showed to him must equal or exceed the public rebuke you gave to him.

If you rebuke someone in relationship or if the church does it, the love that is engaged with that person must equal or exceed the impact of the rebuke, which can be hard if you were hurt by the sin committed against you in the first place. But now you are called to love.

Paul acknowledges, "I wrote for this purpose: to test your character" (v. 9). This idea of testing means to fire up your soul, to see what kind of character you have. Do you have enough character to deal with sin? Do you have enough character to restore a person who has comprehensively repented? Do you have enough character not just to forgive, not just to deal with the issue, but to forgive him and restore him and love him? Paul observes that your character is connected to your response. The apostle's charge is not only for the person who repents but also for you.

Thus, many of us may need to deal with relationships that have been broken. We may have some relationships that have been broken that we ignore, and we haven't done what the Bible says in Romans 12:18—"If possible, as far as it depends on you, live at peace with everyone" (see also Heb 12:14). Have we done everything we can for the person who's hard to love?

God is talking to you from his Word. He's talking to me. Have you pushed for peace and reconciliation? Have you called in a mediator? Sometimes you need a mediator to sit down with the person because you're still angry at each other. You need some help to talk to the person. Have you done that yet? Have you called a trustworthy person who will be impartial in the matter—a mediator who can neutrally communicate on both sides and challenge both sides? The hope is for reconciliation.

But if the person continues in sinful rebellion, you can say, "God, I did all I could do." Then you pray for him seasonally as he comes to mind and check your heart about how you feel about the fact that reconciliation hasn't taken place.

Don't Fall for Satan's Designs by Continuing in Division (2:10-11)

Paul declares, "Anyone you forgive, I do too. For what I have forgiven— if I have forgiven anything—it is for your benefit in the presence of Christ" (v. 10). That powerful phrase, "in the presence of Christ," underscores the church's solemn call. God sees us, and he's going to hold us accountable for how we have dealt with this situation.

Paul expresses all this for one reason: "So that we may not be taken advantage of by Satan. For we are not ignorant of his schemes" (or devices) (v. 11). Satan loves to outwit and manipulate God's people to be against one another, particularly in forgiving one another. He loves to build a case in your heart and mind against people so that you won't deal with them. That's his device. Yet with people who are repentant and everyone's still angry with, Satan seeks to isolate them so he can pounce on them. Too often we let the diabolical lion grab them and do what he will with them because of his commitment to abusing God's people. He's committed to that. He's committed to dividing you from the flock. He's committed to making you feel hopeless. He's committed to making you think the gospel isn't enough for you. He's committed to that. That's one of his biggest devices or schemes.

Jesus is a good case study of forgiveness and restoration. He forgave Peter, a dear friend who betrayed him after he spent three years, around the clock, discipling him. If you count up three years, Jesus spent approximately 26,280 hours with Peter investing in him. Have you ever spent that much time discipling someone? Jesus spent over 26,000 hours investing in Peter, and Peter cursed Jesus. "I don't know him," he said. He denied Jesus. He lied about being connected to Jesus. He avoided the risk of his relationship with Jesus when it got hard.

But Jesus had warned Peter that he would fall. Jesus knew he would fall, and he prayed anyway that he would be steadfast. Jesus went to serve and restore Peter by going to the lake where he was fishing (John 21). He said, "Cast your net." Peter couldn't see who it was, but he pulled up a bunch of fish. Jesus loads his business up with resources after he denied him. He cooked for him on the side of the beach; Jesus grilled fish for him. He didn't give up on him. Peter's apostleship was not lost because of his sin. Jesus told Peter to pastor his people and encouraged him to strengthen his brothers when they fall. Jesus is a master of dealing with people who are hard to love because he deals with us.

Reflect and Discuss

1. In your experience, what makes other people hard to love?
2. What are some ways you yourself are hard to love?
3. Are there some sin issues in others around you that you've been avoiding?
4. What are the consequences of a church not confronting sin? What are the benefits of a church confronting sin?
5. How can you confront sin issues in a loving, humble manner?
6. What is the evidence of false repentance? What is the evidence of true repentance?
7. What are ways you can be reconciled to a person who repents?
8. Do you have enough character to deal with sin? Do you have enough character to restore a person who has comprehensively repented? Do you have enough character not just to forgive, not just to deal with the issue you have with someone, but to forgive them and restore them and love them?
9. Have you done everything you can to be at peace with the person in your life who is hard to love?
10. In what ways has Jesus forgiven you and restored you? How do his love and grace for you motivate you to extend love and grace to people in your life who are hard to love?

How to Leverage Huge Opportunities

2 CORINTHIANS 2:12-17

Main Idea: God wants us to leverage huge opportunities well.

I. Huge Opportunities Must Include Caring for People (2:12-13).
II. Huge Opportunities Must Be Leveraged for the Gospel (2:14-16).
III. Huge Opportunities Must Not Turn Us into Someone Else (2:17).

Everyone wants to have great opportunities. However, often we don't prepare for the opportunity. We must be prepared so that when the opportunity comes and God opens the door, we're able and willing to run through it with his strength and leading.

One famous rapper says that he does "two-a-days" so that he is ready for any opportunity to perform. As believers, we should be doing spiritual two-a-days. We should be in constant contact with our Lord, studying his Word and being in prayer and biblical community so we'll be ready when opportunity comes. But we're going to see that what God calls a huge opportunity, the world may not.

I don't want to squelch your excitement because I know you were thinking, "God's got something for me." Whenever preachers talk about God having huge opportunities for you, a chill hits your spinal cord and your nervous system. You get excited because you think a huge opportunity coming your way means an amazing job and an enormous amount of money. Those are wonderful gifts. However, in God's kingdom, huge opportunities are based on impact, not worldly impression. Considering that reality, we come to a passage that helps us see what our forefathers in the faith would have viewed as a huge opportunity.

Paul is trying to convince the Corinthians that he has a commitment to them. But they don't view him as having a commitment to them because they're not committed to him anymore, since something or someone has taken away their ability to see things clearly from God's perspective. Now they're seeing things from man's perspective, and they begin to have a foggy view of what a huge opportunity looks like. What's huge in God's eyes seems small in man's eyes. That's why the Bible says not to despise the small things. That is, don't underestimate the acorn that's going to be the huge tree. God never works on the huge tree; he always works on the acorn.

God always uses small things in huge ways. That's his way. If we don't recognize the paradoxical disposition of gospel ministry and God's creative work, we may miss out on his gift of opportunity. So Paul tries to help the believers understand how God wants him to leverage huge opportunities. I have three points.

Huge Opportunities Must Include Caring for People
2 CORINTHIANS 2:12-13

Paul states here,

> When I came to Troas to preach the gospel of Christ, even though the Lord opened a door for me, I had no rest in my spirit because I did not find my brother Titus. Instead, I said good-bye to them and left for Macedonia.

Paul is making every effort to communicate to the Corinthian church. He ended up sending Titus there to check on their spiritual condition and response to his message. God opened up wide an opportunity for them.

Now the first place Paul would visit in a city was the synagogue because the Jews generally had some biblical revelation available to them so that they could know redemptive history. When he went there, he didn't have to catch them up in explaining the Messiah. So he would go and preach the gospel in the synagogue.

From there, some Gentiles would get connected. Then they would go into their circles of influence in their neighborhoods, communities, and villages and use those opportunities to preach the Word of God to their friends.

So Paul comes into Troas, a pit stop on his way to Macedonia. He wanted to stop and visit the Corinthians. He said, "I'm not going to go because they're not understanding me right now. And personally, I'm not understanding their response either, but I still care about them." He arrives in Troas and starts preaching the gospel. The door opens wide for him to speak the truth to them. Troas is in the region of ancient Troy, where the Greeks disguised their Trojan horse as a gift and then defeated Troy. The war (actual or mythical, depending on various historians) occurred over twelve hundred years before Paul's visit. However, the people of Troas were still broken by that experience. When Paul arrived, God had already tilled the ground and opened a huge door for him to be able to communicate the gospel. When the opportunity came for the door to be open, he was so well prepared that he was able to walk through the door and maximize the opportunity.

This passage demonstrates that when God opens a door wide to you, you don't have to pray about it anymore. You just walk through the door. Paul didn't ask, "Should I share the gospel with these people?" Yet some of us are so reluctant with opportunities to engage people with the renewing power of the gospel that we don't see that God has opened the door; we don't recognize that we're acting as if we're ashamed of the gospel.

But the gospel is so powerful! The gospel is so mighty; it doesn't depend on us. God enables conversion and transformation from spiritual death to spiritual life. The Spirit, as we proclaim and share the gospel, reveals God's work and is present in his work.

With this open-door opportunity, Titus was supposed to leave the Corinthians and meet Paul in Troas. So as Paul is maximizing his open door, he's not at rest because he can't find his spiritual son and brother Titus. He may have worried that the Corinthians would assault Titus for disclosing their brokenness to Paul. He knew the Corinthians were carnal, so he didn't know if they were going to punch Titus in the face, drag him out of the city, or stone him. Paul was worried about him, and his spirit was not at rest. But he was also worried about the Corinthians, even with this great open door that God had given. He didn't want to add new believers to the roster of his commitment until he had fulfilled the commitment he had made to the Corinthian church.

As God gives you open-door opportunities, you must make sure you don't forget about people. The first thing that happens when God allows you to be fruitful in ministry is you forget about other people because you see yourself as an exalted lord. You can grow, develop, and change over time, but when God opens a door for you, don't let that door be a lonely door. Paul didn't forget about Titus or even the people who hurt him. He didn't forget about them because he didn't see the open door as an opportunity to move on. Paul didn't say, "You don't like me anymore, so I'm not engaging with you anymore."

Paul didn't look at it like that. He didn't let the open door of opportunity make him forget about the people who cared about him, even though they hurt him. That's important. As a believer, many of us are living our lives under the rubric of who hurt us.

We have to be careful about making our lives all about showing up someone who doesn't like us—in other words, centering our lives on "I'm not going to be like you. I'm not going to do like you." When we do that, everything is wrongly motivated by these people rather than by God's approval and blessings. Your life is built around showing someone else what you've accomplished and overcome. So we have to deal with our feelings of hurt toward people who have hurt us; otherwise, when God opens up a door of opportunity, we will barge through that door with bitterness and hatred. We'll walk through the opportunity doing ministry or entrepreneurialism or education or having a family or being a parent out of wanting to prove to them that their hurt didn't impact us. If we have this hurt in mind every time we do something, we have to be careful: it will mess up the opportunity because the root of bitterness crops up and defiles many. We can be doing a good thing out of wrong motives, and the seeds of bitterness can be sown into the good opportunity. We must be careful to let the opportunities God has given us be designed and committed to proving ourselves to those who hurt us, especially when they're not even looking at us. We're the only ones ruminating and being hindered by it.

We must remember that Christ defines us. Also, notice that Paul didn't try to forget about the Corinthians. That's the key. Many of us think overcoming hurts or fears is forgetting them, and that doesn't work. You have to deal with your fears, as Paul deals with his. He affirms, "I want to make sure the loose ends between the Corinthians and me are tied up. The open door won't be as much of a blessing until I deal with my past stuff with the Corinthians. So I'm going to stop what I'm doing, as big as this opportunity is, and I'm going to go back and deal with my issues with the Corinthians."

Huge Opportunities Must Be Leveraged for the Gospel
2 CORINTHIANS 2:14-16

In verse 14 Paul states, "But thanks be to God." He worships in the midst of it. Have you ever been hurting, and you know you have to go ahead and bless the Lord? You don't wait until you feel better because you have to learn to worship the Lord when you don't feel like it. You worship

God with broken feelings anyway. Paul is hurting right now, and he proclaims, "Thanks be to God."

He's giving a sacrifice of praise. He's declaring, "God, I'm going to give praise to you even though I'm hurting." Why? He says, "Because I have to. I have to push past. I have to get my mind out of where it is, so I'm going to have to look to Jesus Christ in a particular way—beyond my hurt and their disposition toward me."

He thanks God who in Christ "always leads us" (v. 14). He utters this rich "in Christ" phrase because he's in a crisis. Whenever you're in a crisis, you have to remind yourself that you're in Christ, not just in a crisis. You can go through a challenge that can so overwhelm you that you forget about Jesus.

That's when worship counts. When you don't feel like it, worship counts. When you're hurting, worship counts. When you can cuss, worship counts. When you can fuss, worship counts. You want to give someone a piece of your mind. But Paul remembers, "Oh yes, I'm in Christ."

He thanks God who did something in Christ. What did he do? He leads us in "triumphal procession." What a powerful expression! This "triumphal procession" (v. 14) would have set off alarms in the minds of the Corinthian church because when Roman generals returned from their conquests, they had huge parades. The Romans celebrated with parades of women and parades of music. But they also paraded prisoners of war including the vanquished kings and their families. Then the conquering Roman kings and princes marched at the end of the procession with their triumphs before them. The parade took place in front of all the people to show off the conquests of the war. The Romans would even take the prisoners of war and kill them in front of everyone to show off the might of a general. Paul uses this illustration powerfully here to demonstrate that believers in Christ are triumphal prisoners of war of Jesus Christ.

Paul recognizes that being led by Christ, our warrior, is a huge opportunity—we are led in triumphal procession into the world. He essentially says, "I'm thanking God for my pain. He leads us out as prisoners of war, not to destroy us in our dying but to build us up in our dying."

Paul suggests that God is using his pain as an experience of death so he can grow. You may be asking, "What's the huge opportunity?" The huge opportunity is to go through something hard and to be awakened. God is using it for your good. Many of us when we look at our lives, especially in times of hardship, don't see God leading us. Paul says that when you go through a trial, God is triumphantly leading you. You've already won, but you have to go through the death experience. When you go through something, you have to worship God in the midst of it because worship reminds you that God is recycling your brokenness for something bigger.

So huge opportunities come along as we endure difficulty. The world doesn't teach that because we are a self-preservation society; we build our lives around not suffering. There's nothing wrong with looking for security, but when insecurity comes, don't be fooled into thinking your security is in the security you've built. Even when you're having natural disaster, you can have spiritual fruitfulness in a natural catastrophe.

Perhaps you've been in a situation where you felt broken beyond repair. You couldn't see beyond your fingertips. But then you remembered the fact that the God of heaven is leading you. That's the paradox of the gospel. Our spiritual death is different. It speaks through us while we're going through it, and it spreads the fragrance of the knowledge of Christ everywhere. Paul declares that God is walking us through brokenness to spread his fragrance through us.

Consider the Roman generals who would kill the paraded victims in front of everyone. The smell of death remained because sometimes those parades would last for days. They would begin to smell the rotting bodies, so they would burn incense to cover up the smell of death.

Let me give another example. Before I knew Christ, I was in my college room, rolling up and smoking things. We would have incense because it would get rid of the smell of weed. I didn't want anyone to smell the death that I was going through in my room. In other words, I was trying to hide the death with a fragrance.

It is the same for us: when you're dying in your circumstances, you also tend to try to hide the brokenness. When you get broken in death, a fragrance comes out of you; God is taking you through something to release the fragrance of Christ out of you. To release his fragrance, you have to be broken. You must be split open so that the glorious aroma of Christ can come forth. So Paul is worshiping and thanking the good Lord for this beautiful experience of being led in triumphal procession.

Paul says that Christ's aroma spreads everywhere: "For to God we are the fragrance of Christ among those who are being saved and among those who are perishing" (v. 15). God puts you in situations to encourage those who are being saved. That means those who are going to get saved as well as those who are already saved, who are growing spiritually. So God strategically puts you in trials for others to take notice.

See, that's why you shouldn't close the blinds and sleep in when God takes you through something. Many of us hide because we want to be viewed as strong all the time. God says, open the blinds, wash your face and everything else, put on some clothes, eat something, and go out in your brokenness because I want my strength to be shown through your weakness. You can't always be seen as the pillar of the family. You can't always be seen as the one who knows everything. You can't always be seen as the one whom everyone confides in. You need to show everyone that the reason you have a reservoir for them is because of the God who is in you.

Paul is encouraging us in this—those who are being saved—but he also addresses those who are perishing. God wants to hold those who are perishing accountable for having smelled his fragrance but not appreciating its aroma. He notes people make two different evaluations. One calls it a fragrance from death to death, the other, a fragrance from life to life. For those who don't know Jesus Christ as Savior, it's a stench because they're dead in sin. Their spiritual nostrils haven't been nurtured to recognize the ambrosial aroma of Christ. God uses the aroma of our trials to hold people accountable who won't trust him. Therefore, they're going from death to death. It only reminds them of their deadness in relation to God and their eternal separation from him.

But for those who are believers, it's from life to life. This is beautiful. One of the best places to see this is at a funeral, when someone's a believer—an actual believer, not a person who's pushed into heaven to make everybody feel good, but a person who's truly a believer. When people stand up to talk about the deceased person and how he or she reflected Jesus Christ, for those being drawn, the aroma hits them in the spirit and shows them their need for Jesus. For those who already believe, it encourages them. For those who aren't given the grace to recognize the aroma, all they see is a dead person and us talking ancient mysticism.

For the believer, brokenness and death should encourage you to smell the aroma of the glorious power of the Lord, Jesus Christ. This aroma is supposed to remind us of the life we're going to have. But it's supposed to tell people who don't have life that there's hell coming for them if they don't submit to the renewing power of God.

Do you remember being in the car with your parents when they told you you're going to get a whupping after dinner? I do, and time sure drags on. Mama cooks everybody's favorite meal in the house that day; the aroma fills the house and everybody is excited, but the smell of the meal just reminds me that it's a sneak preview of the coming attractions. I'm trying to eat my meal as slow as I can eat it because I know that afterwards I'm getting a whupping. The aroma in the house for everybody else is enjoyment of an aromatic meal, but for the one going from death to death, it's great fear. That's what it's like being an unbeliever: the smell makes you think of the punishment that is coming. But for a believer, going through trials should remind you that Jesus is coming back.

God uses trials to make you uncomfortable here. Listen, what you're going through is God reminding you not to get comfortable because if you get comfortable, you'll turn off the aroma.

Huge Opportunities Must Not Turn Us into Someone Else
2 CORINTHIANS 2:17

The text says, "For we do not market the word of God for profit like so many. On the contrary, we speak with sincerity in Christ, as from God and before God." Paul declares that we're not in this for the money. He is alluding to those many who are peddling. Instead, he says, "We're trying to be men of character. Even in the midst of our brokenness, we don't use our brokenness as a means to be about natural things." You have to be careful about making excuses to sin just because God has put you in a trial.

That's a bad place to be in as a believer. Paul observes, "We didn't let this turn us into another person. We try to still be sincere. We're reminded about our identity in Christ. We're commissioned by God." The idea of commissioning here just means God sent you.

Your purpose in life is to die. Being a doctor is not your purpose. Being a lawyer or a teacher—God can use you in those roles, but that's not your purpose. Those are just means that God employs for you to die. Your purpose is not to be a husband. Your purpose is not to be a wife. Your purpose is not to be a parent. Your purpose is to die, and God is going to use all those things to kill you.

You might as well just get skilled at going into the fight. You might as well jump into the ring. You must get used to the fact that God is going to allow you to go through something, but you can't allow going through something to stop you from knowing that you're something to him. You have to get that in your head. But what's beautiful about this idea is that it ultimately points to Jesus leading us in triumphal procession, eternally.

This procession leads to eternity, when Jesus will vanquish his enemies, and his subjects who have trusted him, who suffered for him, who lived for him, who walked with him will be awarded their due. All the subjects of the King's kingdom will then relinquish their accolades to the warrior God and General Jesus because it is his conquests on his cross, burial, and resurrection that provided strength to fight and survive life's catastrophes. Jesus ultimately didn't forget about us. When he received his opportunities, he came from heaven to earth, out of an air-conditioned heaven. He hung, bled, and died and let there be silence all night on Friday, let it be silent all night on Saturday, but early Sunday morning, he got up out of the grave with all power in his hands. And then, forty days later, he ascended into heaven, and he still hasn't forgotten about us because he lives to make intercession on our behalf. No matter how far Jesus went up—he's above the earth, he's above the universe, he's above the Milky Way galaxy, he's at the right hand of God, the Father almighty—he's still thinking about us. He's still praying for us. He's still looking for us.

He still hasn't forgotten us. One day the Father is going to tap Jesus on his shoulder and say, "It's time, Son." Jesus is going to mount his horse. He's going to gather all the saints who have died, along with their horses. And then they're going to come out into the clouds. Then everybody who's living in the depth of their experience, looking for the life, looking for the opportunity—they're crying, they're dealing with bills, they're dealing with debt—suddenly Jesus is going to scoop us up off the planet. We're going to meet him in the clouds because he hasn't forgotten about us.

I'm so glad he hasn't forgotten about me. I'm so glad that one day he's going to come back and get us because they strung him high and lifted him wide. And then he died and dropped his head in his shoulders. But on the third day he got up, and he's coming back for you. And he's coming back for me. I'm so glad he hasn't forgotten about us. I'm so glad he loves us and is working out things that we can't see now. No matter what you go through, don't let what you go through make you forget about who you represent in the midst of your brokenness.

Because God hasn't forgotten you. He's got you! You ought to thank God right now! You ought to shout right now!

Reflect and Discuss

1. How are huge opportunities in God's kingdom different from those in the worldly sense?
2. Why is it important not to live our lives centered on people who hurt us?
3. How do you deal with pain and hurt in healthy, healing ways?
4. How does the gospel encourage you to love and care for people?
5. In what ways do you need to die to self and be more broken in order to be more fruitful in demonstrating and proclaiming the gospel?
6. How does the gospel encourage you to stop hiding and admit your weakness, flaws, and brokenness?
7. What helps you not to make excuses to sin?
8. Why can you be assured that even though you go through trials, God still loves you, cares for you, and hasn't forgotten about you?
9. How does that encourage you to keep growing in Christlikeness even when you go through trials?
10. In what trials are you thankful to God for keeping and watching over you?

Matters of the Heart

2 CORINTHIANS 3:1-6

Main Idea: When God changes our hearts, we are no longer comfortable being what we were.

I. The Gospel Affirms the Sufficiency of Our Value (3:1).
II. Heart Development Is the Deepest Level (3:2-6).

Engaging the heart is of utmost importance in every area of life. Any good counselor will not merely offer you conditioning skills to sanctify your flesh into action. A good counselor will help you examine your heart and what is broken to move toward healing from the inside out. The heart is the most important part of your life. No matter how well you dress, it doesn't cover up your heart. No matter how well you do your hair, it doesn't cover up your heart. No matter where you live, what zip code you live in, it doesn't cover up the needs of your heart. No matter what kind of car you drive, no matter how many degrees—as good as those are to add to your life—that does not attend to the matters of the heart.

If the glory of God and Jesus Christ is the exalted theme of the Bible in relation to its central nature—from Genesis to Revelation—then he is after your heart and my heart. God knows, if you want to change anything, you must change it on a heart level. If you want to change a marriage, it must be changed on a heart level. If you want to change the attitude of a single person, it must be changed on a heart level. If you want to change parenting, it must be changed on a heart level. If you want to change domestic violence, it must be changed on a heart level. If you want to change racism in our world, it cannot be legislated. Legislation is important to bring legal protection, but it doesn't deal with the utmost need for the heart to be changed and the heart to be transformed. People have to believe something different on a heart level on account of seeing a new reality.

Potently put in this pericope, Paul's words help us to be more aware of where our identity comes from and where true change comes.

Paul is addressing the Corinthian church, which is composed of immature believers, but believers nonetheless. Paul affirms that, even in their constant states of spiritual immaturity, their sanctification is worth salvaging. No matter how immature you are as a believer, whether in natural immaturity or spiritual immaturity, it's never too late for your sanctification to be salvaged as long as you have breath and life. So Paul challenges the Corinthians' view of him as well as themselves and the Spirit of God through the gospel of God.

The Gospel Affirms the Sufficiency of Our Value
2 CORINTHIANS 3:1

Paul asks in verse 1, "Are we beginning to commend ourselves again?" In other words, "Do we have to reintroduce to you why we're valuable to you?" The Corinthians had started to devalue Paul and his team's influence and investment in their lives for the gospel. Consequently, they devalued God's investment and began to live outside the sphere of their identity.

Whenever your value in the kingdom of God under Christ's blood begins to lower, it is because of a lack of commitment to recognize where your identity is found. Paul is trying to let them know, "Even if you don't value us, we're valuable."

Have you ever done something for someone? You've helped this person repeatedly, and he acts as if you haven't done anything. You've invested time and poured into his life. You did all this, and it's like you haven't done anything. There's nothing like a person you never can satisfy by giving him something. Thanklessness and a lack of gratitude are signs of deep brokenness. Paul challenges the Corinthians on their lack of gratitude for God's investment in them through him. If they reject Paul, they're rejecting everything he brought with him; thereby they reject God's deep impact and influence on the core of their lives.

So he asks, "Do I have to even go through this again? Do I have to pull out my résumé? Do I have to come to you the way I would have to come to a stranger? But we're not strangers in this."

As we move through this passage, we observe Paul engaging their hearts. He says, "Or do we need, like some, letters of recommendation to you or from you?" (v. 1). Notice Paul is gently rebuking them here.

Recommendations in our day are different from recommendation letters in their day. In our day, recommendation letters are about

25 percent of what secures your school admission or a job. It helps, but it's not the whole of what someone looks at when they consider accepting you to a school or hiring you. It's just a part of the picture. But in biblical times, a recommendation letter was 100 percent of what was used to affirm you (see Keener, *Bible Background*, sub 2 Cor 3:1; Arnold, *Zondervan Illustrated Bible Backgrounds*, 3:209). For instance, when you were traveling, someone would direct you, "Look, go to June Bug's house on Eighteenth and Dauphin, and when you get there, just knock on the door and give them the letter." So the letter of recommendation would accompany you.

In biblical times, you could come to a house at midnight or three in the morning and be welcomed because hospitality was esteemed and guests were honored.

Someone would open the door and say, "Who are you?"

And you would respond, "Oh, here's the letter."

"Oh, OK. Come on in."

This doesn't happen today! These days you could bring letters or subpoenas and still be rejected, but in Paul's day a recommendation was everything. Paul is saying, "After all I've done for you, after all I've invested in you, do you mean to tell me I still need someone to recommend my value to you?"

We must be careful about finding our value in other people's value of us. Many of us are living our lives in the phantom zone—we're living to impress ghosts. So your rubric for your identity is showing someone you're valuable based on your efforts to achieve. As a result, you don't live your life based on the value Christ has given it; you're living your life to prove something to someone who doesn't even care about you anyway. Every post you put out, every picture you put out, every accomplishment you put out is to impress someone.

Paul isn't trying to impress them; he's trying to help them recall, "What I invested in you is enough for you to value me." Paul doesn't find his value in their value of him. However, because he has a relationship with them and a commitment to continue to minister to them, he wants them to value him so he can communicate to them. If they continue to push him away, Paul will walk away.

If someone doesn't let you continue to be an appropriate influence and help in her life, she has a heart issue. Only so much can be done for this person. Now, you can't prove to anyone why you need to be in his or her life. You can't do it. The person has to value your engagement. In fact, what if Paul reversed it and said, "So, do we need a recommendation letter from you?" That is, "Do you need to write me a recommendation letter so that when I preach the gospel, you give me credibility?" He would be lightly doing some rib-punching ministry on them to let them know, "I have done too much for you for you to add anything to me. You don't add value to me."

Heart Development Is the Deepest Level
2 CORINTHIANS 3:2-6

Look at verse 2: "You yourselves are our letter." How beautiful! Paul is telling the Corinthians, "When people look at your lives, based on my impact on them, your lives are a recommendation letter for my value that I've invested in you" (see Guthrie, *2 Corinthians*, 187–88).

Remember, the Corinthian church was broken and confused. But of course, all of us are hypocrites, so don't look down your nose too quickly. In this text Paul is essentially saying to us, "You're messed up, but you aren't as messed up as you were." Some people may look at me and say, "He's a hypocrite!" Well, I am a hypocrite, but I'm not the hypocrite I used to be.

The gospel makes me less of a hypocrite. So any movement in my life is a movement toward not being a hypocrite, and I'm less of a hypocrite because of the work of God. In other words, the gospel is enough in your life to make you less of what you were. Someone may look at where you are and say nothing's happened in your life, but if you gave them a video of the concentrated mess, that's less of a mess than it was before God cleaned it. They don't know how messed up you were, and they don't know that God took you from there and made you better today than you were yesterday. That's the key; that's the gospel. What's most important are the heart issues—and being less of what we were.

Paul is going to emphasize that because he is saying to them, "Look at the investment I made." Look at how powerful this is; he's going to deal with the deep heart issue here.

First Corinthians 6:9-11 says,

> *Don't you know that the unrighteous will not inherit God's kingdom?*
> *Do not be deceived: No sexually immoral people, idolaters, adulterers,*
> *or males who have sex with males, no thieves, greedy people,*

drunkards, verbally abusive people, or swindlers will inherit God's
kingdom. And some of you used to be like this.

Hold on, Paul! The Corinthians are doing this stuff presently, but he
declares, "That's what you *used* to be; you *were* that."

In other words, when you are saved, you are no longer what you
were before you trusted Christ, even though you're still doing some of
those things. Your identity is not in what you do but in what's been done
for you. The key to spiritual growth is realizing that you *were*. The more
you realize that you *were*, the more you'll be able to say, "Now I know
who I am. I *was* this then. . . . Why am I doing this now?"

Then you recognize, "If I'm not this, then what in the world am I
doing here?" The key to spiritual growth is this: realizing the depth of
identity that Christ has given to you. When you plunge yourself into who
Christ has made you to be, you will deconstruct who you were so that
you can, by God's grace, move into being all that God wants you to be.
But you have to embrace the fact that that's not you anymore.

I can remember when I was in college, and I trusted Christ—
November 15, 1992. My life got really weird because I didn't get good
discipleship. In fact, I didn't receive *any* discipleship. All I had was where
I was. So I would go and score some drugs, get with the dudes, and we'd
be in the room, and I would start using, and it just didn't seem the same
for some reason. I was saying, "What's wrong with me? I'm supposed to
get high." I was thinking, *What? What is this feeling I have in me? Why do I
feel different?*

What was going on? It's like someone was literally inside of me,
squishing all my organs and mushing them together. I said, "Why am
I uncomfortable in my sin? This used to be freeing. I can't even sin in
peace anymore. What has happened to me?"

The Lord was saying to me, "You *were* this, but now that you're mine,
I'm here to make you uncomfortable. You can't stay in this mess anymore because what gets you high doesn't change you." This way he takes
me to what I'm hiding from.

I didn't want to go and do all that; I just wanted to go to heaven.
It was, "Let me go to heaven, and I'll see you then. But for now, let me
get at this money, let me spend time with women, and let me get high."

And God was saying, "No, I messed your whole life up." When you
get saved, your life is never the same. Never. If you can remain the same,
you are not his.

Paul comments that this letter of recommendation is "written on our hearts, known and read by everyone" (v. 2). That is, "Listen, I have a heart for you. I love you people." He observes, "You yourselves are our recommendation letter, so that when people see how different your life is, they know God exists." The transformational work God is doing in your life, in the proximity of non-Christians, is to show people that God lives. It's that simple: people should be shaken by the change that happens in your life because God deals with stuff on a heart level. When God deals with the heart, it's not on an external level or an external change. Moreover, he helps us in the process and gives us his wisdom. God's transformational work is written on our hearts to be read by all.

So, how is it read by all? Through our character. When God is changing your character, people are going to read it. You're a letter. You're a living epistle, a living letter walking the streets of your city, on the trolley, on the train, at work, in the classroom, in the pub. Wherever you are, you are different and in process, and people will notice by God's grace the evident redemption taking place every single day as you are being renewed. How beautiful is the goodness of the gospel. Being a Christian is *different*. It's not just an announcement or a piece of paper bringing us into a form of religiosity, but it's brand-spanking newness, from the inside out. So Paul takes us here and he says, "It's read by everyone."

Then he declares, "You show that you are Christ's letter, delivered by us, not written with ink but with the Spirit of the living God—not on tablets of stone but on tablets of human hearts" (v. 3). I want to express in advance that I am incapable of unpacking the pragmatic and theological scope of this text by which God has spoken and breathed revelation. But I will try. This is massive.

Paul says, "You are a recommendation letter written by Christ, worked in us by the Spirit of God." So we see God the Father, God the Son, and God the Spirit—the Trinity working together. It took the whole Godhead to save us! God the Father, God the Son, and God the Spirit work together to obtain us.

Paul continues, "You show that you are Christ's letter, delivered by us" (v. 3). He is saying, "When I preached, I was really a conduit of God making you a letter."

If you will, God gives the believer a hard drive that will never crash. We have to eventually buy a new phone. We have to eventually purchase new technology. Did you know the soul is eternal technology?

Technology is God's work. God has given us a hard drive to download everything he has for us into our hearts. The Spirit of God applies what Christ has done for us to our lives.

Paul declares, "This is done by the Spirit of God." When you are unsaved, you can't see anything. You are blind. Then Paul communicates in the next chapter how the Holy Spirit takes a washcloth, dips it in the eternal blood of Christ, comes to your soul, and scrubs you off. As he's scrubbing you off, you become born again. He takes the veil off your eyes. Then he gives you faith. Then he sends someone to preach the gospel to you, and you're able to respond based on his working on you first. Paul says this is done by the Spirit of God, and immediately you're given a new heart.

Now what happens is, on the download to the drive, he puts in a new operating system. It's in Ezekiel 36:25-27, where it says God takes away the heart of stone and gives us a heart of flesh. How amazing! God downloads the law onto your heart because Christ fulfilled the law. So now the law won't just be something you stare at on a stone tablet, but it's in your heart. Your life is movement toward heart submission to Christ and the law he already fulfilled in you.

Now what happens? The Spirit didn't write on tablets of stone but on human hearts. How did God give the law? The first time when he gave the Ten Commandments, the Bible says the finger of God carved stones out of the mountain and wrote on stone. Then, when Moses saw the people break the law, he threw the stones down, and they broke. God had to write the tablets again because God's people broke the law. Ezekiel says God isn't writing on stone anymore.

You and I had hearts of stone. The stone tablets represented the hard hearts of lost people. And even if God etched on a stony heart, that heart was still unable to keep the law. So instead of ever writing on stone again, he used the sacred nature of the tablets. Where would the tablets be placed? In the ark of the covenant. So now that you've been renewed by Christ, Christ has taken the heart of stone out of you. It is gone. The heart represents value, affections, and will. You're now able to think the thoughts of God on a finite level and have affections for him. You are able to have your will taken out of bondage so that you can obey him. He put his Spirit in you and then allowed you to walk in his statutes. This is powerful!

So now, since you are functionally changed on a heart level—that's your salvation—your sanctification is about your coming to terms with the fact that that's who you are.

Let me try to illustrate. Some people know I hate hummus. But one day I discovered tomato basil hummus. It has the anointing that destroys the yoke of bondage. I get some carrot sticks and cucumbers to dip in it, and it's delicious now. My mind has changed toward hummus because I found a hummus that is tasty. Additionally, it's healthy for me.

When the gospel changes you, God gives you affections for the gospel. He causes you to taste things and do things that you would have never, ever done in your life. God will change your taste buds for you. If you feel weird as a Christian, you're in a good place. You're supposed to be weird. You're supposed to not always try to fit in. You're supposed to feel weird. Stop trying to adjust your heart to a change in culture. Don't try to be a jerk, but it's good to feel uncomfortable. You shouldn't try to make yourself feel good about being around sin so that people won't think you're a jerk. Christian, some of us need to let ourselves bask in the uncomfortable nature of being insulated but not isolated.

Jesus's prayer in John 17:15 was, "Don't take them out of the world, but protect them while they're in it." So God insulates you in a broken world where you're going to feel weird. And sometimes you're going to like things, but then you don't like that you like certain aspects of things because your heart is wrestling with the old nature of the residue of your flesh. And God is saying to you, "Feel uncomfortable." How powerful. God is writing on your heart, and he's downloading truth to stay there. The work of God and your salvation enable you to walk in his statutes.

See, the old heart was heavy from sin, deceitful, and wicked; who can know it (Jer 17:9)? The Bible says it devised evil constantly (Ps 140:2). The heart used to be stubborn and unresponsive to truth. Now you have a new heart. It has renewed thoughts, renewed affections, and renewed commitment to God, and it's lightened by forgiveness through faith. It obeys the Lord. That's the heart you have. You have a heart that can obey. Did you know that you can obey? Well, you can't, but Christ does it through you.

You're supposed to be different. You're supposed to feel weird. You're supposed to wrestle. So when you know in your heart what great salvation you have, no one has to make you pray. No one has to make you get in the Word of God because it's flavorful and tasty to the saint who's been trained by the renewing power of Christ. It's glorious and magnificent, this new heart, and you should invest in it.

Paul says as much in verse 4: "Such is the confidence we have through Christ before God." What is the confidence he has? That a person is able to live a Christian life that honors the Lord and that draws people to him.

That's the confidence. Paul's confidence is not in the Corinthians. His confidence is in God's investment in them as his recommendation letter in the world. So you ought to be a recommendation letter in the world where you proclaim the gospel to people to recommend that they become Christians. They look at your life and watch God's work, and God uses it as a drawing technique to pull them into the faith. This is the confidence we have in our lives. Paul says, "It is not that we are competent in ourselves to claim anything as coming from ourselves, but our adequacy is from God" (v. 5), and we don't need extra Jesus.

Your sufficiency, your value, woman of God, comes from the Lord. Feminism doesn't define you. That's a hyperresponse to masculinity. In other words, it's a hyperfemininity above masculinity because of the oppression men have placed on it—you're a feminist, which is anti-Christ. Instead, find your identity in Christ, and you'll find biblical femininity.

Same with men. You find your identity in being "masculine," and this is as a hyperreaction to not wanting to be gay: *I don't want anyone to see me as being a gay, so what I do is become hypermasculine.* You don't find your identity in how much weight you lift, in how fast you are, in how strong you are. No, you find your identity in Christ. That's where your sufficiency is.

Your sufficiency, woman of God, is not in getting married. Let me apply this: you are not going to be a better woman when you get married. God can make you a great woman without a husband, so stop thinking your desired inclinations will change. God loves to put people in your life that sanctify you, and God is only going to put a husband in your life to show you that your husband is not enough!

Whatever you trust in—that thing you ask God for and he gives it to you—he gives it to you to sanctify you. He gives it to you to show you how empty it is in comparison to him. That does what was supposed to be done before you got married in the first place: it just draws you back to him. If you got more money, you still would be broke. If you got a bigger house, you'd still be broke. If you get more education, but you don't recognize that God is sufficient, that God is enough, that God is your all-in-all, you're going to find yourself frustrated.

God loves to give you what you want so that you can see what you need. He loves it. The all-sufficient, all-powerful, almighty, all-present, all-knowing God of the universe—he is enough.

And your life's work on a heart level is for your heart to meet the Bible.

Enough of anything on this earth is never going to be enough. God's purpose is that you can see the all-sufficiency of God. All he wants to do is deal with your heart, and he wants to challenge your heart because if you change your heart, everything in your life changes.

God told Israel that you build cisterns, broken cisterns that can hold no water at all, but he is the river of flowing water that never ends. God is the God of unending satisfaction. When Jesus tells the woman at the well, "I am the living water," he's saying, "I am enough." And on that experience, she ran and redeemed a city. What an amazing reality! Being spiritually bankrupt is a blessing. Bankruptcy in our world qualifies you for nothing, but in heaven's reality bankruptcy qualifies you for salvation because you know you have nothing, and you know there's nothing you can bring to the table.

Reflect and Discuss

1. What does the Bible mean when it talks about your heart?
2. What has God done in your heart up to this point in your life? Why do you give God credit for those changes?
3. What happens if you try to make a change in your life, but it isn't changed on the heart level? What examples have you seen in your life or in others' lives?
4. Do you know someone who has not shown appreciation for what you've done for him or her? Have you failed to express appreciation for something someone has done for you?

5. Is there anyone who could serve as a letter of recommendation to vouch for your credibility as a Christian? What would make someone that kind of letter for you?

6. Where do you find value for your life? What would need to change so that you only find value in Christ?

7. In what sense are all Christians hypocrites? In what area of your life are you less of a hypocrite than you used to be? What kinds of things do you still do, even though they make your conscience uncomfortable?

8. How has God changed your taste buds? What aspects of Christian life do you enjoy more now than you used to?

9. Have you ever felt weird around other people? What makes you feel that way? Is it a blessing or a curse? Why?

10. What gifts has God given you? Which ones do you now consider worthless compared to Christ?

Experiencing the Unlimited Glory of God

2 CORINTHIANS 3:7-18

Main Idea: Experiencing the glory of God means a drastic decrease in self-reliance.

I. The Old Covenant Laws Expose Our Self-Reliance (3:7-9).
II. The New Covenant Glory in Christ Far Surpasses the Old Covenant (3:10-18).

I tried various religions before I became a believer. I tried almost every single thing that you could think of to figure out what it was. I investigated Buddhism and Hinduism. I examined the Egyptian mystery system. I went into Pan-Africanism. I delved deeply into trying to engage in Islam, all different types of Islam—Nation of Islam, Sunni Islam, Shiite Islam.

When I dabbled in all those different religions, I found the difference between Christianity and the others is that I didn't search for Christianity. I didn't try to study Christianity. Christianity came and got me. There's a difference. I wasn't seeking to understand whether or not Christianity was true. God came and interrupted my scheduled programming, and from that day my life has never been the same. And one of the things that I knew from the inception of my faith was that Christianity was a religion of weighty, robust truth and deep, street-level experience.

I mean, for the first time in my life, I realized that Jesus is the major difference from every other religion. What I began to see is that Christianity is intimately about growing in your experience of God, and in growing in it, you're constantly being freed up through the gospel to encounter God over and over again. When I look back over my life and even look to today, when I am not walking with an intimate sense of God, my life can begin to stagnate. My life can get to the point where I become lethargic, and sinning becomes a whole lot easier. Wandering becomes extremely easy because I'm not living in light of the one who called me out of darkness into the kingdom of his marvelous Son.

I began to grow and to develop in this reality of experiencing him and knowing him. When I say experiencing him, I'm not merely speaking of spiritual gifts, gatherings, shouting, and running around but rather a comprehensive, robust lifestyle by which you live in the manifest presence of God daily. Scripture declares that this is an entirely new way of thinking and an entirely new way of doing things. Paul in this text is trying to help us live in light of experiencing God's presence as a lifestyle.

Now I'm not referring to futile existentialism, gnosticism, or some foolish philosophy that does not find its faithfulness in our Father. I'm discussing the truth that only comes through knowing him and knowing yourself and being able to relate better in this world.

In many ways, I feel burdened in the ability to even communicate the glorious excellencies we find neatly nestled here. Yet we are called to preach it all, and that's what I'll attempt to do. I have one point only: **Experiencing the glory of God means a drastic decrease in self-reliance.**

The Old Covenant Laws Expose Our Self-Reliance
2 CORINTHIANS 3:7-9

Paul challenges the Corinthians because someone has begun shepherding them with unbiblical philosophies of self-reliance, which is characteristic of their Hellenistic society. We also live in post-Hellenism in our pop culture, where you are respected based on hard work. You're respected based on your grind, on how much you can get done, and your ability to have an unbalanced life of working all the time. That's the Corinthians' society. It was no different because their church was wealthy with poor people. But the wealthy were esteemed because they reflected their philosophical constructs of self-reliance.

But Paul presents a paradoxical reality. He challenges their self-reliance and belief that through their self-reliance, spiritual growth occurs. They wrongly believe their ability to grow and show off God is based on all that they're able to produce personally. In verse 7 Paul says, "Now if the ministry that brought death, chiseled in letters on stones, came with glory, so that the Israelites were not able to gaze steadily at Moses's face because of its glory"—and let's stop here. This is weighty. He calls them "stones."

He's broadening our view of the two stone tablets Moses brought down from the mountain. Paul is broadening it in several ways.

Number one, he's making it representative of the whole law, even though Moses came down with only ten of the laws that were written on tablets. And because ten of them were written on tablets, the Ten Commandments were the Cliffs Notes to the entirety of the first five books of the Bible.

Number two, Paul observes what the Ten Commandments represented for us. He says they were "the ministry that brought death." Now he's not speaking of the law being death but rather our relationship with the law. In other words, if you think that by your commitment to the law you will be justified, you're in trouble.

So the law was broken up. Some would say these are distinctions that shouldn't be laid out, but sometimes distinctions are helpful.

Namely, the law has three core elements: the ceremonial law, the civil law, and the moral law. Ceremonial law meant relating to God, civil law pointed to relating to others, and moral law meant relating to self. In all three of the most comprehensive areas in every relationship God created, the law produced in us failure—in our relationship with God, in our relationship to others, and in our relationship to ourselves. The law was given not to make you holy because God knew you weren't. The law was given to weigh you down about your inability to make yourself holy so that you would throw yourself on the mercy of God and say, "Who in the world can do all this stuff?"

Have you ever read through the first five books of the Bible and sat down defeatedly and said, "How are they going to do all this? If you do such-and-such, you have to go get three calves. If a woman is in her time of the month, she has to do this. If you leave your clothes out of the washer too long and they mold, then you have to do this. How in the world do you keep all that?" If you feel like that, that's how you should feel. Because when someone tries to get righteousness by their own efforts, they should feel like a failure. That's the goal. The goal is for you and me to be broken of ourselves.

The goal is not for you and me to become more eternally self-sufficient; the goal is for you and me to see our deficiencies. That's why Paul says it leads fully to death. Look at what Peter says in Acts 15:10-11, when some Jewish Christians were trying to get the Gentiles to live in light of this:

Now then, why are you testing God by putting a yoke on the disciples' necks that neither our ancestors nor we have been able to bear? On the

contrary, we believe that we are saved through the grace of the Lord
Jesus in the same way they are.

So even Peter is saying, "We're not killing it. You're trying to put a yoke around Gentile necks to be committed to the law, as that which grows them spiritually, when we never, ever related to the law like that. And we know we're failing now, and we're trying to act like 'Oh, it's interesting when someone else's failing, and then they try to apply their failure to you.'"

Peter is saying, "Do we really believe this?" He is echoing Galatians 2:15-16.

We are Jews by birth and not "Gentile sinners," and yet because we
know that a person is not justified by the works of the law but by faith
in Jesus Christ, even we ourselves have believed in Christ Jesus. This
was so that we might be justified by faith in Christ and not by the
works of the law, because by the works of the law no human being will
be justified.

So Paul wrote what he wrote, under the power of the Spirit, to give us the level of clarity that's needed to know that self-reliance doesn't work in God's economy.

We wrestle with this idea because our society is in an identity crisis. We're getting lost in gender identity; really it's country identity and cultural identity because America is made up of a bunch of post-slave slaves and immigrants who are now in a melting pot. We're trying to figure out who we are. What we're trying to do is redefine the identity of everything to try to recreate. But when you leave yourself on your own, you come up with some stupid stuff. We don't even know what we're doing. How is it practical to have unisex bathrooms for children? That's not even practical.

So Paul seeks to root God's people in their biblical identity as glory reflectors. He observes, "Now if the ministry that brought death, chiseled in letters on stones"—again, the stone tablets were representations of stone hearts that were unable to receive the law as a permanent marker or to respond to it. He says that ministry "came with glory, so that the Israelites were not able to gaze steadily at Moses's face because of its glory."

Look now at verses 12-13:

Since, then, we have such a hope, we act with great boldness. We are not like Moses, who used to put a veil over his face to prevent the Israelites from gazing steadily until the end of the glory of what was being set aside.

Moses would go up on the mountain and spend time close to the presence of God, and he would talk. The Bible says that he talked with God face-to-face as a friend with a friend while he was in an expression of God's presence.

How massive God is! God's unapproachable presence is in heaven, but God showed up on a mountain in a cloud, in a burning bush with an expression of his unveiled presence, with a minute portion of its revelation in the face of Moses. That was enough to make Moses glow.

You may remember glow-in-the-dark toys. We were excited to take something and hold it up by the lights. And the longer you held, the more the faculties within it were able to glow because it had been in the presence of the light. Likewise with Moses. Because he had been in contact with the light before things went dark, his face was able to glow, but just like the toys, the longer he was away, the more the glow faded.

Paul suggests that when we attempt to do life on our own, we will be brought back to a period that has come to an end to show us not that the law wasn't valuable but that its impact on us could not be permanent. His wisdom helps us because many of us are self-reliant, and it's a fading glory. It doesn't last. It has no strength. And some of us have experienced some bitter things in our past. So we've tucked our hand up under our arm with our pocketbook and put our wallet in our back pocket. We have the wind in our face because "ain't nobody gonna hurt me no more. So I'm going to do everything on my own. I'm pulling myself up by my own bootstraps. Ain't nobody going to bother me." That's a fading glory. You may be responding to your past unbiblically. What can happen is you assume the mentality that Michael McDonald and Patti LaBelle expressed in the song, "On My Own."

However, Scripture reveals that being a Christian is the process of being stripped of our self-reliance. So after you've received your degree and after you've done your internship or your residency, and after you've been fully qualified for everything, and you've written your dissertation, your thesis, and received straight As—after you've received accolades and even magna or summa cum laude—with all that, you still find out that God says, "I blessed you to be qualified, but I want to show you that you still need me! I'll let you have a little bit, but it'll fade away because I want you to know that you need me." That's the beauty of God. God's going to make sure you need him. He's going to make sure nothing works until you are walking in comprehensive attachment to him. You can keep trying to work it out and fake it until you make it, but you'll never get to the finish line. Never. So Paul is challenging the Corinthians because they're relying on themselves and their efforts for the kingdom.

What Paul says next in verse 8 can be translated as "The Spirit has even more glory." Wow! He is speaking of the ministry produced by the Spirit, which we examined in the last section. When Jesus ascended to heaven, he said, "I'm sending another of the same kind, and he's going to come alongside of you. He's going to take from me and give exactly what's from me to you." First Corinthians puts it anthropomorphically concerning the relationship of the Spirit to God the Father whom he indwells. The Bible says that the Holy Spirit searches the depths of God to deliver the depths of God's heart to God's people (1 Cor 2:10-13).

The Spirit searches all things, even the depths of God. So above all that the Spirit gives to the believer is gospel nutrition. In other words, you won't be saved unless he convicts you of sin, righteousness, and judgment. You can't be saved unless he washes you until you're born again. That's what the Bible says in Romans 12:3: "God has distributed a measure of faith to each one"—because without the ministry produced by the Spirit, we can't fully experience the glory of God. Furthermore, the ministry of the Spirit automatically demands dependence.

The Spirit is beyond measure. You can't think your way out of him, but it's not that he doesn't want you to think. He just doesn't want you to think without him. Your life is a walk of faith: he's producing a ministry in you. Your life is the way it is to show that's the Holy Spirit. The Holy Spirit is working in your life to move stuff out of the way to put some stuff into it. That's his way.

So stop rebuking the devil, saying, "I rebuke you, devil." Anyone even pray like that in the Bible? "I come against you, devil. I come against you and all your imps and your whole camp." Why are you praying like that? When you do that, you just sidebar in your prayer and stop talking to the one who can change it, to start talking to the one who's in the way of things being changed.

So Paul observes that the ministry produced by the Spirit produces more glory, meaning it doesn't fade. As a matter of fact, verse 9 declares,

"For if the ministry that brought condemnation had glory, the ministry that brings righteousness overflows with even more glory." In other words, the new covenant has more value than the old covenant in its ability to bring God's glory to reside in your life. That's the Spirit's role.

The New Covenant Glory in Christ Far Surpasses the Old Covenant

2 CORINTHIANS 3:10-18

Paul continues, "In fact, what had been glorious is not glorious now by comparison because of the glory that surpasses it" (v. 10). Listen, the glory of pointing to yourself, self-dependence, is over. Then he tells us to make way for the glory that promotes dependence. And in our society dependence is something that looks weak. It does. I mean, Christ did look weak on the cross, didn't he? Even when he was on the cross, they were saying, "If you are who you say, do this: prove who you are by what you do. Get down with all power if you are powerful."

Paul says, "For if what was set aside was glorious, what endures will be even more glorious" (v. 11). This is wonderful! This idea of endurance, permanence—it's powerful to get this in your head as a believer. What Paul says about the fading old covenant and permanent new covenant is like what the prophets said about the old and future temple: "The final glory of this house will be greater than the first" (Hag 2:9). That was a prophecy that had dual fulfillment because, in their day, the temple they were building was going to be smaller than Solomon's temple. For the first temple, David made elaborate preparations. Then Solomon got rich. They were making pomegranates out of gold and hanging them like ornaments in the temple. They shipped in wood, cedar, from Lebanon; that's the best wood they could ever get. It would be like for us bringing in redwood trees. Solomonic timber was highly valued.

But what made the Solomonic temple powerful? Was it the riches that made up the temple? No. What made the Solomonic temple powerful was when the glory of the *shekinah* cloud of God rested on the temple. The Bible says that as the Levites and the priests were slaughtering lambs on the altar, the glory of God was so thick they couldn't stand to minister (1 Kgs 8:10-11). In other words, they were obeying God's law, but when the glory of God came around, they had to drop everything. Everyone was floored that God was there. He was around them, everywhere around them, all in the temple. Those who were there said, "Wow, God is present!"

Eventually they had to build another one. But the temple they built wasn't going to be as expansive as the one that was built first. God had to give them a promise because those who remembered the glory of the Solomonic temple over seventy years before were depressed (Ezra 3:12). So when they heard the song Solomon's father, David, had written, many of the priests and elder heads of houses started crying while others shouted for joy. Those that wept were thinking that this temple is going to be nothing. But the younger generations haven't seen any other. All they know is that God is back, so this temple is going to be great, and they sang. The Bible says you couldn't tell the difference between the weeping and the worship (Ezra 3:13). God said, "I know this temple isn't as big as the first one. I know it doesn't have as much as the first one, but the glory of this temple will be greater than the former" (Hag 2:3-9).

Regarding Solomon's temple, Ezekiel declares that an angel came down, went into the inner court of the most holy place, lifted the glory of God from the middle of the mercy seat, went out on the threshold, and took the glory back to heaven because the people were self-reliant (Ezek 10:18-19; 11:22-23). But then about six hundred years later, after Herod had built an annex to the temple and rebuilt it, there was a boy about twelve years old who walked into the temple, and no one knew that the glory had returned because the glory was no longer in a temple made with human hands. Lord Yeshua, Jesus Christ, would become the exemplary temple.

God's glory would no longer rest on a building! It would rest on his people. Why does it rest? Because before the glory of God came, blood had to be smeared where it was going to come. So because Christ's blood was smeared on you, the Spirit has brought your life to be a tabernacle of God's presence. So let someone ask you, "Who are you?" You answer, "I'm a tabernacle of the presence of God."

Perhaps you don't yet recognize how messed up you were and are. But if you recognize the foolishness of you and the foolishness of the gospel—that in your life God would take permanent residence—you'll be amazed! If Levitical priests and Aaronic priests could go wild because the *shekinah* glory was around them, then how in the world will those respond who have the shekinah glory indwelling them, living in them? When he says, "I will never leave you or abandon you" (Heb 13:5), it's different from him just being beside you. He's in you! And he stays there! He holds on to you. He stays near you. He loves you through it all, come hell or high water. You are, and I am, a non-earning, non-self-reliant tabernacle and temple that carries the glory of God everywhere.

Now, what if we catch 3 percent of that reality? Most of us are on negative 200 percent. What if we just caught 3 percent? God's right here living inside of you. How would that impact the identity crisis of men? How would that crack open the identity crisis of women? How would that challenge the identity crisis of a person who's consumed with work? How would it change the identity crisis of the suicidal? How would it change the identity crisis of the drug addict, the adulterer, or the depressed? Ultimately, we're healed and changed because God is permanently with us and in us as believers.

Reflect and Discuss

1. How is Jesus the major difference from every other religion?
2. What are the three main categories of the Old Testament law? Explain each one.
3. What is self-reliance? Why is it negative?
4. How does God's law expose our self-reliance?
5. Why are the glory of Christ and the new covenant far better than that of the old covenant?
6. What do you think, and how do you feel, when you realize God is permanently in you?
7. How does that reality heal you and change you?

100 Percent True Gospel Ministry

2 CORINTHIANS 4:1-6

Main Idea: We must be able to discern true gospel ministry.

I. True Gospel Ministry Can Be a Heartbreaking Journey (4:1).
II. True Gospel Ministry Is Not above Healthy Gospel Evaluation (4:2-4).
III. True Gospel Ministry Exalts Jesus above the Preacher (4:5-6).

Nowadays, you can pirate almost anything, such as movies and music. Likewise, the unauthorized production of knockoff designer clothing and sneakers is widespread. I remember a swap-meet sale when I was in Texas working on my seminary degree. The sheriff came in and shut down all the unauthorized dealers. Now many clothing companies in particular have "manufacturing specialists," experts who can detect whether what you've purchased is authentic. For instance, knowledgeable specialists can determine authenticity based on the stitching because they know the genuine manufacturer and can recognize whether the quality of that manufacturer is reflected in the product that's in their hands.

The question is, Do you know the gospel when you see it? Do you know authentic gospel ministry when you see it? Do you know authentic leadership and an authentically committed church when you see it? Today, many believers are hoodwinked by hooligans, but God is calling you as a believer to be a manufacturing specialist.

As a believer, you are supposed to be able to recognize whether something is of God. You should discern gospel truth from a false gospel. You should be able to discern what is the move of the Spirit or not the move of the Spirit, and you should not be afraid to come up against false teaching. You should be a kingdom connoisseur. You should be able to confront, not ignore, when something isn't right.

In our society all this was prophesied. The Bible says in 1 Timothy 4:1-2 that many would fall away from the faith, paying attention to deceitful spirits and doctrines of demons, taught by liars whose consciences are seared. And 2 Timothy 4:3-4 says people won't tolerate or endure sound doctrine. Notice the word *endure*. To hear truth hurts sometimes, so people won't want to hear truth anymore. They don't want to hurt anymore, but truth cuts going in, and it cuts coming out. But it also heals going in, and it heals coming out because wherever the Great Physician works, he's seeking to transform. Wherever God pierces, he wants to heal. Wherever God removes, he wants to put something back in the place of it.

But we will accumulate for ourselves teachers in accordance with our own desires, wanting to have our ears tickled, falling away from truth and buying into a lie. This is prophesied. Particularly in our day and age, people don't love the truth. So Paul comes to Corinth because peddlers of the gospel are entering the Corinthian church. They're coming in as itinerant communicators—not as local shepherds to engage the needs of the Corinthians to make them better—in order to get money from them. They tell them what they want to hear rather than what they need to hear.

Now, any leader who tells you only what you want to hear, you should fear; but a leader who's not afraid to tell you everything is the one to consider following. In this text, Paul vulnerably speaks of what 100 percent true gospel ministry looks like.

True Gospel Ministry Can Be a Heartbreaking Journey
2 CORINTHIANS 4:1

I know this is not a shouting point, but it's a true point. Look at what Paul says: "Therefore, since we have this ministry." The ministry he's alluding to is not the ministry of death and ministry of condemnation in chapter 3. He's speaking of the ministry of the Spirit and the ministry of righteousness: the ministry that is produced by the Spirit and producing righteousness in the people. So the product of the Spirit's ministry is the work of the Spirit in the lives of people. The ministry is a result of what the Spirit has done, is doing, and will do. Paul's point is that the ministry isn't self-motivated or self-initiated, but it's initiated by the work of the Holy Spirit. When Paul ministered, he ministered in the Spirit; he wasn't trying to deceive people as these peddlers did.

The Holy Spirit moved, and Paul bore much fruit through the Holy Spirit's work. Paul didn't do ministry that was forced; rather, the genuine product appeared as a ministry of freedom. Scripture declares, "Where the Spirit of the Lord is, there is freedom" (2 Cor 3:17). The

Spirit produces a ministry of freedom as well as a ministry of intimacy based on 3:17-18. This transformative ministry causes us to look more like Jesus Christ. This is how you know authentic gospel ministry: it's painful because you're being chiseled often. If you feel like God just won't let you go, you're in the right true gospel place. If you can get away with anything, you're not under true gospel ministry. If you always feel good, the sun always shines, and you always get what you want, you may not be under true gospel ministry.

Being under true gospel ministry is for the Holy Spirit to suddenly pierce you at times. When you receive the work of the Spirit, it's not a depressive pain; it is a purposeful pain. When God can pierce you and you still feel his love, that's the work of the Spirit. If you feel cut and left out there, that's condemnation, not edification. The Spirit's pain piercing you is all about edification so that you can get to your godly destination. Thank God pain has purpose in our lives. The Spirit's ministry is a ministry of conviction of sin. That means you feel it when you sin. That's a good thing that you heard—before you were about to sin, when you were contriving to sin in your mind and your heart—the Holy Spirit was warning, "Wait a minute," in your heart. That's a good thing. Listen, if you have an usher instead a bouncer in your soul, you may not be his.

How important that we recognize this: the Holy Spirit also convicts of righteousness. So he's not only telling us what's wrong; he's also telling us what's right. We've been imputed with Christ's righteousness. So the ministry of righteousness pushes us toward what's right and declares that we're already empowered to do it. God doesn't tell us to train for the Christian life so that then he can invite us into it and use us. We're not like a fighter who has to make weight for the fight, as if we have to do all this work, and then the Eternal Boxing Federation will now let us fight. We don't have to make weight. Christ already made weight for us, but he does make us fight.

As the Holy Spirit's ministry produces righteousness, it also produces a redemptive disposition toward God's work in us.

Now Paul says, "We have this ministry because we were shown mercy" (v. 1). This ministry that produces righteousness is a product of a work of the Spirit; it's by the mercy of God. It reminds me of Romans 12:1: "Therefore, brothers and sisters, in view of the mercies of God, I urge you." Mercies of God—the ministry produced by the Spirit who produces righteousness is rooted in the compassion of God. Mercy doesn't just mean God doesn't give you what you deserve. It also means you're experiencing the compassion of God, and experiencing the compassion of God is powerful. That means when God looks at you in Christ and sees your sin, he has compassion for you. Broken people will come to Jesus. And Jesus looks at them and says they are like sheep without a shepherd. See, true gospel ministry doesn't dismiss you for your brokenness. How compassionate is our God! Our misunderstanding of God's ministry of compassion can lead to two extremes. One is a licentious disposition, where you can get away with everything, get drunk, and promote all kinds of foolishness as an abuse of grace. But then the other extreme is at the legalistic end where you earn your righteousness. You feel like you have to earn something all the time. So you're not able to be vulnerable with what's really going on with you because you're going to be judged harshly and not helped compassionately. Paul says it's a ministry that produces righteousness, but it's a ministry that's driven by God's compassion for those he has made and is making right.

In other words, compassion gives you the freedom to tell on yourself. As the Bible says: Get the log out of your eye first. That's called self-snitching. But there's mercy for that. You're not incriminating yourself with the disposition of the judge judging you. You can plead guilty knowing that your lawyer has already made a deal. When you tell the truth on yourself, you can do so knowing that the charges are already dropped.

Then Paul says something that exegetically seems disruptive: "We do not give up" (v. 1). Now, after all we just talked about, how in the world can you lose heart and give up? You can lose heart because true gospel ministry is hard and difficult. Paul is keeping it 100. Paul is opening you up to his pastoral heart of fighting to communicate righteous, Spirit-led, compassionate ministry to people who reject and betray him. The people you love the most have the capacity to hurt you the most.

For Paul, this is not for the Corinthians right here. He's talking about himself and his ministry team. He confesses, "To be honest, sometimes we want to lose heart. Sometimes we want to give up on ministry. We're ministering gospel truth that sets people free, and sometimes we want to call it quits." Now, the majority of men and women I know are not dishonest ministers of the gospel. Most of them are authentic ministers of the gospel, but the ones that I know are dishonest have lavished on them the love of a deceived people.

Let me just keep it 100. The people I know who actually preach the gospel are the most depressed. They're the ones who wrestle when you go after souls and when you minister to someone—when you give grocery money out of your own pocket, when you help with a bill, when you go to the hospital, when you break up a fight in a marriage, when you shepherd someone through something and to the righteousness of Christ—and when they fall away from the faith, you want to lose heart! You want to give up.

Bear with a little bit of my foolishness. Sometimes you want to say, "God, is this thing real? God, are you really at work?" You invest in someone, and they walk away from the faith. I'm not talking about leaving the church. Forget about leaving the church. I'm talking about the faith. I'm talking about, you walked away from Jesus. You can walk away from me all day but not from Jesus.

Let me make it plain. Someone took me to a steak house I couldn't afford. I got the rib eye because I love rib eye. Another person at the table had filet mignon—a grade-A, six-month-aged steak. He pulls out a bottle of A1 steak sauce and ketchup. Anyone who knows steaks knows you only need a little salt, a little pepper, maybe a little butter, and it's good. But he was putting something on it that's below it. It wasn't the quality up to par with the steak itself.

Your response to gospel ministry should be transformation. But if it's not transformation, you're putting something on the truth that's below the truth. You're putting ketchup on eternal filet mignon.

In other words, some people seem to think that the only way we can eat it is if it's drowned in stuff that shouldn't be on it. Nobody should have to drown the gospel for you to consume the gospel.

True Gospel Ministry Is Not above Healthy Gospel Evaluation
2 CORINTHIANS 4:2-4

We twist texts like "Touch not my anointed" (see Ps 105:15) and "Judge not that you be not judged" (see Matt 7:1). But we need to ask, What do the texts really say?

All Paul is doing here is disclosing ministry insight, so we can carefully discern what's of God and what's not of God. Paul says, "Instead, we have renounced secret and shameful things, not acting deceitfully or distorting the word of God" (v. 2). See, there are times when you get to the point where you say, "This is true, so I have to endure, God. I'm still discouraged, but I'm going to press for it." This is Paul's way of talking to us from his heart right now. And he says, "Let me give you the character of my ministry." Paul is angry now—righteously angry. He says he and his team had given up secret and shameful ways. This idea of "renounced" means to express strong disapproval and to distance yourself from it. The idea of "shameful" means dishonor and shame as a feeling that someone would get if you executed the ministry wrong. He said his team was filled with disgust at those who distort the Word of God. You have to be disgusted with anything that would mess up the gospel. I remember my wife and I went to a couple's house for dinner. They were a health-conscious couple. After the meal, they offered us pound cake and ice cream. We were delighted! However, when we bit into it, my wife and I paused. It tasted different from what we were accustomed to. They immediately said, "Do you notice anything different?" They stated, "Yeah, we didn't use butter; we used applesauce." I said, "It's a cake but not a pound cake. Pound cake is called by that name because it has a pound of butter in it." Once you remove that main ingredient, you no longer have a pound cake but something else. Whenever you remove any ingredient from the gospel, it is no longer the gospel; it's something else. You don't tamper with it.

Paul said we don't disgrace ourselves. We renounced those things. We know we can have more stuff. We know we can drive bigger cars. We know we could have bigger houses. We know we can have expensive clothes. We know we can do this. We know we can do that. But we renounce that because of what that could cause. He says we don't tamper. He said we don't practice cunning.

Listen to what 2 Peter says about false teachers:

> *They will exploit you in their greed with made-up stories. Their*
> *condemnation, pronounced long ago, is not idle, and their destruction*
> *does not sleep. . . .*
>
> *But these people, like irrational animals—creatures of*
> *instinct born to be caught and destroyed—slander what they do*
> *not understand, and in their destruction they too will be destroyed.*
> *They will be paid back with harm for the harm they have done. They*
> *consider it a pleasure to carouse in broad daylight. They are spots and*
> *blemishes, delighting in their deceptions while they feast with you. They*
> *have eyes full of adultery that never stop looking for sin. They seduce*
> *unstable people and have hearts trained in greed. Children under a*
> *curse!* (2 Pet 2:3,12-14)

That's in the Bible! Paul is saying, "We refuse to do that. We refuse to tamper with God's Word. We refuse to dilute what God says."

Paul says, "We have renounced secret and shameful things" (v. 2). Paul is saying, "We refuse to practice this type of cunning and working with people to essentially take their resources from them. We would rather do things biblically, honorably, and holistically that reflect the heart of God." See, true gospel ministry is the willingness to take a "loss" so that people can have a "win."

He says, "[We are] commending ourselves before God to everyone's conscience" (v. 2). How amazing! Paul says that we open ourselves up to the godly, not the foolish, because the foolish are people who only want to criticize, but they don't do any ministry, don't join the ministry, don't give, and don't help. So we open ourselves up to the givers, the helpers who are redeemed by the renewing power of the gospel, whether they are infant, intermediate, or mature Christians. He admits, "We open ourselves up in your sight to look in and evaluate whether we're functioning in a 100 percent true gospel ministry. And we invite criticism that is honorable and godly."

If you find any leader who pushes away criticism quickly, you should run. I'm not speaking of dismissing someone who's a conspiracy theorist—that's in a minority—but of rejecting people who really have a heart for whether we're ministering and walking in an honorable way. Paul expresses, "Listen, we open ourselves up to all that because we want you to be trained in knowing what's right and true." He says, "We open ourselves up, not only to you, but we open ourselves up in the sight of God because we almost connect the sight of God to your insight into our ministry. If it's based on biblical godly criticism, that can improve me and improve God's mission."

How powerful that Paul would open himself up. A lot of people say they've seen Jesus, and you can't tell them anything. They say, "I've seen the Lord. He came and talked to me in the basement and asked for some coffee. I saw eight visions of Jesus." Instead, Paul gives a sense in which there's this great openness. He observes, "But if our gospel is veiled, it is veiled to those who are perishing" (v. 3). In other words, it shouldn't be veiled to you. The only people who can't see authentic gospel ministry are people who don't know Jesus.

The point of the verse is that our gospel is only veiled to those who don't know Christ, who are perishing. Every believer, even if you are a babe—you might not have all the diagnostics of a mature Christian, but you still have that little inkling of something that the Holy Spirit is just pinching at you letting you know something isn't right. That's the Spirit talking to you. You may not have a didactic communication from a verse or a commentary or some historic classical texts, but because you have Jesus, you have just enough to ask questions.

You'd say something like this: "I know I'm young in the faith, and I can be ignorant, but can you biblically explain that to me?" And if anyone were to say, "How dare you touch the man of God? How dare you ask the man of God anything," then it would be a problem; run!

Consider how the devil works. He works through false ministers tampering with the text. If you circumvent or add to the Scriptures, you're a liar and disgraceful, and you need to get out of the ministry. True gospel ministers invite redemptive criticism. If you are a Christian, even a new Christian, the veil is no longer over your eyes. Even in your infant state, you're able to see true gospel ministry. That's the point of the verse: you don't have to be a mature Christian to know what's gospel and what's not. If you don't hear for weeks at a time in church or ministry that Christ died, Christ was buried, and Christ was raised; if you don't hear that you're righteous and you remain righteous by Christ; if someone says, "Come to me and do what I say, take care of me, do my stuff," then you're under the wrong ministry.

If you're constantly told that the only way you'll grow is by faith alone and grace alone through Christ alone, and that's heralded; if it's in the songs, teaching, preaching, life group, and Bible study, then you're in the 100 percent true gospel ministry. The gospel must be heralded everywhere.

True Gospel Ministry Exalts Jesus above the Preacher
2 CORINTHIANS 4:5-6

Paul writes, "For we are not proclaiming ourselves" (v. 5). We don't preach ourselves. We don't get up in front of you saying, "I got this. I got that. Be like me." The problem is that's preaching *man*. Yes, in 1 Corinthians 11:1 Paul says, "Imitate me," but then he adds, "as I also imitate Christ." He points you to *Christ*; he's not pointing to himself. He's not like some preachers who say, "Be like me, do like me. My marriage is perfect. My parenting is perfect." That's not the preaching people need to hear.

I'll be quick to say, my wife and I argue every week and need the redemptive faculties of Christ. So follow me in repenting. Paul is saying, "We don't preach ourselves. We don't preach our example." If every illustration points to the life of the preacher, he's preaching himself. If the *Spirit* is not the means for his communication, what can he do for you? Nothing. Paul says, "We are not proclaiming ourselves but Jesus Christ as Lord" (v. 5).

He inferentially communicates something more: we are not to preach to control people.

We preach "Jesus Christ as Lord" because he's *kurios.* He's Lord; he's the sovereign ruler. The goal is to point you to him so that your life can be controlled by his lordship. The purpose of true gospel ministry is exalting Jesus as enthroned at the right hand of God, exalting him who is so majestic, glorious, powerful, omniscient, omnipresent, omnipotent, gracious, merciful, loving, and worthy!

When you see Jesus, you forget about the preacher. "I don't even hear him; all I hear is Jesus." So we don't preach ourselves, but we preach Jesus Christ as Lord. We're only a footnote. Then he adds, "And ourselves as your servants for Jesus's sake" (v. 5). We're a footnote. True gospel ministry has the preacher as the footnote and Jesus as the main body of the text. We need to be pointed to the cosmic Lord who makes all things new. Let us open our eyes and see our Lord.

We had a legendary Chinese carryout in my old neighborhood, known for their egg rolls. The egg rolls were crispy and soft, with cabbage and little pieces of meat inside. People would drive from miles away just for this place. But when you see a picture of it, you're thinking, "You want me to go in there and get some food? You mean to tell me that all the delicacies you're talking about are in there?" They haven't changed the building in fifty years. But people come in suits and sagging jeans to get delicacies they grew up on.

Be careful that you don't judge true gospel ministry based on the external. The question is, What's being cooked in the kitchen?

Reflect and Discuss

1. In what ways is the Holy Spirit at work in your life to convict you of sin?
2. How does it make you feel to know that when God looks at you in Christ, he has compassion toward you?

3. When have you been hurt and tempted to lose heart (be discouraged or depressed)?
4. Does the leadership you're under act in cunning, deceitful ways or honest, transparent ways? If you're a leader, how do you tend to act?
5. Why is criticism hard to receive at times?
6. Is the leadership you're under willing to receive healthy criticism? If you're a leader, are you willing to receive healthy criticism?
7. Does the church you're a part of exalt Jesus Christ and preach the gospel? If you're a preacher, do you preach the gospel of Jesus Christ?
8. What is the gospel of Jesus Christ?

100 Percent Brokenness

2 CORINTHIANS 4:7-11

Main Idea: God wants you to be broken so you'll depend on him and reflect Jesus.

If You're Going to Be 100 Percent Broken, You Must Know This:

I. **God Puts Power in the Vessel (4:7).**
II. **God Puts Pressure on the Vessel (4:8-9).**
    A. God loves to break up your plans.
    B. God loves to break up your will.
III. **God Promotes Jesus through the Vessel (4:10).**
IV. **God Has a Purpose for the Vessel (4:11-18).**

My MacBook, iPhone, and iPad form, in a sense, a technological trinity. Each is designed to be able to be synced. Once you have a new device, it syncs with all your others. The manufacturer makes sure the product is user-friendly. There's nothing worse than buying something and then discovering it's extremely difficult to figure out. You almost feel like you have to get a degree before you can connect with it. The manufacturer makes these products user-friendly. Similarly, God made us to be user-friendly. But because of the fall, we're hard to use. We're difficult to be used in the handiwork of our God because of our mess. But when you come to know Jesus Christ as Savior, you move back to user-friendly status.

However, you're practically unusable. God has to do things in your life to continue to take away the complexities of your mess and my mess so that we may be properly maximized and used for his honor and glory. We come to this text where Paul talks about the user-friendliness of his life. Throughout this book, he's being honest and he's keeping it real. Now, when we talk about keeping it real, it isn't so that we won't walk in holiness. Sometimes when people say they're just being real or keeping it 100, they mean, "I'm going to just show my mess without change or evidence of redemption." But when you keep it biblically real, you show your mess, or your mess is exposed, so that it can be changed in your life.

In this text, Paul is being honest about the difficulties and challenges of his life. Conversely, we'll see in chapter 11 the people the Corinthians esteem as impressive, whom Paul will call "super-apostles." Paul says, "I'm not like them. I don't have their wealth and followers. But let me tell you what qualifies me to be used by the Lord: brokenness." Brokenness is what God uses as a means. That's a consistent state in your life, in my life, that is a disposition God can use. The psalm says, "The LORD is near the brokenhearted; he saves those crushed in spirit" (Ps 34:18). That psalm points to us euphemistically: we are the brokenhearted; we are the crushed in spirit. We can look at it in comparison to Paul's passage because Psalm 34 (and 51) speaks of brokenness. God desires to be near broken people.

Now, what does it mean to be broken? Brokenness in the Scriptures means shattered, crushed, maimed, devoid of arrogance, wounded, contrite, injured, smashed, grieved, anxious, distressed, crippled, wrecked, demolished, fractured, handicapped, and disabled.

No one wants to be in that state. Brokenness is the spiritual state by which one is disarmed of one's self-dependence and pride, leaving us disabled yet enabled. It's a paradox. We're left in desperate need of help. Sometimes God puts you in something desperate to draw out desperation in you.

God Puts Power in the Vessel

2 CORINTHIANS 4:7

If you're going to be 100 percent broken, this is one of the first things you must know. Paul says, "Now we have this treasure in clay jars"—some translations say "earthen vessels"—"so that this extraordinary power may be from God and not from us." So God put treasure in jars of clay.

Why is this significant? We must understand that clay jars were the lowest level of vessels in biblical times. They had gold vessels then. They had silver vessels and bronze vessels. If a thief came into someone's home and saw those vessels, he would believe something was in it because the vessel was valuable. In other words, "Nice vessel, nice treasure." But God reverses that. In fact, clay vessels were vessels used for refuse. That was their toilet. So if a thief came into a house and saw a clay jar, he wouldn't think valuable things were in it. Matter of fact, he would stay far away from it! But God puts valuable things in messy places. When God says he puts this treasure in clay jars, do you know you are a messy vessel? You cannot allow yourself to base your identity on the vessel of your beauty. Your value is based on the treasure that's inside of you.

Now, the question is, what's the treasure? The gospel is the treasure—the death, burial, and resurrection of Christ as the deposit and the work of the Spirit. Remember, the ministry of the Spirit that's produced by the Spirit and the ministry of righteousness are already inside of you. God doesn't work on your life from the outside in. He always works on you from the inside out. The struggles you go through are not around you; they're actually in you. The greatest struggle is not what's around you but rather your reaction to what it does inside of you. So in order for God to get the best out of you, it's not getting the best *you* out of you. God isn't about the best of you. He's about the best *him* in you.

In other words, God sets it up in such a way that the vessel isn't as impressive as his glory. God intends for there to be a gap between what people think about you and what he thinks about you. See, that's the might of the gospel. The might of the gospel is to amaze us to the point of realizing that the Spirit of God himself is in us. Your life's mission is for God to get the image inside of you out of you.

I remember a conversation I had with a sculptor I knew. I asked him, "How do you grab a rock and chisel an image?"

He said, "Pastor, that's not the way I think about it."

I replied, "What do you mean?"

He said, "Pastor, you see a rock. I see an image inside the rock. I'm just trying to get the stuff on top of the rock off of it so that the image that's already in it can be seen."

What God is doing in your life, through the challenges you go through—the chiseling, cleansing, pruning, brokenness, hurt, depression, and shame—what he's trying to do is pull all the stuff off of you so the Christ who is in you can be seen!

Many times in our life we can misinterpret pain. However, a gospel that doesn't have suffering and challenges is not a biblical idea. If you told the early church that gospel, they'd have been in trouble. Some of you don't think you need to be broken. Many of you fake it and act like everything is OK with you. But guess what? That means you need to be broken.

What type of people need to be broken?

Overly independent: The overly independent person thinks he can do everything on his own. The triune Godhead says, "Look at him. He thinks he can live without us. We saved him, and now he needs no one. We have to schedule some suffering for him."

An overly independent person often declares, "I'm gonna do me." And when you do you, God is going to do something to you because the manufacturer never wants what he created to think it can function without him. If you're too independent, you think you don't need anyone. "I don't need the church. I don't need family. I don't need community. I don't need a man. I don't need a woman. I don't need this or that." You have the "I-don't-need-anything mentality" that's quite common in our culture.

Overdependent: This is the reverse. You can be too independent or too overdependent. When you need anyone else or anything else more than you need God, he's going to break you by starving you of the thing you try to plug into that's not him. That's how it works.

Prayerless: You just get on with your day. You don't pray anymore.

Dry-eyed: You don't cry anymore. When nothing can get to you, you need to be broken.

Secretive: Nobody knows you. It's hard to get to know you.

Unteachable: You know everything. When somebody's trying to teach you something, you say, "I already researched that." You just have something to say every time.

I could keep going. Paul says treasure is placed in messy, breakable clay jars "so that this extraordinary power may be from God and not from us" (v. 7).

God Puts Pressure on the Vessel
2 CORINTHIANS 4:8-9

God puts power in the vessel first, but then he puts pressure on the vessel. In their day, when they wanted to get quickly to the treasure in that mess, they would smash the vessel like a piggy bank. God puts pressure on you through life circumstances to smash you. This is what Paul says: "We are afflicted in every way but not crushed" (v. 8). Now all the verbs in this section are interesting. They're present passive[1] participle verbs.

"Present" means it's a present reality. "Passive" means it happens *to* you, not *by* you. "Participle" points to the fact that it's a continuous description of your life. That is, a Christian's life is described by affliction, by crushing. Now I know that's not building your self-worth. God

---

[1] The verbs are formally middle but functionally passive.

is not about building self-worth. He's about showing you his worth. "Afflicted in every way" means surrounded by crisis. It points to everything happening to you at the same time in every area of your life. Have you ever had a point in your life where everything seemed to be going wrong? One of my favorite movie series is the Riddick series— *Pitch Black* and *The Chronicles of Riddick*. Once, Riddick had a hard day. This entire planet dissolved into chaos and was coming after him. Animals and everything were coming after him. And he said, "There are bad days, and then there are legendary bad days." Great statement! Have you ever felt like this is a legendary bad day? This is one for the books. Everything happened today, and it's so bad you can't even cry; you just laugh. You're saying, "God, really?"

God sometimes allows things to all go wrong. As a matter of fact, sometimes it's not the devil. When God sends a trial into your life, it's unrebukable. It won't stop until he says stop. This is "afflicted in every way but not crushed." In other words, we're not smashed apart, but we do have a lot hitting us right now. The things going on in my life right now are frustrating and confusing, but they are all tools of brokenness.

Next, he says, "We are perplexed but not in despair" (v. 8). Perplexity is something happening to you, and you're confused. You don't lose hope, but you just say, "God, why is this happening to me?" That is a normal reaction. Despairing is the loss of hope, though. In other words, when you lose hope, you can't grow. But you can't let what you go through make you lose hope. That's why the Bible says,

> *Consider it a great joy, my brothers and sisters, whenever you experience various trials, because you know that the testing of your faith produces endurance. And let endurance have its full effect, so that you may be mature and complete, lacking nothing.*
> *Now if any of you lacks wisdom, he should ask God—who gives to all generously and ungrudgingly—and it will be given to him.* (Jas 1:2-5)

So perplexity means, "God, I don't know why this is happening." But then if you count it all joy by not losing hope, you ask for wisdom. Wisdom is perspective in the midst of perplexity.

So God won't tell you why. He'll tell you what. Your deliverance isn't being delivered the way you want it. But God's deliverance means getting perspective. David says in Psalm 4:1, "You have given me relief when I was in distress" (ESV). Don't miss the preposition "in." God didn't take David *out of* his trial for him to feel delivered. See, too many preachers preach about your deliverance as removal from hurtful circumstances. I'm not saying don't pray for people to get healed. I believe God heals. However, sometimes deliverance is knowing that God is still good even *in* the trial. The deliverance may only involve holding on just a little while longer. Deliverance may look like clinging to a mustard seed of faith even though God didn't take you out of suffering. Deliverance may look like not losing your mind in the midst of it. Deliverance may just be God's peace in the midst of chaos. It may be only that, but you don't realize that's enough. And the beauty of it is, you can be worked on at that point. You can't be worked on if you are trying to work on yourself. How amazing that God paradoxically allows the mess of life to be the means by which he works on and develops us.

One of my favorite television shows was *Pimp My Ride*. Xzibit would show up at your house, and your car would be a complete mess. But Xzibit would take your car to a place where it would be stripped completely. Interestingly, he always worked on the inside of the car before he worked on the outside, because if you first saw the outside being stripped, you'd become discouraged.

Perhaps you are looking at your life while God is pulling and tearing some stuff out of it. But you have to wait until he finishes. Perplexity says, "God, it's painful, but I see what you have to do. God, it's hurting, but I know it's going to be better. God, weeping may endure for a night, but joy comes in the morning!" (see Ps 30:5). Don't let the process mess up what God is trying to develop in you.

Paul says next, "We are persecuted but not abandoned; we are struck down but not destroyed" (v. 9). All these things happening to you now, this is the persecution, which is the Satan part. Can you imagine going through the God-working-on-you part, then on top of that the Satan part? But God is using Satan as a means. Satan thinks he's trying to destroy you, but God is using Satan as a foolish imbecile, as a means for your spiritual growth.

Satan's desire is to get you to commit apostasy. Satan's desire is to get you to deny God and not see the goodness of God. But because you're renewed by the gospel based on verses 2 and 3, it says you can see now. So the unbeliever is veiled to the work of the gospel, but the person who knows Christ is not veiled. Therefore, you have the visual cortex based on the renewing power of the Spirit to see that God is up to something. Consider some things God likes to break.

God Loves to Break Up Your Plans

God seems most often to break up our plans. Now, we're supposed to plan because God doesn't plan for us. He *has plans* for us, but we need to *make plans* for our lives too. So it's good to have plans, but God likes to break them up because the Bible says, "A person's heart plans his way, but the LORD determines his steps" (Prov 16:9). How good to know we have a divine editor we can lay our plans before.

When I was in my freshman year at college, I wrote a paper in English class. I knew I aced it. I knew I did good on it. I was thinking, "Bam! Take that, teacher!" Then I went back to my seat, crossed my legs, and looked and felt good. But when I got the paper back, I couldn't see what I wrote. That paper was bleeding!

I was depressed, trying to find an exit door. The teacher saw my depression. She said, "Eric, I want you to do something for me. Just correct where you see red, give it back to me, and I'll give you full credit."

When you lay your plans before God, the divine editor edits with the blood of Christ. All he's asking you to do is hand it back to him when you've allowed the blood to be applied to your plan. I'm glad God is merciful in that way. Don't get mad when you see God's edits on your life. Don't get frustrated when you see God working on your life. All you have to do is see the blood of Christ covering your plans.

God Loves to Break Up Your Will

When some of us are stubbornly determined and God says, "I'm going to break it now," how does he do it? Ask Jonah. God said, "Jonah, go to Nineveh." Then Jonah went down away from the presence of the Lord. He chartered a boat. He paid to go away from God's presence. He banked his resources and his will on the boat's ability to take him away from God's presence. God in heaven is sitting on his throne, watching Jonah. The triune God is thinking, "This guy's moving around like I'm not everywhere. I already know where he's going. I know what it's going to take to get there. I even know how many waves there are between where he is and where he's going. And he thinks he can run from us!"

So God the Father stands up off his throne, and he puts on his hat—he puts it on backwards—and he puts his glove on his hand and steps onto the mound. The angels were chanting, "Go, go, go, go, go!" And God spits over here and spits over there. He looks back and goes, whoosh! The text says God literally hurled a storm onto the sea. The

Bible says the storm was so tumultuous the ship began to break apart. The thing that you put your hopes on, God anoints a specific storm to break it apart. He's breaking it so that he can break you. That's what he does. That's his work. But perhaps you may be asking, "Why would God put me through all this?"

God Promotes Jesus through the Vessel
2 CORINTHIANS 4:10

When you are broken, the spaces in your life open to show the treasure that's in the vessel. Where you are when you're broken is where God wants to show Jesus. Exactly where he's hurting you is where he wants to reveal the Son. Look at this text. Notice the active present participle by which we actively in the present identify our lives as this: "Always carrying in the body the death of Jesus" (v. 10 ESV). That means you're always carrying around brokenness. You're always carrying around a disposition to show off Jesus Christ. We need to see that the brokenness God causes in our lives has a purpose.

This passage reminds me of a friend who ran forty yards in 4.2 seconds. He had incredible speed. He could run *fast*. One day in practice, one of the defensive players on his team hit him in a bad way and broke his leg. He's so angry that his leg was broken that he didn't feel the pain of it. And he's angry, angry. Then the doctor works on him, puts the cast on, and tells him he'll be out for the season. He's angry, and he asks the doctor, "Will I ever be able to play again?"

He replies, "It's interesting that you asked that question." He says, "When something gets broken the way your leg did and it heals right, the place where it's broken is stronger after the breakage than before the breakage."

Do you know that your God is allowing you to hurt so badly, to be frustrated so mightily, because he's trying to make you stronger in the place where he pains you? At the place where he wounds you, in the place where he prunes you, in the place that he breaks you, in the place that he challenges you, he's trying to make you better!

There's a "but not" in every section of this passage. The "but not" means God has a limitation on how bad he'll let it get. In other words, you're in pain but not as much pain as it could be. You may be persecuted, but he says, "But not." You say, "I'm afflicted," but God has a "but not" for you.

Look at Job. The devil came before God, and God said, "Have you considered my main man, Job?" He said, "You can touch everything he has *but not* him." Then the devil comes back, and God says, "You can touch him *but not* kill him." In other words, he gets a ticket to the concert but not a backstage pass.

Be encouraged that God is at work. God is going to change you. God is going to build you up. God is going to work it all out for good for those who love him and are called according to his purpose (see Rom 8:28). You can cry. You can scream. You can shout. But I promise you that God has got you! It's hard. But he's got you. It's painful, but he's got you. He's working, but he's got you. It's falling apart, but he's got you! Because of what Christ has done for you, there's a limitation on what this broken world can place on you!

God Has a Purpose for the Vessel
2 CORINTHIANS 4:11-18

The apostle continues to drive home the idea that his sufferings are a sign of his authentic apostleship. He not only describes the nature of his sufferings and the extent of them, but he also talks about the results. The principle of Paul's sufferings and their results are in some sense universal to all believers in suffering. "For we who live are always being given over to death for Jesus's sake, so that Jesus's life may also be displayed in our mortal flesh" (v. 11). Here Paul speaks of the fact that suffering exposes the character of Jesus through our clay vessels. Jesus is the treasure in the vessel, and like a fragile piggy bank full of money, when the vessel is broken, it provides access to the treasure. When we are broken, our Lord is seen through us.

In closing the section, Paul shows that trouble won't last always:

Therefore we do not give up. Even though our outer person is being destroyed, our inner person is being renewed day by day. For our momentary light affliction is producing for us an absolutely incomparable eternal weight of glory. (vv. 16-17)

Paul wants them to be encouraged that God's glory is bigger than the brokenness in their story. One commentator gives an excellent exegetical breakdown of this:

Momentary troubles are "light"—that is, insignificant—
compared to "eternal glory." The Hebrew word for "glory"
speaks in part of weightiness or heaviness. For emphasis,
Paul adds to the word "glory" the Greek word *baros*, which
also could be used to speak of fullness or weightiness, but
also of something being of significance or importance.
He stacks up terms to show the "massiveness" of glory that
makes his suffering seem paltry by comparison. (Guthrie,
"2 Corinthians," 1136)

Suffering at times can feel lonely, painful, and purposeless. It can
take your focus off the purposes of God being worked out. One year my
wife went into the hospital twelve times, adding up to about two months
of hospitalizations. Then 2020 was the worst year of my ministry, and
I got morbidly obese and gained all kinds of illnesses. I had to go to
therapy and go through a ton of healing. I finally treated my weight loss
journey as a spiritual journey versus a fitness goal. It wasn't until after I
was able to change my perspective on suffering that I was able to break
free of my immature responses to my suffering. God breaks us to build
us, not to destroy us.

Reflect and Discuss

1. In your own words, what does it mean to be in a state of brokenness?
2. Why is brokenness a state in which God can then use us?
3. In what ways has God been empowering you through the power of
   the gospel and his Spirit?
4. Are you a type of person who still needs to be broken? If so, in
   what ways?
5. What hardship, pain, or suffering has God been allowing in
   your life to make you more dependent on him?
6. Has God ever broken up your plans? If so, what happened?
7. How have struggles shifted your perspective on God's deliverance?
8. In what ways has what you've gone through allowed Jesus Christ to
   be more promoted through you and your life?

Being Convinced of Eternal Realities

2 CORINTHIANS 5:1-10

Main Idea: Realize that Jesus is the only way for you to understand everything so you can be convinced of eternal realities.

I. **Jesus Is the Only Way to Understand Everything (5:1).**
II. **It's Okay to Be Sick of This World at Times (5:2).**
III. **Our Eternal Hope in Christ Gives Us Courage (5:3-5).**
IV. **We Are Eternally Accountable (5:6-10).**

The inner city in America is part of a complex urban setting often challenged by crime and difficulties.

God has called us to incarnate as local, national, and international missions and leaders to engage these communities from wherever we are. Many times, we don't know the apologetic realities that plague the philosophies of people in such contexts because of the sociological and economic conditions many face. Everyone is trying to work through the reality of identity, but it is not just an African American issue. Even if you didn't have to go through the trans-Atlantic slave trade, you struggle with who you are in the world. As a matter of fact, your parents may have been immigrants to this country, and you're still struggling with who you are. You may have grown up in the best household, you may be getting the best degree you can, but you are still struggling with questions: Who am I? Where do I come from? Why am I here? Is there life after death? What matters the most? What makes me happy? Is there anything out there or anyone out there for me? Is God real?

Everyone wrestles with these issues. But interestingly enough, God has fashioned the souls of human beings, according to Ecclesiastes 3:11. God has placed eternity in our hearts. Now, what does that mean, and what does it have to do with this passage? This verse suggests, as Scripture makes plain elsewhere, that even though we're totally depraved in our sin, we're not fully living out the depravity of our sin. Indeed, God has designed our souls so that we want something or know that something bigger is out there, but we're unable to reach and take hold of it on our own. Thus, we create "eternity substitutes" in our lives. And when you create eternity substitutes, you create mythologies, pathologies, and idolatries that move you further away from the living God.

As a believer, no matter what your ethnicity is, there is nothing wrong with seeking your ethnic identity to understand it and where you came from. I believe that's a part of God creating you artistically to know geographically where you came from—and so that you can know the message you need to be sanctified of in light of your family.

However, Paul is challenging us as believers to let our identity be driven by an eternal perspective. Having this perspective, says Paul, and especially in the midst of suffering, helps shape us and convince us of eternal realities. Moreover, you must know that Jesus is the only way for you to understand life if you're going to be convinced of eternal realities.

Jesus Is the Only Way to Understand Everything
2 CORINTHIANS 5:1

Paul is pointing to the fact that we are in a glorious state of God, giving us the ability in our faith to be convinced of some things. The believer has the ability to be convinced.

Do you remember those mythologies you grew up with? Many of those mythologies were created to distance people and keep them from the church. They were essentially saying that all the church cares about is getting your money and then making you think about the sweet by-and-by—that the gospel doesn't offer any type of enjoyment now, only in eternity.

Paul says that it's about both. The knowledge of eternal realities impacts your mission and commitment in the present. So he states, "For we know that if our earthly tent we live in is destroyed, we have a building from God, an eternal dwelling in the heavens, not made with hands." This idea of "tent" is a play on words because he could have just said "body." But he uses the word "tent" *both* culturally and theologically here.

He's pointing to the Hellenistic understanding of the tent culture of their day. Tents would be put up, tents would be taken down, and they were easily destroyed because tents were always made to be temporary. Tents were not made to be a long-term place where you establish a family.

Tents point back to the tent of meeting in the Old Testament, which was a temporary dwelling place of God. Paul transposes that reality to this text. He's speaking to people who are being beat up by life, who are feeling the impact of a hellacious planet that's not hell. He wants the people to recognize that trouble won't last always. By saying that, he's helping God's people build the framework for recognizing why life is challenging now.

He gives them a footing now that is not about human prosperity on earth. Because if you only promise people prosperity on earth, you miss it. Something in us makes us believe that if we have more, we'll feel better about ourselves. Something in us believes that the quality of our life is better based on our needs being met—if I can experience an overwhelming amount of greed gratification, I'll be happy. But Paul says there's no level of earthly provision that can quench the thirst of an eternal soul.

As Paul walks us through this reality, he's challenging believers not to be worldly in their disposition but godly. He says we have a building from God, a house not made with hands, eternal in the heavens. God has an eternal coat rack in heaven. A rack of outfits called bodies, clothes already on them, just hanging there. Your new body is hanging in heaven. It's eternal, awaiting you proleptically—in anticipation of your arrival.

It's OK to Be Sick of This World at Times
2 CORINTHIANS 5:2

Scripture says you and I have an eternal tent. Because God renewed your soul, it is uncomfortable in this body. In other words, your body and your soul aren't programmed to properly coexist together. So you're going to struggle here because this is not who you really are, and you're going to get sick of it.

Paul acknowledges, "Indeed, we groan in this tent." Now let me ask you, do you groan in your body? Most of us have become so spiritually comfortable on earth that we don't feel the groan that we need to feel here. We may feel complacent. But Paul suggests we should experience a soul discomfort that makes us discontented with being here. Paul says, "We groan"—meaning we vocally express pain, discomfort, or displeasure, which is even inarticulate at times. You make an involuntary facial sign or a groan that shows you're not okay with being here.

What in this world are you sick of? I'm sick of political leaders who refuse to live up to God's Word. I'm sick of the hardship of the poor having no opportunities open to them. I'm sick of racism, the denial of the existence of racism, the lack of unity in the church. I'm sick of bad weather, allergies, and sinus infections. Those should make you groan. I'm sick of divorce, sick of broken relationships, and sick of depression. What makes you groan? Does anything? Every now and then your soul should have sackcloth and ashes on it. The Bible says that creation groans in pain for the revelation of the sons of God. In other words, trees and weather scream, "Maranatha, Lord!" It's as if you're a teenager living in your parents' house and wanting to be out on your own: "I can't wait to get out of here!"

Believers should have a similar feeling being on earth. Paul says we have this passion, "desiring to put on our heavenly dwelling" (v. 2). So our heavenly dwelling is recreated to be properly synced up—the new body with the soul. Your soul is longing for the new body. There is supposed to be this longing disposition. You're not longing for the body. You're longing for the removal of that which impedes full, maximum enjoyment of Jesus Christ.

We're here on earth like the deer and antelope in the wilderness. I don't know if you watch the National Geographic channel. The antelope go to the water hole to drink, and it's real quiet. We are just like them. They go down, they drink, but their eyes continue looking all around. Behind them are lions, and coming toward them are alligators. So you can't even drink—the alligator is trying to get you, and the lions are trying to get you, and you've got to run off. You should be like the antelope. You should be saying, "I'm sick of this. I can't even drink water in peace. Can't have a baby in peace. Can't move the herd in peace." Now I'm not speaking about complaining all the time, but every now and then you need to acknowledge your discomfort with earth.

Our Eternal Hope in Christ Gives Us Courage
2 CORINTHIANS 5:3-5

Then Paul writes, "We will not be found naked" (v. 3). Here he points to two things. One, Greek culture was comfortable with nudity. Nudity was everywhere in Greek culture—statues, art, Olympic Games, and even walking around topless. Jewish culture wasn't as comfortable with pervasive nudity. Nudity became regular because, for the Greeks, being unclothed was natural. But for the believer being clothed was natural.

Two, Genesis says Adam and Eve were naked and unashamed because, even though they were physically nude, they were spiritually clothed. The first thing they did when they fell spiritually was to cover themselves, and what they covered themselves with had to die. Naked and unashamed means free from exploitation, not worrying about emotional brokenness but freely enjoying the covering of God. Paul says, we won't be found naked. In other words, we won't be found lacking the might of God's glory through the Lord, Jesus Christ, in our new bodies. The assumption is that when we become clothed, we're never afraid of exploitation again. We're never afraid of emotional brokenness ever again because of what Christ has done for us.

Paul writes, "Indeed, we groan while we are in this tent, burdened as we are, because we do not want to be unclothed but clothed, so that mortality may be swallowed up by life" (v. 4). Paul encourages us to recognize and contemplate the beauty of this reality. He recognizes that we will be burdened by discomfort in this life. Then he says we don't want to be unclothed, but clothed further, so that what is mortal is swallowed up by life. The idea of the mortal being swallowed up points to God removing everything subject to death again. Anything that can destroy us and tear us apart, eventually Christ is going to get rid of fully.

However, the new body will be truly immortal, as Adam and Eve were not. Because God caused them not to eat from the tree of eternal life and expelled them, they were not eternally damned. Now we don't have to worry about living eternal lives in eternal death, but we get to live eternal life with our Lord because Jesus was raised anew. Our full redemption is practically complete once our redeemed souls are placed in our new bodies.

And Paul says, "The one who prepared us for this very purpose is God" (v. 5). Koiné Greek has a few past tenses, and here the aorist tense is a snapshot of a complete action being done in the past. The middle voice in Greek grammar means something is done for oneself. God has prepared us for himself in the past. In other words, the cross not only affects us, but God enjoys the benefit of redeeming us. God enjoys the fact that we get redeemed, and he likes to watch his cooking work.

When my wife and I were in Dallas, Texas, Wayne and Joann Mitchell took us in as their children. Mama Jo could cook. Best pound cake on this side of heaven, and she made her corn bread with pieces of corn in it. Interestingly, she would taste some of her cooking and throw it away if it wasn't right. But I would want to go in the trash can to get it because it was good by my standards. Once the food was done and laid out, she would sit back and wouldn't eat. Everyone would rush to the buffet, and she would watch and smile because she got pleasure seeing you enjoy what she had prepared for you. What she had created was being enjoyed by the people she made it for.

God has prepared these things for us. God has prepared life for us. God—through the finished work of Jesus Christ coming from heaven, coming down to earth, dying on the cross, being lifted up from the grave with all power in his hands, and then our believing in that reality because the Bible says God was pleased to crush Jesus—enjoyed what he was cooking. When he sees you turn from sin, he's enjoying himself. When he sees you healing from brokenness, he's enjoying himself. When he sees you walking through pain, he's enjoying himself. Your survival is God's pleasure. The Westminster Shorter Catechism says that the chief end of man is to glorify God and enjoy him forever. But the chief reality of God is to be glorified always and enjoy himself and the products of his glory forever.

We Are Eternally Accountable
2 CORINTHIANS 5:6-10

I can't tell you how many funerals this passage has been preached in over the years. I know that it came in handy at many funerals in my time. As a young pastor on staff at a historic church in Houston, Texas, I officiated and preached about thirty-four funerals in one year. So this text came in handy, particularly when there was much grief in the service. At the beginning of the chapter, Paul employed a tent as an analogy for the human body. Paul's being a tentmaker and the Corinthians' familiarity with the terminology would have allowed for him to drive home this great theological and practical point.

As today, tents in the ancient world were both insecure and impermanent. In Isaiah 38:12 the prophet speaks of death in terms of taking down a tent. In verse 2 Paul used the twin images of a "building" and a "dwelling" or house to speak of the resurrection body as a permanent place to live. "Not made with hands" is common biblical language for something only God can build (Guthrie, "2 Corinthians," 1136).

Here he transitions to say "body" instead of "tent." He is letting them know that while we are here on earth our lifestyle should reflect the place and status of our ultimate citizenship, heaven. Paul states, "Therefore, whether we are at home or away, we make it our aim to be pleasing to him" (v. 9). Because of the Corinthians' immaturity and carnality, he is encouraging them to know that their body is a tool for God's glory, not a tool of mischief and savagery. Over and over throughout both letters, he says this to them in different ways: "You were bought at a price. So glorify God with your body" (1 Cor 6:20); "So, whether you eat or drink, or whatever you do, do everything for the glory of God" (1 Cor 10:31). Here Paul elicits accountability. Yes, eternal accountability.

He is clear that "we must all appear before the judgment seat of Christ, so that each may be repaid for what he has done in the body, whether good or evil" (2 Cor 5:10). This is one of the most haunting verses in all of Scripture. Believers won't stand in front of the great white throne of judgment because that is about salvation (Rev 20:11). "The judgment seat of Christ" is about sanctification, not justification.

The *judgment seat* (*bēma*) was a raised platform mounted by steps and sometimes furnished with a seat, used by officials in addressing an assembly or making pronouncements, often on judicial matters. The judgment seat was a common item in Greco-Roman culture, often located in the *agora*, the public square or marketplace in the center of a city. Use of the term in reference to Christ's judgment would be familiar to Paul's 1st century readers. (NET Bible footnote)

In Acts 18:12-17 Paul actually stood before the Roman governor Gallio at the *bēma* in Corinth. I had the chance to tour the Holy Land and was able to stand at this very spot. Paul again uses a familiar iconic location in their city to convey an eternal reality. He wants the Corinthians to feel the weight of having to stand before God and give a play-by-play of their postconversion walk with Christ. His point was to let them know an eternal rewards system is connected to our every choice. The apostle's hope was that the Corinthians would receive this as the nudge they needed to take their walk with Jesus more seriously.

We need this same encouragement in our lives today. In our church culture, we need this nudge and push. We are so temporally bent that it is difficult to understand and feel the need to walk in an eternal perspective. We must use our eternal hope as a means to live with deep commitment here.

Reflect and Discuss

1. In what way(s) have you created an eternity substitute (i.e., lusted after idols)?
2. How do you replace and overcome idols?
3. Is your identity driven by an eternal perspective?
4. In what ways are you sick of this broken world?
5. Does it drive you to Christ and a desire for eternity? If so, elaborate on why.
6. How does it feel to know that God will not leave you unclothed, but instead he covers you in Christ?
7. How has God prepared and secured our eternal hope?
8. How do that eternal hope and reality give you courage and strength here and now?

Where Do You Find Your Value?

2 CORINTHIANS 5:11-15

Main Idea: Rest in the love of Christ and know that your value comes from God.

I. You Can Be Secure: Your Value Comes from God (5:11-12).
II. You Can Make Unpopular Decisions: The Love of Christ Controls You (5:13-15).

A show comes on the History Channel that I haven't watched in a while called *Pawn Stars*. This show has a notable pawn shop in Las Vegas, Nevada, where they assess the value of stuff. People always bring things in that they think are valuable because they're trying to make a quick buck. And sometimes they'll come in with something only to find it's worth nothing. They want to ascribe value to something that has no value at all. Likewise, many times in our lives, we have something we want to take before God as if it were valuable, but when we bring it before God, it has no value at all. But then there are times in *Pawn Stars* when people come in not recognizing what they have in their life. They bring it in to get the value assessed and find they have a priceless possession that was just lying in a closet or attic somewhere. Once the assessors see it, they say, "This is more valuable than you think."

I believe no believer recognizes their value before God. God is calling us to bring ourselves before him and to recognize that only he can ascribe and communicate what our value is. We tend to value ourselves based on persons, places, and things, but God is causing us and calling us to value ourselves based on him.

You Can Be Secure: Your Value Comes from God
2 CORINTHIANS 5:11-12

Paul reasons, "Therefore, since we know the fear of the Lord" (v. 11). This idea points back to verse 10, where he talks about standing before the judgment seat (or the *bēma* seat). Every one of us as believers will stand before Jesus Christ at some point, not to be evaluated on whether we will spend eternity with God but rather to determine the rewards we will be able to receive that we can throw at Jesus Christ's feet. Most people think rewards are about how much heaven you enjoy. I believe all of us will equally enjoy heaven. However, we won't be able to equally enjoy what we're able to throw before the Lord as an expression of something he did through us and to us—something we can give right back to him. When I get before the Lord, I want to have a lot to throw at his feet. The throwing of our crowns at his feet is a designation of our dependence on and submission to him and how much we've placed value on him above ourselves. You want your life to have so much value that you say, "God, everything in my life is for me to enjoy you enjoying me enjoying you."

"Since we know" (v. 11) points to living our lives aware of the day of accounting and living our lives knowing that God's eyes are upon us. When we only look at the transcendence of God, we may not recognize his immanence—he is knowable and here with us up close. Transcendence means he's up above everything, enthroned, and the earth is his footstool. However, his eyes are immanent in that they see everything up close. God sees your whole life—past, present, and future. He sees actual and potential decisions you can make. He sees the beginning and end of those decisions and where they can land you. If you had married this person, he can see the type of children you would have had. If you took that job instead of this one. He knows all that at the same time and can mentally handle it, yet he looks in your individual life and knows you intimately on a deep level. The people who know that God looks deeply, with detail, at the internal matrix, down to the atomic structure of our decisions, live their life a different way.

I remember when I was little, and I was doing something I had absolutely no business doing. My dad or mom would call me in. I could tell by the way they said my name that I was in trouble. I would know it was over because they would say they saw me. If I had known they were looking at me while I was acting a fool, I would have behaved differently.

Knowing you're being watched changes your integrity and your disposition. We need to recognize and realize and know that God's eyes are on us. One of my favorite verses in the Bible on God watching us is "For the eyes of the LORD roam throughout the earth to show himself strong for those who are wholeheartedly devoted to him" (2 Chr 16:9). God loves to support people who are willing to die to their selves in order to see the glory of what he wants from them. Knowing the fear of the Lord means you're intimately knowledgeable of what it means to stand in the presence of God because you know his eyes are on you.

Knowing the fear of the Lord, Paul says, "We try to persuade people" (v. 11). Paul has a chip on his shoulder here because he doesn't have credibility with this flock he's ministering to. But Paul says we persuade people with the gospel. In persuading them with the gospel, he has to do things he wouldn't normally do to persuade them that he has gospel credibility so they can hear the gospel.

He says we persuade other people, but we are known to God. Paul affirms that he is knowledgeable of God's omniscience in such a way that it affects how he does ministry. It affects his commitment to the gospel, and he hopes it is known to them.

You need to have leaders you're confident in and who fear the Lord. You may not have lived long enough to have been under hellacious leadership. Some of us will complain about the leaders we have, not knowing what's out there. In order to appreciate what God has given you, you have to know the substandard disposition of selfishness that exists in the realm of the ecclesiastical order. Paul is saying, "I shouldn't have to persuade you. I have walked with you from spiritual infancy to spiritual maturity." He is fighting for them to see their value. He didn't just say, "I hope you know this," but, "It is also plain to your consciences." This is knowing on its deepest level.

The church discovers its identity in Christ through those who proclaim their identity in Christ and who live a particular way before them: repenting of sin and walking in commitment to the gospel and proclaiming the truth of the Word. But you and I don't get our value from our leaders or anyone else. I am not my flocks' mediator. I didn't die on any cross and get up from any grave for them or for you. So you don't find your identity in me. But what you should discover in pastoral leadership is the identity that we proclaim: Jesus Christ, in whom you find yourself.

Therefore, you must find your value in nourishing what reminds you of your true value. Paul communicates the excellences of Christ. He is saying, "We're not commending ourselves or writing ourselves a résumé to you for you to value us based on how we value ourselves. We are not building ourselves up but giving you proper cause to boast about us." Paul wants the believers to boast about what he preaches.

He's saying, "Boast in what God has done through me for you." Boasting about your pastor—where your pastor lives, what he does, or what he drives—is worthless. He insists, "Boast that we suffer well, we go through hardship, and we hang in there; boast in the fact that we preach the gospel every week; and boast in the fact that, when you were in a dark place and heard a sermon, it took you out of that dark place." Many times in ministry people tend to meet with you when they have an issue with you. They will write a discourse when they have an issue with you but give a clause when they want to encourage you. When you get fifteen discourses and one medium-sized thank you, you begin to wonder what value you are to God's people. Leaders need to know that what they are teaching, disciplining, and shepherding is making a transformative gospel impact on your life. A church and its leaders develop a healthy relationship when they know that God is up to something. We want to know that someone's marriage stayed together because we preached the Word. Paul is trying to help the church in its value to have healthy congregational-pastoral relationships because it has missiological implications for lost people. It is important that you love and like the church, not just put up with it because that's what you're supposed to do. He wants you to boast about impact so that you will be able to answer those who boast about outward appearance. Don't brag about facilities, but brag about what is in the heart.

This encouragement points to you and me. We have to nourish the place where we are reminded about our value. The church doesn't give you and me value. The preacher doesn't give you value. Outreach, retreats, men's and women's retreats don't give us value. They only affirm the value Christ already gave us at the cross.

You Can Make Unpopular Decisions: The Love of Christ Controls You

2 CORINTHIANS 5:13-15

You know your value when you make unpopular decisions. Paul writes, "For if we are out of our mind, it is for God" (v. 13). This means going into a spiritual state of insanity. To a person looking at some of the decisions you make—as you're walking with God, and God's telling you biblically to do something that goes against the grain of your flesh—you look foolish.

You know you're growing as a Christian when you don't make the popular decision based on the fleshly comment feeds on social media. As a believer, as you find that your value isn't in the opinion of the world, you begin to turn down what you could have had. You may get a job offer, and it may pay you $250,000 a year, but 10 percent of your duties lack integrity, and you are able to walk away from it. When you know the Lord and you fear him and you love him, it is repulsive to your spirit. When you make a decision based on the Spirit, and your flesh is crawling with another decision for you, then you say to yourself, "I know I'm a Christian." When you make a decision in the flesh, you're going to regret it because you can have everything you want in the flesh, yet your soul is uncomfortable.

Paul observes, "If we are in our right mind, it is for you" (v. 13). You should have a rubric as a Christian, based on your value, that if Christians are making biblical decisions, you should affirm them. When your brother and sister are making decisions that their flesh is calling them to do, you just grab them by the hand, and you pray for them that they would walk in the right decision and not compromise. Paul expresses, "You should be encouraging me when I'm making these unpopular decisions."

You see, for the spiritually immature, there is a thin line between sacrifice and stupidity. That person is making a stupid decision by motives birthed in the flesh—selfish ambition, stubbornness, immature and inexperienced counsel, and not counting the cost. But for the spiritually mature, you know you're walking sacrificially if it's birthed in prayer, the Word, gospel principles, wise counsel, and counting the cost.

You find your value finally in being defined by the love of Jesus. Paul declares, "For the love of Christ compels us" (v. 14). Our value isn't defined by our love for Jesus because our love for him wanes. In order to be controlled by Christ's love, you have to know it is Christ loving you, and his love for you compels you. This idea of "compels" means holding within bounds so as to manage or guide you. It means that the love of Christ guides you.

You must be careful of defining Christ's love based on your ups and downs. Many of us say, "If I'm doing well financially and I'm not sick, then God loves me." That's not where your value is. Then when things are falling apart, you conclude, "Christ must not love me." You have to know that God's love is everlasting. God is so committed to you in the gospel that he loves you when nothing is happening in your life. God loves you when you're at your worst; it doesn't stop him from loving you. You will exhaust yourself if you allow circumstances to be the barometer for how you feel that God feels about you. You must learn to find your value in Jesus.

Paul breaks it down further. He says the love of Christ compels us—controls how I make decisions, controls my yes and controls my no. He says, "Since we have reached this conclusion, that one died for all, and therefore all died" (v. 14). He's speaking of dying in Christ. Those who are putting their faith in Christ, die. Why do you die in Christ? "And he died for all so that those who live should no longer live for themselves" (v. 15). When God buys you, he buys the rights to your soul. You may already need a massage because you have knots in your back. Why do you have knots in your back? Because of your view of God. You may think that God having control of you is restrictive. You don't realize that your demonic "freedom" is actually a straitjacket. But in Christ you're free. God telling you not to do something you want to do is true freedom. When God tells you no, you better realize he's not stopping you from nothing. You need to stop being so cat inquisitive. Some of us are like cats when God tells us no. We want to sneak in and see what's up. But sometimes, just trust in our God. I don't even want to know why he said no. Thank you for saying no; I'm a little mad, but I'm not going to go over there. Man's rejection is God's protection.

On that same show I mentioned earlier, *Pawn Stars*, sometimes people have had heirlooms in their family for years that they've treated horribly. They bring them in to the pawn shop, and the assessor looks at them and says, "Man, do you know how much this is worth? Where did you keep this?"

And they'll say, "In a box in the garage, but someone told me it may have value."

The pawnbroker says, "It would have been more valuable if you had taken better care of it. This is a mess, and it's been in the hands of so many people and thrown around. But I'm going to buy it, and I'm going to restore it. It will be more valuable after I buy it and invest in it than it was before it was in my hands."

I'm trying to tell you your life is a mess. It's been in many people's hands. It's been in some dark places. It's been in some broken places, and it's been treated horribly. However, you need to take it to heaven's pawn shop because, when you take it to the Lord, he'll buy it back. And when he buys it back, he'll restore it back to everything he wanted it to be no matter where it's been, no matter what it's been through, no matter how much hell or how many fires it's been through. Because when you put it in the hands of the Master, it is restored to its value. You've been raped. You've been molested. You've been beat down. You've been looked down on. You've been talked about. You've been the brunt of people's jokes, but if you would just learn how to take yourself to the King of kings and the Lord of lords, he'll take care of you, and he will restore you.

Reflect and Discuss

1. How does knowing God's eyes are on you change your disposition and how you act on a daily basis?
2. Why do we tend to base our value on other persons, places, or things?
3. What does it mean for your value to come from God?
4. What helps you reorient yourself to the fact that your value comes from God?
5. Why is Christ's love for you not based on your work or performance?
6. How does the reality of Christ's unconditional, gracious love for you motivate you?
7. In light of that, how then should you live?

100 Percent Reconciled

2 CORINTHIANS 5:16-21

Main Idea: The gospel reconciles us to God and others.

I. Gospel Reconciliation Impacts How We View Jesus and Others (5:16).
II. Gospel Reconciliation Frees Us to Operate Differently (5:17).
III. Gospel Reconciliation Is the Primary Ministry of the Church (5:18-21).

Relationships can be difficult. Have you ever expressed to someone you love, "I'm going to love you from a distance"? I don't know how that works, but maybe you just post something on social media—"I love you"—and that's as far as you go. But how well does that work if that's your only interaction with this person? Being a Christian doesn't remove relational conflict. Sometimes becoming a believer increases it. When you weren't a believer, you didn't know anything was wrong. But now you look back, and you don't know how you operated in all the mess in the first place. That's the reality of becoming a believer.

The challenge is that God doesn't give you the freedom to just acknowledge what's wrong with the relationship. The question is not just, Do you know what's wrong with the relationship? Rather, the question is, Are you willing to deal with the breaches that are in the relationship? Paul is helping us avoid two extremes. One extreme is barricading ourselves in relationally, where we create chasms so we don't have to deal with anyone. When we don't like certain people, some of us will do things to irritate them to push them further from us. The second extreme is "easy believism" or cheap grace, where you ignore the issues for an appearance of peace, but there is no practical disposition for conciliation. Neither one of these is the gospel: barricading yourself against dealing with folk or kissing and smiling but cussing about each other behind their backs.

The Bible calls for a deeper sense of community, a deeper sense of commitment, a deeper sense of reality. You are not really real until you become a Christian. Real realness comes from being really changed by

Jesus. When you're changed by Jesus, you will know what keeping it 100 really means.

So we come to a passage in which Paul conveys, "I'm not going to slight words with you, but I'm going to give you a robust, theological idea that has potent practical principles that can push you out for his glory." As a matter of fact, I'd like to park here for a moment so that we can see the power God offers us as he proves this reality in this text. Paul, a gospel globe-trotter, is again finding his spiritual children in the faith resisting him because his commitment to them includes engaging them about their sin. And because they're too spiritually immature to respond properly to a rebuke, they go on a hater-raid, and they begin to undercut his identity as an apostle. When someone challenges you, you want to change his identity so you can ignore the truth. The whole book is about Paul reestablishing his spiritual authority and his right in the gospel to rebuke them.

So here he says, "I'm going to prove to you that you can't run away from engaging me." This idea is rooted in the Paul's words in 2 Timothy 3:1-3, where he says that selfishness and rebellion among believers will be prevalent going into the last of the last days.

> But know this: Hard times will come in the last days. For people will be lovers of self, lovers of money, boastful, proud, demeaning, disobedient to parents, ungrateful, unholy, unloving, irreconcilable.

In other words, people will create things that say we don't want to be together, called "irreconcilable differences." Nowhere in the Bible is that given as a way for people to end their marriages. The idea just creates a fogginess that says we don't want to deal with our differences. Paul is breaking the code by saying the gospel can reconcile anything. Still, reconciling anything is hard.

Gospel Reconciliation Impacts How
We View Jesus and Others
2 CORINTHIANS 5:16

In verse 16 Paul declares, "From now on." That is, now that you are a believer, there should be some "from now on" in your life. When you become a believer, some things should stop and some things should start. You don't really know you're a believer until you have a "from now on" moment. You must get to a point as a believer when you realize you need a "from now on" moment that shows that you're not going to live under the deception of the flesh anymore.

He continues, "From now on, then." He's using transition words. He uses double transition language to talk about your transition. That means he's emphasizing how much you transition when you become a believer. He could have just said, "therefore"; he could've just said, "from now on," or he could've said, "similarly," "moreover," "in short," or "in conclusion." No, he doubled it by both transition positions to let you know that your life has made a structural, positional, practical, and comprehensive transition when you named the name of Jesus.

As he considers this reality, he acknowledges, "We do not know" (v. 16). Here the word *know* implies "regard" or "value." The word means "appraise" or "hold close to your chest." We no longer regard anyone according to the flesh. Before you became a believer, you made decisions based on "a worldly perspective," fleshly inclinations, and you no longer do that.

I remember when the Lord showed me in college that Yvette was going to be my wife. I was thinking, "Lord, she's fine, but she's not my type." Back in the day, I liked a gum-popping, bamboo-earring wearing, tight-jeans, halter-top type, right? Yvette came in godly, and she loved the Lord, and that was not what I was used to. I said, "She's fine, but she's not what I'm used to." And Yvette ended up telling me that I wasn't her type either. But God was showing me that he was going to put things and people in my life that would upgrade my view of him.

God is after you to look at things not with your eyes only. As a matter of fact, Paul is talking about looking at things with your flesh. We have repeatedly made dumb decisions because of fleshly inclinations. But Paul says this is not how we do things anymore. A Christian looks beyond the flesh and values the core principle—the biblical, theological, Christological, soteriological, exegetical, expositional reality of core Christian teaching in every area of life. You're on a trajectory to see everything differently. So God is committed to you doing that, even if it frustrates you, because sometimes God will make sure he gives you what you don't like in the flesh so that he can give you what you do need in the spirit.

Most of us don't think anything is authentic in our "like" taste buds unless we like it in the flesh. We don't think real "like" is spiritual. We think in order to like something we have to like it fleshly first and ask the spirit to catch up. But the kingdom doesn't work like that. The kingdom is backwards to the flesh. Therefore, God does spirit work, then shows you the physical. It's like when you know what's inside your car and you have a fine interior. You know because you're riding in it most of the time. You can enjoy the inside, and you forget about the outside. Even though you know there's an outside, you can appreciate the outside because you've been all through the inside.

Paul asserts, "We do not know anyone from a worldly perspective" (v. 16). He is talking about leaders. Paul says, "You like impressive leaders. You like people who preach themselves, who promote themselves." In other words, they have a spiritual disposition that wants leaders who nurture their fleshly fantasies. But that's why the Bible says,

> For the time will come when people will not tolerate sound doctrine,
> but according to their own desires, will multiply teachers for themselves
> because they have an itch to hear what they want to hear. (2 Tim 4:3)

Paul is fighting against that already and helping them to avoid that.

Next Paul observes, "We have known Christ from a worldly perspective" (v. 16). The way you view everything is rooted in how you view Jesus. You can't fix the flesh with the flesh. That's why John says, "Whatever is born of the flesh is flesh, and whatever is born of the Spirit is spirit" (John 3:6). You don't fix flesh with flesh; you fix the flesh with the Spirit. Therefore, your root transitional reality only can be viewed from Christ. Now, what does it mean to view Christ according to the flesh? It means Paul, pointing back to his preconversion state, looked at Christ from a nonrespectful perspective. But he's talking to Christians. Therefore, according to Paul, you can be a Christian yet view Christ in a fleshly way.

For example, if the only time you can say "amen" is when it's about providing for you financially or doing something in the physical realm for you, then you view Christ as a cosmic genie rather than a change agent. There's a difference between the two. Some say, "I want God to change around me but not in me." When you regard Christ according to the flesh, all you want him to do is change stuff, not change you. To be a Christian is to wrestle with being changed and to always be in transition. God is going to confront your flesh—that's what being a believer means. Now we may have an immature idea of a fly-by-night scene of strolling in a field with a gentle Jesus. We want the Jesus in the beautiful pictures, with some lambs around him, looking all soft. We don't want the Jesus with the flaming eyes and the burnished brass ankles, with the linen ephod and the golden bulletproof vest. We don't want the dude who was up in the temple turning over tables with a whip in his hand, tearing into people. He's the same person. Don't get it twisted! When we regard Christ according to the flesh, we create our own Jesus—which is an idol. We say, "God is love," and we swim in that. We don't recognize what love is. Because love disciplines us; love doesn't just do for us what we want. Many of us in our minds have an idol; it's not the real Jesus. Paul is confronting our view of Jesus. When our view of Jesus is confronted, our view of everything is confronted.

Paul is saying, "Yet now we no longer know him in this way." He's speaking to believers inclusively, declaring that's not how we live. That's why the Bible says that when you go to make disciples, you teach them everything (Matt 28:19-20).

See, the problem with some preachers is they only teach some things, but you have to teach it all. As the old church used to say, "Preach it all, Reverend, preach it all!" That means everything. Everything that God has for me, even if it's difficult, I want it. All of it is going to make me look like the Lord God through Jesus Christ.

Gospel Reconciliation Frees Us to Operate Differently
2 CORINTHIANS 5:17

This passage is powerful. Perhaps we have viewed this verse anthropologically, or from a human perspective, but I want us to view it Christologically. Paul writes, "Therefore, if anyone is in Christ, he is a new creation; the old has passed away, and see, the new has come!" Again, we tend to have a reductionistic view of this passage and believe Paul is only speaking about self-renewal. In other words, "I'm new now. I'm a new creation; hallelujah, praise God!" But that view ignores the center of the text. The center of this text is a short prepositional phrase that sums up the excellencies of why things are made new. "If anyone is *in Christ.*" That may be the most beautiful doctrine in the world!

Being "in Christ" is the great doctrine called "union with Christ." This foundational doctrine helps us as believers to know who we are. But being "in Christ" is not just knowing *who* you are because that's not enough. You must also know *where* you are. Being in Christ is about knowing where you're located because where you're located changes how you act.

For instance, I remember when I would go over to my grandmama's house. She had a living room that didn't get used much. In fact, she had wrapped the furniture in plastic, and I never understood that. If you ever sat in there in your Easter suit after a Sunday morning, you felt as if you were in a sauna.

However, when you were in grandmama's living room, you acted a certain way because of where you were located. Now, you can be in the backyard and do what you want, but when you're in the living room, your disposition must change because your location engages your activity. See, when you're in Christ, you're now covered like that couch. When you're in Christ, your location tells you something totally different based on your operation, and it's not constriction—it's freedom.

The Puritan theologian John Owen viewed our union with Christ as "the cause of all other graces." Owen believed that all the benefits of redemption flow from the believer's union with Christ. Union with Christ, Owen wrote,

> is the cause of all other graces that we are made partakers of; they are all communicated to us by virtue of our union with Christ. Hence is our adoption, our justification, our sanctification, our fruitfulness, our perseverance, our resurrection, our glory. (From *An Exposition of the Epistle to the Hebrews*, 21:149–50; in Fesko, "John Owen")

Union with Christ, therefore, is the all-encompassing doctrinal rubric that embraces all the elements of redemption. So being in Christ is the mechanism by which God funnels all of heaven's blessings through him. Only if you're in his locale do you get the benefits of salvation.

We encounter this idea when Jesus describes himself as different things to the seven churches in Revelation. One of my favorites that John reports is "the one who has the key of David" (Rev 3:7). Jesus having a key communicates that he unlocks something. And the only way to experience what he unlocks is to be in him. (For further study, Hawthorne, et al., *The Dictionary of Paul and His Letters* addresses Pauline semantic domains and the existential, theological, and spiritual realities of what it means to be "in Christ"; see pp. 433–36.) In essence, to be in Christ is to be covered by him.

In Christ you are recreated. David in his sin prophetically wished, "God, create a clean heart for me and renew a steadfast spirit within me" (Ps 51:10-11). David is expressing, "I feel so bad about my sin; I wish you could give me a brand-new heart. Is it possible, God?" The Holy Spirit was using him to give him a prophetic nudge of the beauty of things to come in Jesus. Because ultimately in Jesus Christ, he would create in you a clean heart, he would renew the right spirit in you, and he would make you brand-new. Right here we see David's prophetic wish coming to reality in Jesus Christ. That's why Jesus can say, "Abraham, Moses, and all others looked forward to the day I came." They had to wrestle with redemption that they could only look forward to, but now we get to live in.

"Therefore, if anyone is in Christ, he is a new creation; the old has passed away" (v. 17). In other words, old operational realities have dissolved. "See, the new has come!" Now, in our walk with the Lord Jesus Christ, we're in a new disposition. Paul gives us the foundation. But now Paul is about to sucker punch us with why he was giving us all that rich doctrine. He'll have you saying, "Amen," until he says, "I've got you now." Notice what he does.

Gospel Reconciliation Is the Primary Ministry of the Church
2 CORINTHIANS 5:18-21

Paul declares, "Everything is from God" (v. 18). All that he just said is from God. We didn't trigger our salvation; God did. So you weren't looking for him; he was looking for you. He wasn't lost; you were. All this is from God—all the workings of salvation, giving us the faith, giving us the ability to see the gospel, the ability to confess the gospel, the ability to be transformed by the gospel. All is under the hand of the living God. Everything is from God. Boom! Paul compounds that into this multivitamin pill and drops a gospel bomb. He says, "Everything is from God, who has reconciled us to himself through Christ and has given us the ministry of reconciliation" (v. 18).

You must understand that Adam was our federal head. His sin DNA came to all of us. Not only is our nature sin, but we practice sin in concert with our nature. One sin is enough for God to pour out all his wrath on us. I want you to feel this. But God did something different. God was able to hold his peace on us, even though he aimed an eternal fully automatic rifle—fully loaded with full metal jacket ammo—at the soul of every one of us to eternally gun us down. Every single sin fills up the cup of wrath. More sin, more wrath. But God is compassionate, full of loving-kindness, blessing sons and daughters to a thousand generations. So at the same time he holds back his right, his holy right. He has a right. I don't care who you think you are, God has a right to kill you forever. He has the right, but he's not just wrath. He's not just tough love.

He's not just holiness. He's not just justice. He's also grace. He's also mercy. However, his wrath must be satisfied. His grace can put up yield signs before himself. Jesus's death on the cross yielded the wrath of God so that it stopped it, so that it could be poured fully out on Jesus instead. Now, why is that important? Because God has every right to destroy us, but he held it back to send Jesus to reconcile us. Jesus is the bull's-eye.

Who in your life do you need to reconcile with? God is fully righteous. If he can pursue reconciliation with us with all the issues he has with us, what's wrong with us? Paul said God has given us the ministry of reconciliation. Paul says, "In Christ, God was reconciling the world to himself, . . . and he has committed the message of reconciliation to us" (v. 19). Our first priority is to spread the message that people can be reconciled to God through Christ. But there's a corollary to that: because of Christ, people can be reconciled to one another, and we can help make that happen.

I've had relationships that have been strained. I remember when God was specifically talking to me about people I needed to reconcile with, and I didn't like it. God said, "I need you to go handle that."

I came back, "I ain't feelin' it." I'm honest with God when I talk to him. You have to pour out your heart before the Lord. I'm honest without being disrespectful. I say, "God, I'm not really feeling reconciliations."

And God comes back, "I don't care what you're feeling. So until you make a motion toward reconciliation, I'm going to lean on you. I'm going to lean up against your soul and make you uncomfortable." You know you're a Christian when God says, "All right, you're going to do you; I'm going to do me. Now I'm bigger than you, so I'm going to put you in this terrifying submission hold in your heart, not in your body." When you get hit in the soul, it's ten million times more painful than the flesh because the soul is the real you, and the nerve endings of your soul, based on the conviction of the Spirit, are robust. So what he did was headlock me, arm bar me, and choke me all at the same time. What's mesmerizing about the Holy Spirit is that when you try to run, it's almost as if your running makes his grip tighter. When the Holy Spirit is holding you and he won't let you do anything, you finally say, "Okay, okay, God!"

I remember setting up this reconciliation meeting and trying to sit down, feeling frustrated with the whole situation, and pursuing and doing all that I needed to do on my end. God says, "When you go in here, it's not about the other people. It's about you obeying me. Don't worry about the response; you go in and you obey me."

And I'm responding, "All right, I'm gonna roll in here. You know I'm not feeling this whole situation, but I'm going to be obedient because I'm sick of this headlock."

I went in; it was a thunderstorm. I sought reconciliation. I was frustrated. I held back words I hadn't said in years. I'm just being real. We wrestled and fought. The reconciliation didn't happen, but the headlock ended. God said, "You did what you were supposed to do. You can't worry about their response." That is why the Bible says, "*As far as it depends on you*, live at peace" (Rom 12:18; emphasis added). You can't force peace. There is no peace like God-sent peace.

That means you may have to face some people you hate. Many of us are the haters. We're not the hated on. Some of us have been hurt by some people beyond repair. God is about your holiness even when you're uncomfortable. If you dwell on your hatred for them—how much they hurt you, how much they frustrated you—you're not trying to get with them. If you dwell on them, you're not going to reconcile. As a matter of fact, when you see them, it's almost as if a demonic boiling system just hits you and you're feeling, "I just want to kill them, God." Just that disposition—when you sit on that—causes what Hebrews 12:15 calls the root of bitterness. It sprouts up and becomes the rooted tree for everything in your life. Now you're not operating on being *in Christ*, but you're operating on being *in anger* with them. So the rubric for your life becomes impressing people who aren't looking at you anyway. The rubric of your life now says, "Exalt me, God, so I can denounce them and show them I was right!" Your life is now motivated by your bitterness, your unforgiveness, and your anger, and Christ is no longer the center, but how you feel about them is. The only way you feel good about yourself is knowing that they feel bad about where you are.

But the truth has nothing to do with that. It has everything to do with you walking in gospel holiness.

So if someone raped you, molested you, abused you, or abandoned you, you may still need to engage them. You have no right, even though you're sinned against, to sin against them. Their sin against you is light-years away from how you sinned against God. Until you believe your sin stinks too, you'll never reconcile with anyone. You're going to have to deal with it. And I pray that the Holy Spirit leans into you like a heavyweight boxer, to tear your soul apart until you become obedient to walk in holiness and face your bitterness, face your anger, face your fearfulness of this. And guess what? You're going to find the greatest amount of freedom.

Consider what Paul says: "That is, in Christ, God was reconciling the world to himself, not counting their trespasses against them, and he has committed the message of reconciliation to us" (v. 19). "Committed" doesn't mean God is committed to us. It means he appointed us a duty. Reconciliation is our appointed duty, and he entrusted the message of reconciliation to us. Wow! We invite people to be reconciled to God, and we do our part to reconcile people to one another.

Interpersonal reconciliation involves three main elements.

Number one, you both must acknowledge the breaches you have between each other because a hug and a "like" on social media don't mean reconciliation. Reconciliation is admitting this has been an issue and acknowledging the sins.

Number two, you must repent of the sin. That means you have to agree with God and embrace that reality because there can be no reconciliation without repentance. That would be false peace.

And number three, sometimes you have to own up to things you didn't realize you did. Sometimes you say, "I didn't do that!" But if you make it all about you, it's a breach.

Sometimes you need a mediator. Let the mediator point out the problem. Oh, this is real practice! You can't be the one to point out stuff. That creates a greater breach. You've got to let someone who is in between you say it. You must have an objective participant who is on neither side to stand between you to help you broker reconciliation. That means you may hear information that you totally disagree with, and the person may view you extremely falsely. Then you say, "That wasn't my intention, but will you please forgive me?" You don't know what that can do for reconciliation: "That wasn't my intention." Do you find that hard to say? If Jesus could take on sins that he didn't even commit, can't you verbally communicate that you didn't mean to sin against someone? Jesus didn't do any of it. He lived the perfect life and took on all our sins and died. And now you can't admit something that you don't feel like you are wrong of, that they feel like you were wrong of, in order to bring reconciliation? That's not the gospel.

So we must do what Paul says: "So that in him we might become the righteousness of God" (v. 21). What does that mean? First, it means that when people hear our message and accept our invitation to be reconciled to God, he gives those people righteousness. It's called imputed righteousness. We give Christ our sinfulness, and God gives us Christ's righteousness. That's the great exchange.

Second, whenever you reconcile and fight for reconciliation with your brothers and sisters, whether it happens or not, God holds you up as a trophy of what righteousness in him looks like. Because at the center of the gospel is bringing two opposing sides together that you would not think should be together.

I was watching a cooking show segment about oil and vinegar. Have you ever noticed how oil and vinegar, when put together, just move around each other? They don't really mix with each other. I mean, they really don't like each other—oil and vinegar. They never mix. So the culinary scientist took an egg, cracked the egg, put it in the mix, stirred it up, and oil and vinegar couldn't help it anymore. They had to unite because the egg was present. What the egg does on the molecular level is it grabs the oil; it says, "Come here!" It grabs the vinegar and says, "Come here! Let's get together." You see, the only way they could coexist is because the presence of an agent brought them together. The only way reconciliation happens is because Jesus is in the mix. If you're feeling all that other stuff, it will keep oil and vinegar hitting each other. But if you let Christ, who is the eternal emulsifier, get in the middle, he pulls together the un-pull-together-able.

Reflect and Discuss

1. What are some hardships and issues you've experienced with relationships?
2. How do you usually respond to relationship conflicts?
3. In what ways have you regarded Christ and others according to the flesh?
4. How does the gospel change and shape how you view Christ and others?
5. What is union with Christ? What are the benefits that come with it?
6. How does union with Christ and its benefits make you act differently in relationships?
7. Are you honest with God in your prayer life when it comes to relationship issues and struggles? Why or why not?
8. Whom do you need to face and reconcile with in your life? What relationships do you need to improve on?
9. How do the cross and the gospel of Christ compel you to do that?

Living a Commendable Life, Part 1

2 CORINTHIANS 6:1-5

Main Idea: There are things you must know and do to live a commendable life.

I. **Favor Flows from the Gospel, Not from Us (6:1-2).**
II. **God Does His Best Work in Less-Than-Ideal Circumstances (6:3).**
III. **Focus on the Evidence of God's Grace in All Areas of Life (6:4-5).**

My kids turned on the TV and *Good Times* happened to be on. They love *Good Times*. They think J J is the best comedian that ever existed on planet Earth. We decided to watch a couple of episodes. In one, J J is the Picasso of the ghetto. He is using some landmark paintings from the famous artist Ernest Barnes who actually draws those. But he's given credit in the show for Barnes's elongated soulful paintings from the late sixties and early seventies. Then the character Sweet Daddy Williams sponsors J J in an art exhibit at a famous hotel in Chicago at that time. J J's exhibit painting is supposed to be of Sweet Daddy's (they don't say this anymore, but they said it back then) "main squeeze." Sweet Daddy likes the way this painting is coming along. His main squeeze finally comes into town. Of course, everyone has on fur coats, rings on every finger, and all different types of chains. She walks through the ghetto doors of the Chicago projects at the Evans household and makes her entrance. She walks around to the painting and says, "What is this?" She goes off about J J's interpretation of what she looks like. She and J J go back and forth, and she keeps going off. And of course, Sweet Daddy is embarrassed, and he begins to walk out of there. As he walks out, he's frustrated, and J J says, "You liked it at first!" They are all angry. J J is looking at the painting, and everyone is telling the girl, "But that's you!" But she didn't think it represented her because the painting depicted circles around her eyes and other things that she refused to see when she looked in a mirror.

That's how some of us can respond when our lives are painted one way in our minds but painted accurately in the eyes of God. When God paints our lives and we get to see what our lives are really like, it can be shocking and really disturbing. I would even say our view of the Christian life must always be evolving because I believe most Christians have a skewed view of what a real Christian life is like. Most of the Christian life is obscure. Most of the Christian life is daunting, long seasons of sowing and reaping, seasons of brokenness, seasons of enjoyment, of frustration, of excitement. In fact, Christian life is summed up in Ecclesiastes 3: there's a time and season for everything.

However, the disposition of Christianity communicated through many corridors of mega-edifices is of a Christian life with little suffering and few challenges. Instead, your sanctification is based on how good your life seems to be—without any seams or imperfections. If your life gets closer to perfect, it's because you're growing spiritually.

But when I look at the Bible, I see a different narrative. I see this paradox of the coexistence of enjoyment, of joy, of comfort with brokenness, with loss, with pain, with frustration, and the two sides simultaneously hovering like helicopters beside each other, shooting at each other, and stopping the fight to stay in orbit together. Many of you struggle with wanting the Christian life to be the TV Christian life that's communicated by false teachers. However, if you continue to allow yourself to be put on an unredeemed trajectory of the Christian life, you will find yourself frustrated and moving toward apostasy. But if you recognize the beauty of the tension you can never get rid of, the beauty of the brokenness you can't shake off, the beauty of the ailments you can't pray off, you will find that God sometimes delivers, God sometimes doesn't, but most of the time—as a matter of fact, all the time—he's up to something.

So Paul challenges the Corinthians. This is nothing new. They believe they deserve their best life now. They believe they deserve to be rich. They believe they deserve no sickness. They believe they deserve no suffering. They really believe Paul is an irritation when he starts to talk to them about the reason they reject his apostleship. They reject his apostleship because his apostleship doesn't look like the Christianity they believe. Yet when opposition arises, the encouragement we discover as believers is the gospel's power in every challenge.

Favor Flows from the Gospel, Not from Us
2 CORINTHIANS 6:1-2

Paul writes here:

> *Working together with [God], we also appeal to you, "Don't receive the grace of God in vain." For he says: At an acceptable time I listened*

to you, and in the day of salvation I helped you. See, now is the
acceptable time; now is the day of salvation!

Paul begins this section after communicating that we are ambassadors on a mission for the Lord, that our salvation is based on what Christ has done for us in taking on the wrath of God, and that our ministry is to promote that reality every single time we get an opportunity. He transitions in chapter 6, yet he stays on the same track and begins addressing favor or grace when he talks about the "acceptable time." He puts favor in context when he quotes Isaiah speaking about Israel. They would go through a difficult time, yet God would provide a favorable opportunity and acceptable time. Paul observes that this favor has been released through the messianic death and resurrection of Jesus Christ. So this favor has been inaugurated.

We hear favor isn't fair, and all of us love favor, but the question is, What does the text say favor looks like? To begin, it doesn't look like our best-looking pictures on social media.

In other words, you can put your best foot forward, but you do have to live real life. All of us get to post the best pictures we can take to give people the appearance that we're beasts and everything's okay, but the selfies in this passage tell a different story. This passage speaks of different means that God works through to challenge us. So as Paul quotes Isaiah, he challenges us to consider an authentic Christian life. He works through this day of salvation, what it looks like, and how God has helped us.

God Does His Best Work in Less-Than-Ideal Circumstances
2 CORINTHIANS 6:3

Paul states, "We are not giving anyone an occasion for offense, so that the ministry will not be blamed." The New Living Translation puts it this way: "We live in such a way that no one will stumble because of us, and no one will find fault with our ministry." Paul recognizes that when you become a believer, your life is not your own. And your life not being your own is the greatest freedom you can experience because when you were owning your life, you always messed up your life.

In your hands, your life is foolishness. In your hands, your life is a plumb mess. In your hands, I don't care how long you spent in the mirror doing your hair, in the beauty shop, or in the barber shop. I don't care if you go get the pedicure, the manicure, the best gear on the planet. Best perfume, best cologne, best workout—did all your Pilates, P90X, or whatever you did. I'm just telling you right now, your life in your hands is a mess. Paul recognizes that. So Paul says, "Because my life isn't my own, I have to live my life with a gospel vibe to it." A gospel vibe is wanting to live in a way where nothing in life gets in the way of communicating who Jesus Christ is. That means sometimes some of the stuff I want to do, I don't do.

This moves on to meddling. There are some things in your life that you have a right to do that you have no right to do. Many of us operate in the era of contemporary, upgraded Christianity. We love to push the envelope of saying that we're still in the faith, not really caring about the outside of the envelope that people will open and see. We'll do what gives us a "like" from others and not live in light of "I have to fall back from some stuff if it's going to best reflect the heart of God." Sometimes you must fall back from some things you want to do, adjust the timing, or change where you do it in order not to become an obstacle to someone.

I remember when Nehemiah, my middle son, first started walking, and he loved to run around our ottoman. That was Nehemiah's thing. And Manny, my oldest son, would always have his stuff everywhere around the ottoman. That was Manny's thing, and he had the right to do it. Nehemiah would trip because he wasn't a strong walker and wasn't able to gallop over stuff. So he would hold onto the ottoman, and when he fell, he would try to get back up. I said, "Manny, you have to move all the stuff around the ottoman so that Nehemiah has freedom to learn how to walk, so that he can strengthen his legs, so that he can have the mobility that we have." Many of us don't want to move the obstacles from our life that get in other peoples' way. Some people in your life are barely holding on, and there's a bunch of stuff that you—not someone else, not their past—have in their way that is an obstacle to their being able to be strengthened in their legs, like Hebrews says, and to be able to hold on to the living God and move forward. Paul says that I live in such a way that I'm so free that I don't have to have everything I want. If it's an obstacle to someone else, I'm not going to have it.

Some of you need to watch where you show your liberties. Some of you are too flagrant with your liberties. Moreover, when someone says something, you're going to give them a theological treatise on why you're free to do that. Let me say, if you have to give a theological treatise on why you're free, you're immature spiritually. The fact that someone is wondering must have put you in a mindset of falling backward versus pushing forward. It's not your job to push the immature to maturity in looking at your liberties maturely. So sometimes you have to say, "You know what? I'm not going to have the enjoyment when I go out with my friends. I'm going to fall back from some of this, some of what I would normally do, because I know this environment. It could bother someone and make things look a little weird in relation to how they would look at the faith, and when I begin to share the gospel with them, they won't see the gospel; they'll see the meme of my liberty."

So Paul says, "Listen, what makes my life commendable is I'm not doing me." See, that's our problem. Too many of you want to do you; when you become a believer, "you" is over. Okay, I know that's not proper English. I'm just letting you know that you're over. I'm not telling you that you can't enjoy liberties. I know you may like to drink. I know you may like to puff a cigar. There's nothing wrong with that every now and then. I know you may be an older Christian, and you're thinking, "Oh no, no." It's liberty. However, taking a picture with a group of folks with some cognac in your hand and a cigar talking about "wrecking crew"—I'm just giving you an example. Everyone can't handle this. That's not how we roll as believers, to promote our liberty in a way that could crush someone. Do that by the firepit in the backyard with the closed fence up without getting drunk and without getting high.

Paul says a commendable life lays stuff down and doesn't feel constricted. He suggests we don't feel constricted by it because "Christ is my freedom; I'm not my freedom." See the difference? Being free isn't about your enjoyment of a sublevel desire and enjoyment of freedom. Christ is your freedom. So even if you feel fleshly constricted, you should feel spiritually liberated because you're diving into the freedom and joy of what God has given you the grace to experience in Christ. Because he's bigger than that thing, you can say, "I'll fall back from that right now."

Guess what happened when Paul let go of his liberties? I'm going to give you a list. He shut down idolatrous businesses. He freed people from human trafficking. He confronted racism. He shattered legalism and religion. He crushed licentiousness. He unveiled false intellectualism. He preached Jesus as the living God. He was countercultural and transcended culture. That's a serious list! God gives us the grace to transcend liberties. Indeed, as Paul contends that no one can find fault with his ministry, notice what he says: "We are not giving anyone an occasion for offense, so that the ministry will not be blamed. Instead, as God's ministers, we commend ourselves in everything" (vv. 3-4) or present ourselves in a commendable way. As servants of God, we should present ourselves in a commendable way to provide evidence of a personal characteristic or claim or action that demonstrates God's gospel.

Focus on the Evidence of God's Grace in All Areas of Life
2 CORINTHIANS 6:4-5

Now Paul asserts, "This is what I deal with, and this is what makes Christianity commendable." He's not preaching himself, yet he's giving an exemplary example in practical terms in his life. Not just his life but his crew—the people he walks with also walk like this. So if you understand this letter, he's not speaking about himself. He's speaking about the type of people he journeys with, submits to as an apostle, and allows to hold him accountable. In other words, he has people in his life that he invites to be a community of challenge to him. He wasn't too apostolic to let Titus or Timothy or Silas or Priscilla or Aquila or Phoebe question him. He wasn't an untouchable apostle up on some high horse who couldn't receive a challenge from someone he perceived as less spiritually mature than he was.

Paul's words are aromatic and fragrant. He's trying to help us see that we need one another. You and I need to be in community with people who are willing to go the same direction, people who challenge you and you challenge them. He's trying to build that idea. Let me tell you how much I need that. I need the elders on my back challenging me. I need my wife challenging me. I need my friends challenging me. I need my flock, if they see something, say something: "Pastor, what's good with this?"

Look again at the list Paul gives. Pauline lists are interesting because he only gives you a glimpse. Here, Paul is the most vulnerable he has been in this letter. Three times he gives several lists of fights, of difficulties he's working through as an apostle. Anyone who's not vulnerable, I'm scared of them. I'm scared of people who don't ever show some of their heart. If you're a fortress, you're the weakest person on the planet. If you're open, you're strong because you let God strengthen you rather than let your appearance of who you present yourself as strengthen you.

Look at what he writes: "Instead, as God's ministers, we commend ourselves in everything" (v. 4). Every way, in everything, it's all open. Everything's fair game for judgment. Christians don't say, "Only God can judge me." Really? Who wants God to judge them? Think about it. I want you to judge me, to challenge me and tell me how I'm wrong, so that when I get before the judgment seat, I can say that I have dealt with the mess in my life with others. I want to be judged rightly. So Paul states, "I commend myself in every way." In other words, "My life is open to challenge as well as commendation or affirmation." He hopes to be confronted and encouraged.

He says, "By great endurance" (v. 4). Guess what that assumes? Hard times. Hard trials. He's not bragging about his ability to endure. If you understand God's Word, you know endurance is done by faith in what Christ has done, and the Spirit gives you gospel perseverance to stand in difficult times.

Paul writes in Romans 5,

> *Therefore, since we have been justified by faith, we have peace with God through our Lord Jesus Christ. We have also obtained access through him by faith into this grace in which we stand, and we boast in the hope of the glory of God. And not only that, but we also boast in our afflictions, because we know that affliction produces endurance, endurance produces proven character, and proven character produces hope. This hope will not disappoint us.* (Rom 5:1-5)

What hope-filled foundational truths!

The commendable life is not how issueless your life is. Nothing is commendable about everything going well all the time. Rather, "great endurance" in verse 4 speaks to the glory of the gospel. This is mind-boggling. "Great endurance" points to the fact that Paul has gone through hellacious circumstances and needed the Holy Spirit to keep him beyond his willingness to give up. He's saying, "My situation was so bad that God had to grab me and hold me in place to stay there through the whole thing." Lord, have mercy. What a good word from the Bible. God helps us in these ailments of brokenness to strengthen us in the might and beauty of who he is. In chapter 1 Paul said that he wanted to give up, that God did put on him more than he could bear—contrary to Christian clichés. He said that it was to show that God raises the dead.

Notice again what he lists: "by great endurance, by afflictions, by hardships, by difficulties" (v. 4). Listen to the hardship he endures. Who says this? He says, "By beatings" (v. 4). Plural. He's not speaking about his mother and father beating him. He's speaking about enemies inflicting outrageous wounds. One time Paul got stoned on the outside of a city and left for dead; they just left him there. I mean, have you ever been robbed? Paul's been robbed on the road because they carried all their money. It's not like they could put it in the bank and Western Union it over here; he didn't have any of that. They had money on them. Dudes were running what in Washington, DC, we call "capers"; dudes were robbing dudes that were on journeys. And some beatings—this is crazy! And look: "By imprisonments" (v. 5). He went to jail for things he didn't do. "Riots" started because he preached the gospel, and it disagreed with the philosophies of the environments where he was communicating the gospel.

"By labors, by sleepless nights" (v. 5). He says he's had insomnia. They didn't have sleeping aids back then like turkey or warm milk, so you just had to deal with your sleepless nights.

What am I saying with all this? As a shepherd, I'm talking to myself because I go in and out of understanding the Christian life well. Sometimes you'll get in a mindset where you get angry at God because you think you deserve something he hasn't given you. Hardship is happening in your life that doesn't align with what you expect from God. So you assume, based on bad thinking, that God is inactive. You begin to create intimacy distance from God because he hasn't given you what you want when you want it and how you want it. Then you look at other people who appear to be doing better, and you argue with God about his doing something for them that he didn't do for you. "God, I've been waiting for you on this. God, I've been wanting you to do this." But you don't realize that what you're experiencing places you in the right place. You're right where you are supposed to be. It's okay if you're not on the cover of a magazine. It's okay if your business doesn't become a Fortune 500 company. I'm not saying I don't want that to happen. I know that I don't receive that; so what?

What I'm saying is whether normal, hard ups and downs—being kept by God, taken care of, yet things working out, things not working out—all of this is normal. And it's good for you. That's why David said, "It was good for me to be afflicted so that I could learn your statutes" (Ps 119:71). If God had given you everything you prayed for, you wouldn't be the Christian you are today. Prayer isn't really about God answering your prayers. Prayer is about your heart being exposed and God aligning you with his will through wrestling.

Some of you are wrestling with the Lord right now. And the Lord says, "I know you don't feel like I love you. I know you don't feel like I'm blessing you. Where your bank account is, is my will. The jobs that didn't open up is my will. The thing that did open up is my will. The school you didn't get into was my will. The spouse you didn't get was my will. My will. And you need to not embrace your circumstances. Embrace me and it will make all that other stuff fade to black." And you'll be in another place again when you're wrestling.

Most of us think spiritual maturity works like this: "I'll just get to a place where I'm okay." No. Spiritual maturity is you continuing to cling to the fact that you know you won't be okay and that you need to keep grabbing hold of God to help you in your lack of okay-ness.

Reflect and Discuss

1. Why do so many people have unhealthy, unbiblical views of the Christian life?
2. What is your view of the Christian life?
3. How does this text influence your view of the Christian life?
4. What is favor, and what does it look like in the Christian life?
5. Is there anything in your life that's getting in the way of your communicating the gospel to others?
6. How has God worked on you and in your life during less-than-ideal circumstances?
7. What is some evidence of God's grace in your life right now?
8. How does that evidence help you through your issues and struggles?

Living a Commendable Life, Part 2

2 CORINTHIANS 6:6-10

Main Idea: There are things you must know and do to live a commendable life.

I. Characteristics of a Commendable Life (6:6-7)
II. Empowerment for a Commendable Life (6:7)
III. Struggles of a Commendable Life (6:8-10)

A fairly wealthy family had plans for their children. One of their plans: they set them up to win from the youngest of ages. They hired a tutor at the early ages, and then they put them in the best Montessori schools, if you will, to help them develop, grow, and get the best education they could possibly get.

Even during the summertime, they hired people to give them three hours a day of education so that they wouldn't be off schedule. During the summertime they had to do book reports. These parents were setting their children up to win. Junior high school, high school, they pushed them forward to some of the most exclusive schools that were almost the cost of a college tuition. But that's how committed these parents were to their children's development and growth. So when it was time for college, of course, the scholarships were coming in from all over the place. The parents had a trajectory that they wanted their children on. They wanted them to go into specific types of crafts and fields. They didn't want them to pursue any crafts that didn't align with their clear plan.

One of their children happened to be artistic. The parents didn't like the disposition of that child. After all the education they provided, they didn't like the child going into an area of "I don't know if you're going to get a job" education. They said, "I don't think that pays anything." The child was distraught; she appreciated her parents' gift of education, but she wanted the freedom not to live under their expectations. Her parents had created a trajectory and life journey that didn't match her heart's desire.

So the child said, "Give me two years to dig into it. If it doesn't work out, then I'll do whatever you want me to do." Yet these parents kept pushing what their ideal of a stable life could be. What the parents realized later is that just because they set up their child for success on a particular educational track didn't necessarily mean that their child would pursue that particular field.

One of the things we must be careful of as believers is letting people dictate to us what life should look like. We have to be careful that we don't take some of the memes that sound good on social media as a principle for spiritual life. I started following some of the memes on one Instagram site that offered principles everyone should believe. You know, work hard this way so that you can get these results; while everyone's asleep, you work. Or this is the type of relationship you need, says one star, and she's looking over a man's shoulder. As beautiful as many of those memes and hooks look, many of them don't align with the nonideal life that happens when you're under the power of the Spirit. Indeed, if you're not careful, you will embrace a worldly philosophy of life and almost make it equal with a biblical philosophy of life. Then when you face real life, you're confused. But when you recognize what a real Christian life is, then you won't be confused because a real Christian life doesn't mean seamless pursuits and nothing bad will happen to you if you do everything right. Sometimes you can do everything right, and everything still can go wrong.

Now, if you're not a stable believer, you will view the Christian life in a weird way because you think A plus B equals C. But God is the one who orchestrates and who is sovereign over your journey. Everything isn't necessarily going to work out the way you *want* it to, but it'll work out *for* you.

Paul wants the Corinthian church to see that his own "ideal Christian life" has come about by nonideal circumstances. So Paul's presents a list of "everything" from "patience" to "slander" and says that these dichotomous experiences represent normal Christianity. Yes, these experiences may be confusing. And you may have had a confusing week and a confusing month. In fact, someone may have given you a pleasant phrase forecasting what this year was going to be like, and it hasn't turned out that way. And now you're wondering, "God, what's wrong with you?"

But the problem is that God's design is not for him to be aligned with us. God's design is for us to be aligned with him and with everything God is using as a junkyard for our sanctification. Everything's a junkyard for our sanctification. So what we're going through—and it's not working out the way we thought it was going to work out—is God working out things in us and for us but not necessarily for what we think we want and need.

In this text Paul describes a commendable life. A commendable life focuses on the evidence of grace in all areas of life. Earlier Paul expressed, "I want to live a life that doesn't put any obstacles in anyone's way from their seeing Jesus in my life." In other words, if something gets in the way of Jesus being glorified, I'm willing to fall back from it so that Jesus is clearly visible through me. That's the big idea. So he says, "We commend ourselves in everything" (v. 4). The way we show ourselves as commendable is by saying that what we are doing is commendable. Paul's list depicts the regular Christian life and authenticates if we're on track. Now most of us would look at such experiences and conclude we're off track, but the Bible would say we're on track. The Christian life continually challenges our expectations.

Again, Paul says in verse 4 that the way we commend ourselves is through "great endurance." "Great endurance" introduces the descriptive list recorded in verses 4 to 10 and implies many afflictions. This list represents the real Christian life, which turns constantly like a roller coaster ride. Great endurance means the ability to be strengthened to withstand difficulty.

I love powerlifting. I especially enjoy my first day of working out after some time away. Have you experienced this too? You feel excited about that first day because you believe you're back in your routine, and you do a little bit more than you were ready for. Then it is not the next day that gets you; it's the day after that. You wake up in pain because your muscles are all tight. You're thinking, "I don't want to feel sore anymore." But as you work out more and more, and you remain consistent under the adversity of working out, your endurance increases, and you experience growth without the soreness you had in the beginning.

God gives you the ability to be strengthened under the might of the gospel—to have a greater sense of endurance so the afflictions that happen in your life don't make your soul as sore as it usually would get. You're growing when the stuff that used to get on your nerves doesn't get on your nerves like it used to. When you sit back and realize, "That could have really gotten on my nerves today, God. But you know what? I know I'm a Christian. I know I'm growing. I know I'm doing better because that would've set me off about two months ago. It wasn't that long ago, but I'm growing." You ought to celebrate when that happens in your life.

So Paul names the experiences of great endurance in verses 4-5: "By afflictions, by hardships, by difficulties, by beatings, by imprisonments, by riots, by labors, by sleepless nights, by times of hunger." But then he transitions, saying, "This is how we commend ourselves."

Characteristics of a Commendable Life
2 CORINTHIANS 6:6-7

Paul has just described various situations. Now we're going to see the characteristics of what happens when the Holy Spirit is working in our lives and we're growing. We might not know it, but he's growing us. Paul has gone through this life cycle over and over again.

He declares, "By purity" (v. 6), meaning sincerity or authenticity. As you go through difficulty, the Christian life becomes more real to you. It becomes real in difficult situations because you can't really know "real" in good situations. If God lets everything be okay in your life, you're not going to pray. You know you're not. But you're going to get up when you feel the grace. Have you ever felt that peace from having a real good time with God on Monday, and now it's Thursday. You're thinking, "Man, the time was so good this week, I'm just going to fall back for a couple of days." You know what I'm saying? But the Christian who is committed to purity doesn't allow good times to fool him into the notion that he's okay in his soul. You must be careful of letting situational freedom make you think you're spiritually okay.

We're proven by purity. During these difficult times, we demonstrate our commendation by purity, which happens because of God's work through us. So this is that purity where God heats up your life on purpose and lets the impurities come to the top, like a smelting pot for metals. And he pulls the dross of that mess off. Then you get to experience in that season and area of your life a level of purity.

Moreover, Paul doesn't just say purity or sincerity or authenticity. He says "knowledge." Knowledge here is not just the deposit of information. In context it means growth and discernment. It's a sign of spiritual growth when you see what others don't see. Discernment means to look beyond what you see to perceive the core of what God wants you to see. That means you can look beyond the externals. That's how you know you're growing. You would have accepted certain things; you would have become involved in some relationships, but God purified your discernment. So you're not accepting stuff and taking jobs because they offer a high amount of money. You're not just engaging in a relationship because the person is pretty. You're not just moving over here because the grass looks greener. In other words, you begin to ask gospel questions. This is how you know you're growing. You begin to ask, "God, where do you want me?" If you just speedily make decisions, you're not walking in discernment. You are saying, "I'm just gonna do this!" That would be foolish. Instead, you're meticulous about wondering whether something's of the Lord. Real, commendable Christians function this way. Do not take everything on face value, but take things based on gospel value.

Now here is the true test to show whether your life is commendable: "patience." God is working on me in this area.

I confess: I hate patience. I hate waiting. I want what I want, when I want it, how I want it. I say, "God, please. All this waiting stuff is for buffoons. You know I love you. I've been walking with you twenty-some years. Just give it to me and quit all that spiritual growth stuff right now. Give it to me!" Yes, I know I'm preaching to myself, but every now and then you're just praying, "God, can't you just give me something now?" But that's not the way the Christian life works.

Rather, patience is not expecting everything to come quickly but settling into the fact that some things take time. Now there are some things I've been wanting God to do, and God just keeps taking his time. What I'm finding is that God is showing me something, and he's using patience as a form of suffering to build enduring patience. His purpose is basically to show me what I neglect in the now because I'm living in the future.

See, sometimes we are living in a mental future, when God wants you to be faithful in the now. And when you're living in a mental future, you can't focus and nurture now. That's why Psalm 37:3 says, "Dwell in the land and cultivate faithfulness" (NASB 1995). The psalmist is frustrated because God isn't doing some stuff quickly, and God tells him through the Spirit, "Sit yourself down, dwell in the land, and take care of where you are. I'll take care of the future." The key to patience is that God won't move you on until you begin the process of nurturing where you are. I don't care what you want to do; it's going to take some time.

Patience and contentment are key components of our life. We must honor God in whatever season he places us. See, patience says, "God, I'm not going to look at where I want things to be. What I'm going to do is focus on where you've placed me and what you've placed before me." If you always focus on the future, you can't appreciate the Lord. Your appreciation is not some big feature film of your life. You must be able to appreciate the grime and the grit of where God placed you and be faithful there. So I told myself, anything worth building takes time; therefore, patience is needed.

Courageous fortitude, which endures adversity without murmuring or losing heart, now that's what I need! Even in the times when you're waiting, you can't murmur and lose heart, and that's what's powerful about this reality.

Then Paul goes from purity to knowledge, and from knowledge to patience, and from there to kindness. Usually when God makes us wait, we're not very kind. Most of the time when we're going through something, we're snappy. How interesting that in this list one thing falls right after the other thing. That's intentional. So after patience he says, "Kindness."

What's kindness? Kindness means generosity and treating people in the way they should be treated—even the ones you don't think deserve to be treated that way. The test of your sanctification is to be kind to the people you don't think deserve it. That's commendable. When someone asks you about someone else, you say, "You know, that's a good brother, man; God bless him! I'm glad for what God is doing in his life." On the inside you're thinking, "Man, if you ask me about this person again, I'm going to go off." But sanctification pushes you to say kind things. That's how you know you're growing: kindness.

But Paul doesn't stop there. He doesn't just give the situation. He doesn't just give the characteristics of a commendable life. He also gives the empowerment that drives us. If he only said, "Be patient and be kind," we would feel helpless. Because no one can do that without some help. We need help from heaven to be all that.

In studying this passage (I read it once a quarter to help me), I noticed something striking. And almost every commentator I consulted mentions it, which is Paul's exegetically intrusive placement of the Holy Spirit.

Notice this: "By purity, by knowledge, by patience, by kindness" (v. 6), then suddenly he puts the Holy Spirit in there. Now why in the world would you put the Holy Spirit in the middle of a passage? Because that's who you need to help you live a commendable life. In other words, Paul says, "What makes this happen is the oiliness of God's presence." One commentator talks about the Holy Spirit being the rock or the bedrock that holds the passage together. It's as if, with these characteristics up front and these characteristics on the backside, the Holy Spirit is the one who's saying, "Listen, you're going to have to coexist." Let's look at where the Holy Spirit is. The Holy Spirit is between two things: kindness and sincere love. The Holy Spirit is there because kindness and sincere love are the two most difficult characteristics to offer others when you're facing difficulty. The Holy Spirit supplies us with the power to execute because he's the superintendent of our sanctification. He's the superintendent who oversees and even applies the gospel to our spiritual growth, and he's there to help throttle us up in that particular area to develop us. Paul is saying, "This is the empowerment." Paul says what has marked his apostolic ministry is the power of the Spirit. Nothing he does will work unless the Spirit is blowing on it. Nothing in your life will work, family of God, unless the Spirit is blowing on it. So Paul is nurturing us and helping us understand what biblical commendation looks like.

Then he adds "sincere love" (v. 6). This is authentic love for people you don't like. Not mere acts of love but sincere love. It means love that likes. So he wants to nurture love in us and help us realize that, as important as this entire list is, these two reflect its outworking. Kindness and sincere love are not only at work in us through the Spirit, but they also impact others though our outreach.

Finally, he says, we commend ourselves also "by the word of truth," authentically communicating the truth, not flattering people with what they want to hear.

Empowerment for a Commendable Life
2 CORINTHIANS 6:7

Now, how do we live such a commendable life? Paul offers an encouraging balance here; he speaks of divine dependence and its characteristics. He says the commendable life is done "by the power of God." How is this accomplished? In two ways: "Through weapons of righteousness for the right hand and the left." In your walk with the Lord, there are times when you must play both offense and defense. The right hand signifies a weapon you would use to be on offense, like a sword, and the left hand usually held the defensive weapon, a shield. Both point to chapter 10, where it says the weapons of our warfare aren't carnal but spiritually powerful for the destruction of fortresses. Also, in Ephesians 6 Paul talks about the sword of the Spirit and the shield of faith. Now he assumes you have on the full armor of God. Sometimes we are to fall back as Christians, but falling back doesn't mean apathy and a lack of activity. So he communicates that there are times as a believer living a commendable life when you will know how to fight. He's speaking of the spiritual warfare activity that discernment lets you see so you can fight when you're supposed to fight and defend when you're supposed to defend.

Interestingly, the shield in biblical times was a large shield that protected the whole body; the shield represents faith. Paul is fighting discouragement at this point. How do you get discouraged? The flaming arrows of the devil.

The devil loves to hit us as believers while we're going through trouble because he wants us to exalt what we're going through instead of exalting God. Paul says we must defend ourselves because we're most vulnerable to the attacks of the enemy when God's working on us. When God is doing surgery, we're most vulnerable, and so we must have defensive weapons. We are the only people anointed by God to fight during surgery. God doesn't put you and me to sleep during surgery. God keeps us awake during surgery. This is a surgical passage. What he's telling us to do, while he's working on us, is to defend against arrows. God gives us the grace to defend ourselves. He doesn't always practically defend us without our doing anything. Moreover, God may be saying, "Because I've caused you to go through it doesn't mean that the war is over. It may mean the war has just begun."

These weapons in the right hand and in the left suggest divine dependence. In this act of divine dependence, by the power of the Spirit, we are called to walk in biblical faith. And when we hold the shield out, we don't have to stab anyone because the shield covers everything.

Struggles of a Commendable Life
2 CORINTHIANS 6:8-10

Then Paul discusses what we do this "through." Namely, we defend ourselves based on God's empowerment "through glory and dishonor" (v. 8). Glory is when people want to magnify you, and dishonor is when they want to minimize you. Paul says a commendable life doesn't let situational ups and downs impact our identity in Christ. That's powerful. Whether "through glory," when people are praising us and we're feeling good about ourselves, or in the midst of dishonor, we have been empowered to live a commendable life. In other words, we must not use our fluctuating feelings and circumstances as an open door to walk away from our responsibility as believers.

Paul goes on, "Through slander and good report" (v. 8). Slander is when people say untrue things about you and it hurts you, but you have to keep going. Slander is one of the primary tools of the devil. The way he got kicked out of heaven was slandering God's throne. And if you look through the Bible, you'll see how he has constantly used slander as a way to direct God's people away from where they're supposed to be. So they use slander to say untrue things and praise to say true things. Paul says, I stand in all of this.

He expresses, "I'm treated sometimes as an impostor. I'm authentic. People say I'm not authentic in my Christianity, that I'm not an authentic apostle. Yet I'm found to be true." So he's encouraging himself right in the midst of that. I've seen seasons of my life when God has to override the lack of affirmation I receive from my surroundings.

So Paul observes, "As unknown, yet recognized" (v. 9). He says, I may not be popular, but I'm known by God. Then Paul declares, "As dying, yet see—we live" (v. 9). He continues, "As being disciplined, yet not killed; as grieving, yet always rejoicing; as poor, yet enriching many; as having nothing, yet possessing everything" (vv. 9-10). Paul is fundamentally identifying what affirms his ministry and how a Godward perspective emphasizes the spiritual reality versus the natural reality. In life, you are in three phases: going into a trial, in a trial, and coming out of one. With that framework in our journey, we can understand that we will constantly experience these dichotomies. Therefore, we need tools for what it means to be consistent in the midst of adversity. The perspective Paul gives is the means.

How do we apply this to the Christian life? We may not have everything we want, but we have everything we need. In fact, we possess everything that makes us who we are, says Paul. Our identity in Christ and empowerment of the Holy Spirit provide us with everything we need to live a commendable life. He is communicating, "You may be poor in popularity, you may be poor in wealth, and you may be poor in opportunities, but guess what? Based on God's rubric, you possess everything." Conversely, a noncommendable life seeks everything outside of the Lord.

When you become a believer in Christ, your view turns upside down. Scripture declares that in plenty and in want, you're kept through every situation. That should encourage you where you are and where you're going, that God's activity doesn't end in all types of difficulty in your life. Therefore, your life and walking in these things are applause before God's throne, a big praise before the living God. Why? Because he's the one working and willing in you his good pleasure.

Reflect and Discuss

1. Have you ever experienced a time when you felt like you were doing things right, but everything was going wrong? If so, describe it.
2. How did that shape your view of God and the Christian life?
3. Out of the characteristics of a commendable life that Paul names, which ones do you most need to grow in? What are some ways you can grow in them?
4. What is God's empowerment to help you live the commendable life?
5. How does that encourage you to live the commendable life?
6. What are some of the struggles of the commendable life Paul named that you've experienced the most?
7. What allowed you to overcome those struggles?

Being a Community of Distinction

2 CORINTHIANS 6:11–7:1

Main Idea: God calls us to be a community of distinction.

I. **A Community of Distinction Must Develop a Godly Affection for the Church (6:11-13).**
II. **A Community of Distinction Must Be Particular about Who Has Access to Our Souls (6:14-15).**
III. **God Identifies Himself with Us as We Identify Ourselves with His People (6:16–7:1).**

In the early part of the twentieth century, there was a theologian, activist, and Christian pastor who in some people's view was a controversial and polarizing figure. He was polarizing in some ways because of his commitment to deradicalize Christianity. That is, his desire was to see that what the Bible communicates is not a different type of Christianity that needs an adjective like "radical" to describe it. In other words, he used the word *radical* to mean something other than what's normally communicated. He observed that *radical* is actually the reality of what's in the Bible. He challenged the body of Christ on the cost of discipleship. He challenged the body of Christ by saying that coming into the faith is free by faith alone, through grace alone, through Christ alone, because sanctification, although it's paid for too, does cost you a commitment of sacrifice. He found himself coming to these United States. His name is Dietrich Bonhoeffer (for this and the next few paragraphs, see Metaxas, *Bonhoeffer*, 108–9).

Bonhoeffer left Nazi Germany at its height, when it was moving toward World War II. He came here in 1930 to attend seminary in Manhattan at the great Union Theological Seminary. He expected to get robust biblical theology and robust systematic theology. He expected to learn exegesis and inclusive multiethnic church history. His desire was to be blown away by an exalted and cosmic commitment to Jesus. Yet he found himself in the corridors of apathy. He found himself under the pillars of simplicity and idolatry and playful Christianity that was

135

substandard. People needed to quit taking Scriptures for granted and start taking them seriously.

A friend of his, who was a sociologist, was doing some work at the great Abyssinian Baptist Church there in Harlem, New York. His friend said, "Let's come from these churches in Manhattan. Let's roll over here to hood Harlem to just chill over here and see what's going on at the Abyssinian Baptist Church." So there, under the leadership of Dr. Adam Clayton Powell Sr., he found something in that hood church that he did not find in the ivory tower of a seminary. He found a man who preached great intellectual truths from the Bible, not dumbing it down, to people from public assistance to the boardrooms of Manhattan. He was committed to saying that he wanted to bring the weightiness of the Christian faith there. And there Bonhoeffer finally found the gospel. There he finally found biblical theology and systematic theology. Not only did he find a powerful pulpit, but he also found a commitment to street engagement.

The Abyssinian Baptist Church was one of the first churches in the boroughs to build a community center, which impacts and transforms the community even to this day. But beyond the great intellectual realism, biblical theology, and systematic theology that shaped him—and even the social action that was connected to regeneration (not just the social gospel, as people would say)—Bonhoeffer discovered that the gospel changes everything. The gospel offers regeneration, which impacts the social implications of life in the city. The gospel changes everything. He not only saw that, but he entered homes of older Black folk in that neighborhood. And he found himself, as a man whom God raised in a racist Germany, now being theologically trained in racist America in homes of people eating fried chicken, collard greens, black-eyed peas, rice, and corn bread, yet being embraced as part of the community. He saw Christianity for the first time as seen through these poor yet transformative, committed people. They were not exalting their Blackness; rather, they were incarnating the eternal realities of Jesus Christ in the corridors of a broken inner city after the Harlem Renaissance. And he said that he finally found the faith!

When Bonhoeffer found it, it was a deep embrace and hug from the community that had accepted him. And I wonder today, if he were here, if he stepped into our inner cities, if he stepped into some of our churches and he stepped into some of our fancy and not so fancy edifices, what would he find? Would he find this type of community where the people of God take the Bible seriously? Where they take the moving of the Spirit seriously? Where they take biblical commitment and connection and accountability and submission and love seriously? What would he find if he came today? We now arrive at a text that is spectacularly glorious. In these verses 2 Corinthians 6 reaches a climax in Paul's desire for the believers to stop erring on the side of carnality and start pouring themselves into Christianity.

A Community of Distinction Must Develop a Godly Affection for the Church
2 CORINTHIANS 6:11-13

Paul pours out his and his colleagues' love for God's people—so much so that he wants to show his open commitment and affection toward them at the expense sometimes of himself. He says, "We have spoken openly to you" (v. 11). In other words, he's been straight up with them. That's what Christianity needs. Christianity needs truth tellers. He didn't say, "I'll just put you on blast." What he says is, "I've spoken plainly to you. I didn't hide anything from you that you needed." I don't know about you, but that's what I need in my life. I don't need people to talk *about* me; I need them to talk *to* me. When Paul mentions speaking openly, he inserts the government name in the middle, "Corinthians." Then he says, "Our heart has been opened wide" (v. 11)." He didn't put an *s* on "heart," but he does use the plural pronoun, "our," pointing to the unified desire of his crew to love as one group, one person: God's church.

A heart wide open means emotional freedom. We find something powerful here. We find someone who's willing to tell you off but hang out with you.

The Bible says that we should be "speaking the truth in love" (Eph 4:15), right? The truth without love is condemnation. The truth with love is edification. Truth left alone is constipation. So I'll have the center instead of the outer because I want someone in my life who isn't afraid of me or intimidated by me. I want people in my life who love me enough to tell me off but to lick my wounds after they've given me a verbal beatdown. Paul expresses, "Our heart has been opened wide." The embedded idea exegetically is that he is emotionally open. What hurts the church many times is we have so many emotional issues that we can't open up to anyone.

Often, we insert our past experiences into our present experiences and miss out on the expansiveness of what God wants to do through us in the current experience. That's why we have to be set up to heal from some stuff so that, as God moves us forward, we can receive all that God has for us. But you and I can't get all that God has for us if we are allowing ourselves to be emotionally broken by the past, over and over again. Rather, we must deal with it in a way that we can open ourselves to receive from God in the present. So he says, "We have spoken openly to you" (v. 11). That's what we need.

You know, I'm going to be scared of you if, when I say, "Hi, how you doing?," you say, "I'm blessed and highly favored of the Lord, hallelujah!" Yet you're walking with your baggage under your arm, and nothing is ever wrong with you. I don't want to spend any time with you because you can't be honest.

I need some people in my life who will speak freely and who will open their hearts wide to me. I need people in my life where I can hear their story. See, you won't pass judgment on someone if you know what they've gone through. So one of the beautiful gifts of biblical community and opening your heart wide is sitting down with them and listening.

You know what I like to ask people? "How did you come to know the Lord? Where did you grow up? Talk to me." You might have thought someone was a bit crazy, but after you hear her story, you realize, "Oh, she isn't as crazy as I thought!" Because you listen to what she went through and see where she is now. True healing takes into account what others went through.

That's why it's important to listen to God's narrative trajectory in people's lives. Listening gives you a wide-open heart to people who have major issues. Now I know you think it's just for them, but it's also for your crazy mess. You need to be in a place, as well, where you tell your story in a nonjudgmental environment and people can hear and understand you better. Then, if someone else comes into community saying, "So-and-so is crazy," you can say, "Hold on, hold on now! You don't know. You don't know them like that. Fall back, chill out, join the church, get serving, and get in a life group, and then come talk to them. But don't say that until you know." You must be able to do all that.

You can hear their hopes. You can cry together. You can hear their disappointments and let them pour out their heart because the Bible says, "Confess your sins to one another and pray for one another, so that you may be healed" (Jas 5:16). What's your hang-up? That is, what is your kryptonite? You need to have a couple people in your life who know your kryptonite. I have people in my life who know my kryptonite, so they know how to redirect my GPS. I have people in my life that I invite into my crew. You need to be willing to invite. Now you may say, "Everything is not for everybody." What you have to do is give out elementary, then intermediate, then advanced information about yourself. Give someone a little information about you. Stand back and see what he does with it. If it comes back to you through channels, then you say, "Right. Off to the next one." In other words, "You can't handle a nugget; your social media post was about me without my name. So I'm not fooling with you anymore." But if he could take the elementary and honor it, then you give him some intermediate. Soon you discover he can handle that intermediate. Wow! Then you just let it all loose. But you can't do that with everyone. You can't be hypervulnerable because the Bible says in Proverbs 18:24, "One with many friends may be harmed." That means you've got to get a tight formation of a few people you trust. And it may not even be the people you grew up with. You need this type of community around you to be able to encourage you, to check you, and to strengthen you.

Look at what Paul says: "We are not withholding our affection from you, but you are withholding yours from us" (v. 12). "Withholding" means to be emotionally narrow—not narrow in the good biblical sense but narrow in a sense of being almost fully closed off and emotionally unavailable to the body of Christ. So he is calling them to emotional availability.

I can remember when my wife and I finished seminary years ago, and I would exclaim, "Hey, man, I finished seminary!" I knew everything. I *knew*. You understand: two and a half years of Greek, two years of Hebrew, a semester of Aramaic, a little bit of Ugaritic up in that mug. You know what I'm saying? I translated books of the Bible. I translated Obadiah. I translated John. I translated Romans twice. So, you know, I thought I was going to come to the church and help the church out because I was a beast at twenty-five years old. I was going to help people who have been walking with Jesus longer than I'd been living. You know, I just knew more than they did because I spent four years in seminary, and they'd been walking with Jesus for sixty years.

I ended up going to Good Hope Missionary Baptist Church in Houston, Texas, where I took an assistant pastoral role. And God bless my little young wet-behind-the-ears heart. So my wife and I are there. They gave me the midday Bible study on Wednesdays, and the average age was eighty-five years old. I'm bringing Bible study methods for seminary students. I was going to teach them everything I knew about the Bible. I stepped in there with my chest out, and they're looking over their glasses at me like I'm crazy, but you know what I love about them? They had seen it before. Because they had seen dumb young preachers before, they knew the trek of patience. So they let me teach, God used it, and it blessed them. But they did more for me than I did for them. And guess what they started doing?

They knew my wife and I were new to Houston. So they introduced us to the cuisine of Houston because a lot of them were from Louisiana. They would bring big old pots of dark gumbo. I'm talking about that murky gumbo, and the claws are hanging out of the gumbo, and the chicken is all shredded. They would make us homemade corn bread with jalapeños and cheese and corn. They invited us into their homes and accepted us and nurtured us. They began to talk to me and slide little things in on me, and without my knowing it, it began to open me up to not just wanting to talk to the church but to love the church.

Have you ever been to a church where, even if there are no ushers and no hospitality, you feel a hug from the congregation without their touching you? That's a gift. So as Paul lays this out and challenges us with this idea of restrictions and affections, he wants us to be opened up to the Lord.

A Community of Distinction Must Be Particular about Who Has Access to Our Souls
2 CORINTHIANS 6:14-15

Paul says, "Do not be yoked together with those who do not believe" (v. 14). Now, many of us have heard this scores of times, and we've interpreted it in relation to dating. But in context, the interpretation is richer. In their day, they would use bulls or oxen to plow fields so they could plant seeds. It would be strange to them if they saw two different species of animals under the same yoke plowing because different species of animal have different strengths and different purposes. So you wouldn't put a donkey beside an ox. It would look foolish. They would have said, "Why would you put them together?" The yoke doesn't even fit because an oxen yoke is this size and a donkey yoke is that size.

Paul is pointing back to Jesus where he says, "Come to me, all of you who are weary and burdened, and I will give you rest. Take up my yoke"—there it is—"and learn from me, because I am lowly and humble in heart, and you will find rest for your souls" (Matt 11:29). In his context, Jesus is talking about people who have tried to do stuff on their own, people who have tried to live under the law, have failed at the law, and felt the heaviness of their self-failure. He says, take that yoke off; put on my yoke instead because it "is easy and my burden is light" (v. 30). He is saying, "I'm giving you freedom from doing stuff on your own. Therefore, since you're getting freedom from doing stuff on your own, you can plow more effectively because now you're yoking up with me. I'm not yoking up with you. I fulfill the law. You take off the law and put on my blood. You take off your own efforts, and you put on my divine life. You take off your ability to be legalistic in all your effectiveness and ineffectiveness and put on my death, burial, and resurrection."

So, what is Paul communicating? When you yoke up with an unbeliever for soul stuff, you're putting yourself under a yoke that will always weigh you down. Now, I'm not saying you can't be around unbelievers at all. That's not what I'm talking about. They can tell you how to buy a car. They can tell you how to buy a house. They can tell you how to put a résumé together, but they can't help you to get emotionally free from a broken relationship. You ask, "Tell me how to get over this relationship." And they're going to tell you all kinds of crazy stuff.

Our problem is we are being pastored by the culture and not being pastored by Jesus. Many of us find our hope and our ideas and our counseling off the *Breakfast Club* and *Power 97*. Many of us find our relationship and business advice off of *Empire*. Most of us find our view of singleness off of that other show—yeah, you know what I'm talking about. In other words, we are being culturally pastored versus biblically pastored.

Paul expresses, "Why in the world would you want to yoke yourself to mess again? Why not yoke yourself to the Bible and to biblical community?" When in the world are you going to really believe that this actually works? I'm telling you, you get with some godly believers and some food, you're going to get it! It works. What is the first place you go for answers when you've got a struggle? What's the first place you go when you have frustration? Many of us wing it when it comes to decision-making. God is trying to nurture you to be distinct, not foolish. And how many times do you have to fail before it will work? So Paul tells them not to put themselves in situations where they're opening up their souls to people whose souls are dead.

Paul asks, "For what partnership is there between righteousness and lawlessness? Or what fellowship does light have with darkness?" (v. 14). What is Paul talking about here? He uses the words *partnership, fellowship,* and *agreement.* This idea is summed up in the word *agreement,* which points to worldview and ethics—to who shapes your way of thinking and how you walk in what you're thinking. So when he asks, "What agreement does Christ have with Belial?" (v. 15), he's essentially telling them, "Stop trusting yourself by yourself." Don't think you can handle something when you can't.

Back in the Corinthians' day, their clubs were different from ours. They had a mixed temple, which was used for both spiritual and pagan activities. So their temples had idols, and they worshiped the demons through praying to the idol, with the presence of the food being sacrificed cooked for everyone. But then nudity and orgies were happening everywhere. So the Corinthians were so spiritually mature, they said, "Hey, man, you want to go get something to eat?" "Yeah, let's go get something to eat." So they go down to the club acting like they can handle that.

Let me just be pastorally straight up: some of you need to stop acting like you can handle what you aren't able to handle. You can't handle your ex: "I'm just going to friend him on social media, and it's not going to be anything with that." Or you say, "Oh, I haven't seen that fine woman in a while. You know, I'm going to send a friend request and maybe share the gospel at some point." You must know what you can handle. You have to be smart enough to say, "Man, let me just block every connection that has anything to do with that situation." See, being distinct isn't your asserting yourself. Being distinct is admitting what you can't handle. You know you're ungodly if you say you can handle what you can't handle. Godliness is admitting weakness, not asserting strength.

That's why all my intimate friends know my stuff straight up. We get on the phone: "How are you doing?" We immediately talk about our need for the Lord. And we say things like "Man, why you doing that? Man, stop tripping!" We're going off on each other, loving each other, praying with each other, and challenging each other. That's what you need in your life.

By the way, be careful that you do that in a unisex environment. I don't think men and women can be friends like that. You can say what you want, but you can't go to the movies with an opposite sex buddy. Just let me give you my testimony. I've been there. I'm thinking everything's copacetic. You know, I'm just oblivious because I'm a dumb dude. I'm not knowing, "Let's go to the movies; let's go out to eat." We're just buddies. Go and get in the little booth in the mall and take a picture together—you know, not knowing that Shorty got a collage in her apartment.

You understand what I'm saying? When you're talking Bible and you're godly, that's attractive. I'm telling you something. "Hey, we're just friends. That's my sanctified bro." No, no, no, no, no! I've seen best friendships end up with estrogized testosterozation with epinephrine mysticism. You can't handle it! "This is my buddy." No, we can be buddies in community with other people around. And don't go driving them home because if you park outside of the apartment and you're talking, an hour goes past, then two hours go past. Then she goes into the house, and he goes into the house. Man, I'm just telling you!

Ladies, you need to tell them, "I can't emotionally handle this. Do you have any intentions for me? What are your intentions?" I remember a girl asked me that, and that thing was like Dracula and garlic. And fellas—this is free pre-relationship series—don't be just calling and texting verses randomly to women without it being a group text. I'm just being real practical. "I just wanted to show you that the Lord loves you." In their mind they have picked their dress; ladies you need to be honest.

God Identifies Himself with Us as We Identify Ourselves with His People
2 CORINTHIANS 6:16–7:1

Look at what Paul says: "And what agreement does the temple of God have with idols? For we are the temple of the living God" (v. 16). Notice that Paul says *we* are the temple, not *you* are the temple. Notice the unity of community. He's applying the death and resurrection of our Lord centrally to help us understand the nature of biblical community. How does he point us to this reality? "We are the temple." That means we together are now a temple, and we have different uses and utensils within us. The way God uses us is different now. That should give you godly esteem in him and good knowledge of self.

Then Paul quotes Jeremiah: "I will dwell and walk among them" (v. 16). Because of the gospel, God makes his dwelling among us, here with us. And, quoting Isaiah, he says, "Come out from them and be separate" (v. 17). Being separate means that we shouldn't have fellowship with darkness, but we should be a witness to all. Paul writes, "Do not touch any unclean thing, and I will welcome you" (v. 17). Then, quoting again God's words through the prophets, he says in verse 18, "I will be a Father to you, and you will be sons and daughters to me, says the Lord Almighty." Or, in today's language, "If you get in community with one another, you'll realize you're mine. You'll have my presence and my paternity." Practically, God is always present and wants to be continually present in our lives. God is not like someone trying not to own that you're his. He's not a deadbeat dad who pushes back. "I don't need to see a paternity test." God has already saved you through gospel adoption. Christ's blood runs through your veins. Therefore, you already have his paternity.

We affirm the paternity of God in our lives when we get around people of our bloodline. How do you know you are part of the family if you don't ever get with the family? You say, "Hey, we're family." We can't tell that if you don't ever come to any family reunions. Every time we get together, it's a family reunion with Christ at the center.

Look at what Paul says in 7:1: "So then, dear friends, since we have these promises." Yes, we have promises. That's what makes us different. Promises are things God says he will do; he will keep his word. He says you can bank on these. So he declares we have these promises. What does God promise? What does he confirm? That you'll have my presence, that I'll continue to affirm no matter what that you're mine, and that I'm demanding that you be distinct. I'm demanding that you walk in awareness of my presence.

Therefore, "let us cleanse ourselves from every impurity of the flesh and spirit" (7:1). In other words, "Whatever in your life is clogging your ability to experience me, get rid of it." Paul communicates that cleansing yourself means confessing sin, repenting, and experiencing the place of biblical community.

And then finally he says we should be "bringing holiness to completion in the fear of God" (v. 1). "Fear of God" means standing in all the reality of God. Bringing holiness to completion is our sanctification process in which we arrive closer to where God wants to expand us to grow spiritually to look more like Jesus Christ.

I remember when I first saw a man working with pizza dough. I was young and was watching him work with this little piece of dough. I asked my mom, "How much more dough is he gonna put with it?" And my mom said, "Baby, he's not going to put any more dough with it."

I'm looking, and he takes some cornmeal, he takes some flour, he lays it out, presses the dough, and it's still small. Then he begins throwing that dough in the air. Suddenly, it starts to expand and expand and expand. It gets real big. I said, "Mommy, that's too big to put stuff on." And she said, "Watch him, baby, watch him." Then he put it down, and it had expanded to just the right place. He sauced that dough up, dropped some mozzarella cheese and other stuff on, and boom! He put it into the oven. I was blown away.

Something so little, when it got into the hands of the baker, was able to get bigger because it submitted itself to being stretched. It submitted itself to being pushed out further in the hands of the baker than it could be by itself. And when it got to its place where it was stretched to its borders, ingredients that it didn't have on it in the first place could be added to it because it submitted itself to the handiwork of the baker. What I'm trying to tell you is to submit yourself to the Lord and biblical community. Allow yourself to be stretched; allow yourself to be pushed; allow yourself to be thrown in the air. God and his community will add things to you that you can't receive on your own.

Reflect and Discuss

1. What is your view and emotional disposition toward the church?
2. How can you grow in godly affection for the church?
3. Do you have a community of people around you who will speak the truth in love to you? Why or why not?
4. In what ways are you being more pastored by the culture than by Christ?
5. Is there anything or anyone in your life you're unequally yoked to right now?
6. How does it feel to know that you've been adopted into the family of God?
7. How does gospel adoption encourage you to be stretched more for what God is calling you to do?

How to Work through Church Hurt

2 CORINTHIANS 7:2-13

Main Idea: God empowers you with all you need to deal with your church hurt.

I. **Dealing with Church Hurt Involves Joyful Optimism (7:2-4).**
II. **Dealing with Church Hurt Involves Coming alongside One Another (7:5-7).**
III. **Dealing with Church Hurt Involves Authentic Repentance (7:8-13).**

I love spending time engaging people with the gospel—just talking to people who have a lot of challenging assumptions about the church and particularly about pastors. One time I was engaging a guy with the gospel, talking to him about Jesus Christ, and trying to strengthen him and engage him. Everything he brought up, the Lord was dropping a little answer on me for him.

Every time, over and over again, I was able to respond to his different assumptions. Then it occurred to me that no matter what question I answered, this guy was just determined to be an antagonist toward the faith. As I listened to him and answered some questions and engaged him, I realized that the questions I was answering weren't his issue. The questions I was answering scientifically—the questions I was answering intellectually, historically, and epistemologically—were not his issue. In the background, these things were merely fog covering some of his church experiences.

What I learned is that everyone who has an issue with the church isn't necessarily wrestling with gender questions. They're not necessarily wrestling with their understanding of the historical Jesus or their view of the resurrection. Many times, the root of people's disposition toward Christianity trails back to a season when God gave them an opportunity to come among the people of God and to be engaged by the people of God, and they had high hopes for Christianity. But sadly, they didn't run up against the truth. They ran up against us.

When they ran up against us, something happened. Now I'm not condoning apostasy. I'm not condoning a disposition toward the church that is antagonistic. However, I don't care how long I live on this planet, most people I know who have been in the church and who have an issue with the church have dealt with church hurt. I don't know what it is about church hurt, but church hurt is worse than family hurt. I'm talking about a person who sat across from people for over two decades. I've dealt with people's family issues, and they were optimistic about getting over the humps of some of the most broken family issues, but when it came to church hurt, it was almost like shut-down ministry.

Some research has been conducted over the last few decades. Every year more than four thousand churches closed their doors compared to more than a thousand new churches that opened. Forty-five hundred new churches started between 1990 and 2000 with a twenty-year average of nearly a thousand. Every year 2.7 million church members fall into inactivity (Krejcir, "Statistics and Reasons"). This is in the United States. This translates into the realization that people are leaving the church. It says, from the research, they are leaving as hurting and wounded victims of some kind of abuse, disillusionment, or just plain-old neglect. It's interesting that they do a study, and they find out that people aren't leaving the church because of doctrinal reasons. People aren't leaving the church because we're not doing social justice. It's because of some type of hurt from coming up against the body of Christ and its leaders in some way that has pushed them away from being in the local church.

At first it was hard to get my mind wrapped around this passage because Paul sometimes has such complex language in his communication. It seems like he's dumping subjects together. But as we step into the passage (even though we know this is the "Keep It 100 Series") and look closely at it, we discover that this is probably the most vulnerable passage Paul ever wrote. His vulnerability is based on the Corinthians feeling hurt by Paul and Paul feeling hurt by the Corinthians. That's what's going on in this passage. What he's trying to do here is to face those hurts with the gospel so that they won't turn into relational inactivity with one another and so that he can encourage them and strengthen them—and so that they could even strengthen him.

We're going to find out in this passage that church hurt is both for people in leadership and for those who are in the pews. Most of us think we are the ones who get church hurt, but both leaders and parishioners, because all are part of the body, experience hurt and pain.

The question is, What do we do about it? How do you handle church hurt? Do you run? Do you avoid confrontation? Do you just vote with your feet? Or do you commit yourself to a gospel that put God on the cross, where God shows through Jesus the most effective way to deal with hurt is through his hurt.

Dealing with Church Hurt Involves Joyful Optimism
2 CORINTHIANS 7:2-4

Paul says, "Make room for us in your hearts" (v. 2). "Make room" means to extend the emotional borders. Paul is telling the people of God, "Listen, I know I hurt you and you hurt me, but the only way for reconciliation to happen between us is that you extend the borders of your hearts that are closed off to me." He's challenging God's people.

I remember when my wife and I lived in an extremely small apartment with one bedroom. We had a kitchen that was on the wall, and it didn't even have its own area. It was smaller than an efficiency. We didn't have that much furniture, and when you put in one couch, the whole apartment seemed to shrink. But it was funny because people always wanted to fellowship at our place. And I was thinking, "Why do you want to be over here? Some of you have massive homes. Let's go over to your house!" They loved our house because, even though the house was small, we were willing to press in to allow as many people in there as possible in order to experience the joy, community, and fellowship the gospel brings.

Paul is saying, "I want you to open up your heart in the way that the God of heaven has made it available. Even though it's crowded with hurts, even though it's crowded with frustrations, even though it's crowded with brokenness, I don't care what's in there. I want you to excavate and declutter whatever is in your heart stopping you from experiencing comprehensive *shalom*, restoration, comfort, and strength that only Jesus Christ can bring." Some of you need to learn how to do that.

Some of you are so closed—not closed-minded but closed-hearted. Closed-hearted is different from closed-minded. The mind is a part of the heart spiritually. That's why you may be tight-lipped now. It's some people in your life in the church—I'd forget about your family right now—the local community, the local church, that have hurt you so deeply you have shut down your ability to ever be hurt again because you believe that if you open your heart up again, if you let someone else in again, if you let some leader shepherd you again, if you let the body of Christ be the body to you, then someone is going to hurt you. Let me give you the answer to that: Yes! They will! But you can't grow unless you open yourself up. You're not going to grow.

Paul starts off the passage with this challenge. Because the Corinthians didn't want to talk to Paul, he had to send Titus (we'll see that later). You have to understand, Paul led them to Jesus. He was their spiritual father. So Paul didn't hurt them intentionally; rather, they had a bad interpretation of what he had executed to them lovingly as a leader. Instead of receiving it as a spiritual means of rebuke and development, they came against the character of his leadership in order not to deal with the conviction of their sin.

He says, listen, can I talk to you? "We have wronged no one" (v. 2). Wow! He says he has "corrupted no one" (v. 2). This is church hurt language. In other words, "I didn't live my life trying to co-opt you to get at your gear, to get at your clothing." Paul's saying, "Do you know how much I gave up to pastor you?" He communicates, "I'm getting my tail whupped for the gospel. I'm not no super-apostle." But some such false teachers had come in. Since they wanted natural things from the people of God, the false teachers turned them away from the gospel. The people's hurt stemmed from a false view of the gospel and not a true view of it because they had allowed themselves to be drawn away by the foolishness of those who nurtured them in their church hurt.

You have to be careful of people who nurture you and provide a greenhouse for your mess. You have to be careful of the person who's listening to your mess too much and never challenging you. That's not the person you want in your life. Such persons are false teachers. Every now and then you need someone to say, "I've listened to you; now can I say a few things?" You need someone like that in your life who's going to talk to you about your stuff and not nurture you in your foolishness. This is so powerful!

Paul says he has "taken advantage of no one" (v. 2). It's interesting: Paul's expressing, "You love leaders who take more advantage of you than the one that loves and leads you." As a pastor, many times you feel as if you're fighting a ghost. We have a new member class, and I love the class because I learn a lot about people. But one of the things I've heard more in a new member class than anything else is church hurt. I can't tell you how many times I've heard, "At my old church . . ." And they'll name the church and name the pastor. I'm uncomfortable—this should have been a counseling session, not a group therapy thing. Then they'll say, ". . . but here you are different." I've been on the earth for a little while, and the same way you're publicly denouncing him, just let me do one little thing and I'll be on the other end of your denouncing in five seconds. So I don't take compliments that are based on the detriment of someone else; I only take compliments that are just free. If you want to encourage your pastor, just let it be free from where you came from.

Verse 3 says, "I don't say this to condemn you." Look how loving Paul is. He means, "I'm not saying this just to make you feel bad." He says, "Since I have already said that you are in our hearts" (v. 3). Wow! He is saying, "Open up your heart to me, but you are already in our hearts." Do you know how deep that is? They were publicly rejecting him, and he didn't let that dissuade him. That's why you must have the gospel.

Nowhere in the world as a leader can you get slandered by an entire congregation and then tell them, "You're in our hearts." You have to understand the cross. Christ on the cross had to allow himself to have this same disposition, or he'd have come down from that device. Even in your life—and this is the issue—what makes church hurt different is that the people are in your heart, and the hurt takes place in the same place. You can't get them out of it, so what you try to do is to excavate them from your heart and barricade it.

Paul is saying, "Even though you're in my heart, and my friends and I feel the hurt (it wasn't just Paul; it was also his missionary group), we're still good to get in it with you." Look what he declares: "To die together and to live together" (v. 3). He is saying, "I'd rather die with you." That was first in the Bible; "ride or die" is not new. He expresses, "If we're representing this gospel together and we get persecuted, I'll gladly die at your shoulders as we're persecuted together as a unified unit for Jesus Christ, or we can live together. If we're not under persecution and we live together, this is not mere existence; we can flourish together." So Paul conveys, "I want reconciliation with you!"

In verse 4 Paul admits, "I am very frank with you." He's saying, "I know I'm saying some things to you that you're not used to anyone saying to you." He adds, "I have great pride in you" (v. 4). This is not ungodly pride; this is godly pride. He says, "I am filled with encouragement; I am overflowing with joy in all our afflictions" (v. 4). He's going to tell you why in a second. The affliction here is not the sufferings he's going through in Macedonia and in different places, which he's going to explain soon. The greatest suffering he's going through is his relationship with the church. Paul is saying, "Nothing hurt me like being hurt in the local churches." God is using Paul to face his church hurt. When people come to my church and they have church hurt, I send them back to their church. We think the increase in disciples is great, but they're not going to be healthy here—not just *here* but *period.* I'm not so excited to let them warm a pew to the detriment of their dealing with their past. I would rather they be healthy and not here than to be here and we nurture them in a lifestyle that's unhealthy. They should drop their sacrifice at the altar, and then go be reconciled to their brother.

Okay, what if they don't respond to your overtures? "If possible, as far as it depends on you, live at peace with everyone" (Rom 12:18). You're not sovereign. You can't control the response of people to your repentance and your commitment, and you can't make them deal with the hurt you've caused them or they've caused you. All you can do is repent and engage, share your heart, and deal with it. If they don't respond properly, it's between them and God now.

Paul is trying to do that with the Corinthian church because he has joy for a reason.

Dealing with Church Hurt Involves Coming alongside One Another
2 CORINTHIANS 7:5-7

Paul continues, "In fact, when we came into Macedonia, we had no rest. Instead, we were troubled in every way: conflicts on the outside, fears within" (v. 5). They feared for their lives, basically. He says, "But God, who comforts the downcast, comforted us by the arrival of Titus." I love the way the New American Standard translates verse 6: "But God, who comforts the depressed." Paul struggled hard with depression. One of his depression triggers was his relationship with God's people. Every person I know with depression has a trigger. Can you imagine dealing with depression through the experiences he faced?

Paul is depressed in Macedonia, getting beat down on all sides, extremely depressed. Titus, the guy he led to Christ and discipled, came and had a counseling session with him. Let me just say this: you know you made a good disciple when your disciple can turn around and give you therapy. That's good Bible right there, that God so worked in Titus that Titus could encourage Paul.

I remember a few years back going into a difficult church meeting. People were standing up against me, and I can remember standing my ground—God keeping me. I walked into a corner, and tears started rolling down my face. One of the elders walked over to me and grabbed my shoulders, looked me in my eyes, and began counseling me. Other members came over ministering to me, quoting Scriptures, standing with me, praying with me, quoting theology to me, and ministering to my soul. And through the depression I was feeling from being attacked, from being frustrated and going through church hurt, I felt counseled by the flock.

The leaders don't just need that; we all need that. That's what the body is for. This idea of comforting is the same word used of the Holy Spirit, the Greek verb *parakaleō*, which means "come alongside" and hold up. That's what we have to do with one another. During the time of brokenness and church hurt, we must come alongside one another and strengthen one another. We must nurture one another and preach the gospel to one another because we serve a God who fills people with his Spirit to give us a word in season.

Paul continues: "And not only by his arrival but also by the comfort he received from you. He told us about your deep longing, your sorrow, and your zeal for me, so that I rejoiced even more" (v. 7). You see, some were responsive when they got the previous letter Paul sent them, and they began repenting and wanting relationship and community with him again. This tells me that it's possible for breaches to be healed among God's people. That this is possible means church hurt doesn't have to last forever. Look at what he says. There was "longing," their desire to be with him; "sorrow" over the issues that they had among one another; and "zeal," which was exceptional fervor to accomplish God's purposes in dealing with the issues of church hurt between them and Paul. Beautiful!

Dealing with Church Hurt Involves Authentic Repentance
2 CORINTHIANS 7:8-13

This is the difficult one. Confrontation we love because we love to give people part of our mind. But when we must own something, it's totally different. Look at what Paul says: "For even if I grieved you with my letter, I don't regret it. And if I regretted it—since I saw that the letter grieved you, yet only for a while" (v. 8). When you get rebuked or challenged on the front end, it grieves you for a while. But if you're a believer who's sensitive to God's Spirit, you should be thinking, "Maybe someone has a point." Do you see what I'm saying? Whenever someone challenges you amid a church hurt situation, you have to consider, no matter how right you feel, that you may be wrong. In verse 9 he says, "I now rejoice, not because you were grieved." That is, "I don't want you to be comprehensively hurt." He explains, "But because your grief led to repentance." Repentance isn't acting as if everything's okay or putting on a front. Rather, repentance is to change your opinion and mind in relation to the breach between you and someone else. It literally means a change of mind, not about individual plans, intentions, or beliefs but rather a change in the whole personality away from a sinful cause of action toward God. You can't even get saved without repentance. If you're a believer who never repents, you should doubt your salvation because you can't separate repentance and faith. They're like conjoined twins—they're together.

Now Paul explains the difference between two kinds of grief. He says, "For godly grief produces a repentance that leads to salvation without regret" (v. 10). Godly grief means you've examined things from God's perspective. That means you're not examining it with that other person in the foreground. If you let your feelings toward the person get in the way, you can skate your way around godly grief because you're looking only at that person. But the question should be, Is what this person said biblical and part of the heart of God? If you consider that, it leaves you to lean into God and say, "God, deal with me."

So godly grief leads to repentance. It literally means "grief according to God." I call it "hopeful sadness." It's the change that focuses on God's interests; it's grief that is driven by the interest of God being reintroduced to the soul of the believer. It's authentic repentance versus counterfeit repentance.

Then Paul says, "But worldly grief produces death" (v. 10). What is worldly grief? It's "hopeless sadness" or sorrow. Hopeless sadness is bitterness and anger without resolution. It leads nowhere. Worldly grief just says, "Nah, I'm not fooling with them ever again. I'm going to treat them like vampires." Ungodly or worldly sorrow always focuses on self, not God. I like the way Puritan preacher Thomas Watson explains counterfeit repentance:

Another deceit about repentance is resolution against sin.
. . .

We see by experience what protestations a person will make when he is on his sick-bed, if God should recover him again; yet he is as bad as ever. He shows his old heart in a new temptation. (*The Doctrine of Repentance*)

Counterfeit repentance just wants to be out of the hurt of the situation and not deal with the situation. That's why David in Psalm 51 shows us what authentic repentance looks like: godly sorrow. David did four things: he threw himself on the mercy of God, asked to be cleansed by God, expressed the impact his sin had on others, and asked God to change him from the inside out.

Finally, Paul says,

> *For consider how much diligence this very thing—this grieving as God wills—has produced in you: what a desire to clear yourselves, what indignation, what fear, what deep longing, what zeal, what justice! In every way you showed yourselves to be pure in this matter.* (2 Cor 7:11)

In other words, they weren't inherently innocent; the gospel made them innocent. They began dealing with the false teachers. They began repenting and dealing with the issues. When he said "diligence," he meant they committed to making things right. "Indignation" meant they dealt with the offender. "Fear" drove them to a passion for God. And "zeal" and "justice" were evident.

Lastly, Paul writes,

> *So even though I wrote to you, it was not because of the one who did wrong, or because of the one who was wronged, but in order that your devotion to us [really, to the gospel] might be made plain to you in the sight of God.* (v. 12)

He says, "For this reason we have been comforted" (v. 13) because you gave us an opportunity, essentially, to close the gap in the thing that caused a division between us. The beauty of being a Christian is that we get to experience the solutions of the good Lord that he brings through Jesus.

The Bible says in Isaiah 53:3-5—it's just so plain—

He was despised and rejected by men, a man of suffering who knew what sickness was. He was like someone people turned away from; he was despised, and we didn't value him.
Yet he himself bore our sicknesses, and he carried our pains; but we in turn regarded him stricken, struck down by God, and afflicted.
But he was pierced because of our rebellion, crushed because of our iniquities; punishment for our peace was on him, and we are healed by his wounds.

Jesus experienced church hurt. He experienced church hurt while he was about to get crucified. His closest friends went to sleep while he was being carried away by godless men. His dear friend, Peter, who said he'd never leave him, cursed him. The Bible says we didn't want anything to do with him. He experienced the greatest amount of hurt: dying for people who rejected him while he was dying for them.

Jesus experienced church abandonment. Jesus experienced betrayal by the people who were supposed to love him. You may have experienced this. While dying on the cross, he said, "Father, forgive them, because they do not know what they are doing" (Luke 23:34). The one who has the right to hold a grudge didn't hold it. That's the gospel! The gospel is letting people go, not counting their sin against them. My Bible teaches that he didn't let his bad experiences turn him away from the mission God had placed on him. He died for those doing him hurt. He suffered for those who brought him sorrow. He was bruised for those who tried to break his spirit. And he was a propitiation for those who persecuted him. Jesus's death on the cross heals all hurts, all pains, and all betrayals. He is able to rebuild the most broken and fragmented of hearts.

Church hurt is the most painful kind of hurt you can experience. I guess it's because it's the place where we have the highest expectations. Even the world holds us to "You're supposed to be a Christian." So it's a high standard because of who Jesus Christ is.

In 7:13b-16 we see a glimmer of light. It would seem that Paul doesn't view the Corinthians as a lost cause, but he perceives a level of teachability. Their reception of Titus is evidence of grace: "And his affection toward you is even greater as he remembers the obedience of all of you, and how you received him with fear and trembling" (v. 15). They received him with reverence, and his authentic love for them was known to Paul. In verse 16 Paul voices his optimism concerning this conflict being resolved. As hurt as Paul is by their actions and disposition toward him, he is pursuing peace with them.

One of the most difficult things to do in relationships where you are wounded, especially by believers, and something that takes an enormous amount of maturity, is seeking gospel resolution. One of the things that is painful in pastoring is people having no regard for the impact of their actions on the pastor's emotional and spiritual health. Although people talk a lot about church hurt, few know pastor hurt. Most pastors deal with a lot of conflict with congregants that never gets resolved. Over the years, I've experienced people causing conflict in the church, and when you try to help resolve it and seek peace, if they don't want to deal with the truth, they leave. And when they leave, they spread carnage in their wake that has to be cleaned up. Many times it can affect your perceived credibility and personal relationships.

Paul felt this deeply, to the point where Titus had to minister to him and engage the Corinthians as well.

Reflect and Discuss

1. What is church hurt?
2. Why is it so hard to open your heart with love for others after you've been hurt?
3. How does the gospel of Christ help and compel you to deal with your church hurt?
4. What does it look like for the people of God to come alongside one another in times of pain and hurt? Have you ever experienced that for yourself?
5. What's a way you can encourage your pastor and/or ministry leader?
6. How does false repentance differ from authentic repentance?
7. Why is authentic repentance necessary for reconciling with others?
8. How does meditating on church hurt and the abandonment that Jesus experienced help you to heal of your own hurt and to forgive others?

Having a Lifestyle of Generosity

2 CORINTHIANS 8:1-7

Main Idea: Generosity is a part of the core DNA of a mature disciple.

I. Giving Comes from God's Grace and Joy (8:1-2).
II. Giving Has Three Characteristics (8:3-6).
III. Giving Should Continue to Be Done (8:7).

Do you know people who view the church as a money-laundering scheme? Have you had contact with churches that have been just about money? Have you have seen preachers who are just about money? Sadly, when many people think of the church, they think of fraudulent activity or someone wanting your money. But when we examine this passage in chapter 8, we see a different perspective.

Even for many believers, money-hungry and miracle-promising televangelists are their framework for Christian giving. However, we are called to surrender all things to God's glory—not just our income but our lives—and to the lordship of Jesus Christ. Our spiritual lives should mirror this calling because we are the church body. And therefore, Scripture gives us parameters to measure where we are spiritually, and one of those is prayer. Are we praying and surrendering our lives to God daily? Another measure of where we are spiritually is our investment in the Word. Further measures are how we deal with others and whether we're sharing the gospel. And another one is our giving. We must understand what the Bible says about giving so that we can grow spiritually, and not just in generosity toward the church but also in comprehensive stewardship with everything we have. God has given us everything so that we can use it all to honor him; we must honor the Lord God with everything in our lives.

Paul's words in this passage are contrary to what we might expect. In the first part of his letter, he exhorts the Corinthians about their need to grow as Christians in different areas of their lives. Then he asks them for money after that! Most preachers would take a different approach: "God's going to do this for you." Then they give all these false claims, so that by the time they ask for money you feel good about believing that what they said is coming to pass—and it is connected to the resources you're going to give. However, we see a different narrative in the Bible. We need to understand this narrative and see how God uses our stewardship to engage the world.

Giving Comes from God's Grace and Joy
2 CORINTHIANS 8:1-2

Generosity is a part of the core DNA of a mature disciple. Paul says, "We want you to know, brothers and sisters, about the grace of God" (v. 1). He's just talked to them about reconciliation with him in the last part of chapter 7. Now he's going to talk to them about the grace of God. "Grace of God" here is God's unmerited favor that comes through what Christ has done for you and me. The Greek word *charis* can be translated not only as "grace" but also "favor." Favor is always about God giving you something to lift him up with.

Most of us, when we think of favor, think of what we can get. "God's hand is on me. God's going to do something through me. All my haters are going to be looking up at me." We think of favor in the sense of self-glory, but in the Scriptures, favor has to do with God giving you something to leverage it for him. When you hear "favor," you should not hear your exaltation; you should hear God giving you an opportunity for something bigger than you. That's what favor means.

Varying levels of favor are given to believers based on God's choice to use them in their sphere. Receiving God's favor is not about being a better believer or lesser believer. Rather, it's about what God has decreed for each believer. Paul says, "We want you to know, brothers and sisters, about the grace of God that was given to the churches of Macedonia" (v. 1).The Macedonian churches are probably Philippi, Thessalonica, and Berea. They are all distinct, inner-city churches.

Now, you couldn't just enter the Berean church and say anything you believed. In fact, the Hebrew Israelites[2] wouldn't go there. If Hebrew Israelites entered, the Bereans would demand, "What you need to do for us is open up the Scriptures and prove what you say. Give us

---

[2] Hebrew Israelite culture is a Black Religious Identity Culture (BRIC) that emerged from the vacuum in the American church as it preached and proclaimed a broken image of Blackness (Mason, *Urban Apologetics*, 93). Hebrew Israelites believe that Blacks, native Americans, and Hispanics are the original tribes of Israel in the Bible.

knowledge, wisdom, and understanding!" The Philippian church was a persevering body that endured through God's resilience, whereas the Thessalonian church was eschatologically minded. It wanted Jesus to come back quickly and didn't want to deal with now. The congregants would start working, and when they heard that Jesus is coming back, they'd say, "I'm quitting my job!"

God was at work in each of those churches, and Paul begins to walk with them. But how did Paul receive his call to go there in the first place? One day Paul and his friends were about to go into Asia, and the Holy Spirit told them no (Acts 16:9-10). Paul went to sleep, and God gave him a vision of a Macedonian man crying out, "Come over to Macedonia and help us!" Paul woke up and said, "I think God wants us to go to Macedonia." The Holy Spirit opened the door. They went to Macedonia and preached the gospel. In all these cities, Paul started reaching people, and they began coming to Jesus Christ. Then they became supporting churches for the future of the mission of God through Paul so that Paul could continue to promote the gospel of Jesus Christ.

Verse 2 begins, "During a severe trial brought about by affliction." This affliction is severe, next-level suffering. Trials point to character development. When God tests you, the Bible says, "Consider it a great joy, my brothers and sisters, whenever you experience various trials, because you know that the testing of your faith produces endurance" (Jas 1:2-3). The work of the Smelter is to heat up your life on purpose to bring the impurities to the top so he can scoop the dross off and see his face when he looks into what he's creating. In other words, God decided to use the difficulty that his people were going through, and not take them out of it, for the sake of their character development. Likewise, sometimes the reason God doesn't deliver you and me from affliction is because he's still working on us. So God let the trial get worse. It wasn't just a trial. It was a severe test through affliction. And whether in biblical times or now, God uses affliction as a way not to show *him* who you are but to show *you* who you are. Affliction is meant to show you who you really are and who you're not—not to leave you there but to work on you so you can be who God wants you to be. That's the goal.

Although affliction may have affected the atmospheric pressure of the Macedonian churches, Paul exclaims, "Their abundant joy and their extreme poverty overflowed in a wealth of generosity on their part" (v. 2). Wow! How in the world are believers going through hell and high water with joy? Because being a believer is unending satisfaction with God no matter what.

What is amazing about being a Christian is you can go through excruciatingly painful circumstances—loss of job, sickness, relational frustrations, all different types of pain—but you endure because God has given you some joy. You'll say, "God, I'm in pain, but I'm satisfied with you even though I don't have everything I want."

Paul says that they have joy in extreme poverty. Look at the adjectives: *severe* trial, . . . *extreme* poverty" (v. 2; emphasis added). How in the world, in between severe trials and extreme poverty, can you have joy? Paul situated joy between the two. To be held together, you need some joy in the midst of all that.

They have extreme poverty. Where did that poverty come from? We must understand that in their culture, only 5–15 percent of the people were wealthy; everyone else was poor. No middle class existed. Even today in most third-world countries, there is no middle class. There's poor and then there's rich. What you had in their day was believers who had businesses. I want you to imagine this. You went to school, you took tests, and you graduated magna cum laude. You have your MA, you learn how to do app development, and you start a little business. You have a GoDaddy and your little websites set up. You've been working hard at Starbucks because you need insurance until you get the business running. You did all the work to get everything up and running. The business is struggling the first year; then, all of a sudden, you have investors, and the business starts building up. Now you're in this big corner office, Picasso on the wall, a flat-screen TV under the see-through table. You have a receptionist who brings you teas and coffees from Teavana and overseas.

Then you become a Christian, and no one wants to work with you anymore.

That's what happened to these people. They lost everything because they became believers. And rather than denounce Christ, they said, "I'm OK to lose my business." Some of these people were already poor, but some people got poor by becoming believers. The severe affliction was coming from being a believer. Can you imagine one day being at the top 5 percent of the wealthy people in your country and the next day being at the bottom 5 percent of poverty? Yet look at their hearts. Look at their minds. Look at what happens: They "overflowed in a wealth of generosity on their part" (v. 2).

They wanted to give to an opportunity Paul had shared with them. He describes them as overflowing with wealth. In connection with joy, your giving is a reflection of your satisfaction with God. If you're not satisfied with the Lord, you don't give. Their giving flowed from joy, not manipulation. If you don't give to the gospel mission, you aren't experiencing satisfaction with God through Christ.

Jesus saw a woman. He was in the temple with his apostles, the Twelve (Mark 12:41-44). They were on the back wall looking while people were tithing. People were throwing stuff on the altar. You know how they do it in some of these places. Dudes running all across the money. And then this old woman comes up looking like a hobo (we used to call them bag ladies back in the day), and she drops two little coins in. And Jesus says, "Look at her; she's given more than everyone else"—because generosity is based on the heart, not the amount.

Giving Has Three Characteristics
2 CORINTHIANS 8:3-6

In verse 3 Paul says, "I can testify that, according to their ability and even beyond their ability, of their own accord." "According to their ability" means they didn't give emotionally.

I remember one time back in college we went to see this preacher, and the Holy Spirit was in that place. People were laid out and all kinds of stuff. They took up the offering. People were running up there dropping it on the altar, running up there when he gave a word. Then they got to the parking lot, and the Holy Spirit left them: "Man I just gave my rent money!" So Paul is essentially saying, "It's according to your ability; you don't just act a fool trying to be with everyone else."

I remember in one church that you had to have something in your pocket to give. Scripture says give according to your ability, in your pay bracket, not beyond it. Don't get into debt giving to God's ministry because it wasn't your money. So it wasn't generosity.

Nonetheless, Paul adds that some were giving "beyond their ability." Why would he say that? Because there are times when the Spirit will tell you to give sacrificially. There are times when the Holy Spirit will prick your heart, and he will push you to give. And you're thinking, "But God . . ." Give. Now, that's not the preacher leaning on you real hard. God will lead you when you are presented with an opportunity. Pray about the opportunity, and don't just say you're going to do it. Watch your mouth. Ecclesiastes 5:1 says, "Don't be bumping your gums when you come into the house of the Lord" (that's the Eric Mason translation). Instead, wait, pray, and let your yes be yes and your no be no. But then it says that they gave "of their own accord" (v. 3). That means they freely gave. Why is this important? Because these people were poor.

What was the spirit of their giving? The spirit of their giving was, Paul says, begging us "earnestly for the privilege of sharing in the ministry to the saints" (v. 4). So that means Paul didn't ask them to give; he simply presented the opportunity. He probably communicates, "Let's pray for the saints of Macedonia, particularly in Philippi. I had to write them a letter talking about what they're going through: to live is Christ and to die is gain."

He was keeping it real with the believers, and they asked, "What's going on in Macedonia?"

"Man, you can't believe it: because of the persecution they are losing their homes and businesses."

So everyone got together to give money for relief. And Paul actually said no. How do I know Paul said no? Because they begged him. They insisted on participating, and guess what they called it? Paul says they called it "the privilege of sharing in the ministry to the saints" (v. 4). Or, as the New English Translation puts it, "the blessing and fellowship of helping." In other words, they were saying, "I want in on this kingdom investment. When I look at the investment of that thing, I want to be able to say, eternally, that what I gave helped God's work to increase."

Our church has planted eleven churches in Malawi, Africa, and as a result, hundreds of Black girls are now able to go to school in their neighborhood. They no longer have to walk two hours away in fear of getting raped and molested. Because the opportunity was presented and the sacrificial giving was offered, we helped God's work to increase. In light of that, Paul said, "And not just as we had hoped" (v. 5). We didn't even expect them to act like this, but "they gave themselves first to the Lord and then to us by God's will."

Giving Should Continue to Be Done
2 CORINTHIANS 8:7

In verse 7 Paul observes, "Now as you excel in everything—in faith, speech, knowledge, and in all diligence, and in your love for us." He says they should see that they "excel also in this act of grace" (v. 7). He's challenging the believers to give. Giving should be seen as flowing out of what Christ has done for us on the cross. For thirty-three years God let God the Son not be in heaven with him. That was generous. He not only gave his Son, but God gave us everything to enjoy. And in light of that reality, our giving flows from his giving to us.

Reflect and Discuss

1. How do you view the church with regard to money?
2. What does God's grace or favor mean?
3. How does God's grace lead to our joy?
4. What is joy, and how can you have it in adverse situations?
5. What are the characteristics of giving?
6. Why is it important to not be emotionally manipulated into giving?
7. How does God's grace compel you to keep on giving to gospel mission?

Impact of Jesus Money

2 CORINTHIANS 8:8-15

Main Idea: Jesus has generously given to us, so we should generously give to others.

I. Generosity Isn't Done under Pressure, but It Must Not Lack Commitment (8:8).
II. Jesus Sets the Tone for Generosity (8:9).
III. Generosity Counts on Follow-Through (8:10-12).
IV. Generosity Has a Reciprocal Effect (8:13-15).

There is a young man who has captivated minorities and others in inner cities through his messaging and communication. He grew up in Philadelphia, and he calls himself the Prince of Pan-Africanism. His name is Dr. Umar Johnson, and a few years ago he posted a video about white Jesus money, and it went viral. He's challenging the church on what he perceives as a lack of helping inner cities, in particular, to experience a comprehensive socioeconomic transformation through the money that was given. He argues this money is handed over to white banks, which promote redlining that doesn't positively impact the fabric of the inner-city community.

I've listened to him and many others, and I hear their heart in many ways. On the one hand, I agree with their sociological and economic concerns yet take note of the historical, spiritual, and socioeconomic fallacies that pervade their interests. On the other hand, I believe the church must take more seriously the need to construct more than just buildings to make up for the failure to impact the fabric of communities. Practical redemption needs to occur on every level. That doesn't mean we leave out gospel preaching. I'm speaking of both spiritual justice and social justice because I don't see them as two separate things. I see them as two sides of the same coin. Most revivals happen in middle- to upper-class white evangelicalism. That's documented. However, inner-city revival is not really documented, and there's a desperate need for inner-city revival. My theory is the next revival that is going to happen among ethnic minorities in cities is going to come from a clear connection between what's put in the plate and what happens on the block.

I believe it is going to take prayer. I believe it is going to take Holy Spirit movement. I know what the reformed revivalists say. However, there has to be a connection between the social and the spiritual. Indeed, it's a fallacy to think inner-city churches have not impacted the fabric of ethnic minorities in lower socioeconomic communities.

In this powerful text, Paul is challenging the church at Corinth, who has the money, not just to make a claim of what needs to happen in ministry and in missions but also to come through with their promise. If you pledge that you're going to give something, then give it. Paul is telling them, "Don't complain about what's not happening if you're not contributing to it."

Generosity Isn't Done under Pressure, But It Must Not Lack Commitment
2 CORINTHIANS 8:8

In verse 8 Paul says, "I am not saying this as a command." Paul isn't saying that this is apart from the word of God or even that he doesn't have the right to give a command to the flock on this matter. Rather, he wants to take a different approach when asking them to resource gospel mission and help move God's kingdom forward. This is firm gentleness. Paul is careful how he approaches the Corinthians on generosity. He wants them to show maturity by not having to be commanded. He doesn't want to have to push them extremely hard. I believe many ministers of the gospel have messed up people's view of money because they expect people not to be generous. These preachers believe it's their work, not the Spirit's work, to make people give. Paul is doing something here that is totally the opposite.

He doesn't create a false prophecy to help people give. He does something more powerful. He appeals to spiritual Christian maturity. You know you are a babe in the Spirit if you're not generous. He says, "Rather, by means of the diligence of others, I am testing the genuineness of your love" (v. 8). He wants to use the Macedonian church's inordinate generosity as a motivation because the Macedonian church was the inner-city hood church with no money. They didn't have money, but they begged Paul to let them participate in gospel mission—not for what they could get out of it but for what they could see happen based on their economic and spiritual participation and God's involvement. Paul acknowledges that he wants to prove the Corinthians' genuine love. In other words, "I want to show you the Macedonians so that I can show you what earnestness looks like." Remember, the Corinthian church had substantial money. So he is saying, "Look at them who had no money, and they begged to give. But when it comes to you—a year ago you made pledges, but I haven't seen anything in the account yet." He's using the generosity of the Macedonians as a way to test the authenticity of the pledge of the Corinthian church. This is powerful.

I visited Progressive Baptist Church, Chicago, where I was shown two pulpits. Dr. Martin Luther King Jr. helped foster the movement of civil rights and social justice in Chicago from one of the church's pulpits. Other unknown people made significant sacrifices to help promote resourcing, not only in the Civil Rights Movement but also for comprehensive care of needy people in the neighborhood. They helped sustain lives in the midst of racial segregation and injustice. That flowed from the local church.

We stand on the shoulders of those who sacrificed. If we would look back and see God's historical-theological narrative of the church in the city, we would have to recognize the church's amazing sacrifices. Still, we are called likewise as members of Christ's church today. We shouldn't just want to come hear a word or to have a place for our children or for air-conditioning. We should also ask what our presence helps to do here besides people saying, "I see people going in and out of there, but nothing's happening around here." Paul offers a challenge and test of our character.

I'm a foodie. I like food, and I *love* reduction sauces. I especially like a port wine reduction, which is used as a demi glaze on a good steak. The sauce starts as a thin liquid, and as it's heated, it reduces down. Even though it's less sauce later, it has more body. It has more richness. And it has more flavor. What Paul is trying to do is reduce the liquid of God's people who are watered down by too much stuff. He's trying to reduce them down to the bare minimum of what makes us the salt of the earth. What God is calling us to do as the church is to be reduced. Sometimes God can do more with less.

Paul is challenging the Corinthians' understanding of giving. As he says, this is not by command. Although Jesus received commands from the Father, you rarely in the four Gospels hear him talk about being commanded by the Father. His motivation for what he did stems not from command but rather devotion, which you hear in his "I must" statements. For instance, Jesus told them that it was necessary for him to suffer many things from the elders, chief priests, and scribes (Matt 16:21). Christ was passionate about what his giving was going to do in our lives. We must also be passionate in our giving as his followers. We must have this mindset in our entrepreneurial society where everyone is building a brand for themselves. At the end of the day, what does God's kingdom get out of our desire to make a name for ourselves? Let us heed Paul's challenge to the Corinthians: "I believe that your love is genuine, but your love can't be genuine through verbiage. I need to see that something happened because of your resourcing it and your affections for Jesus Christ."

I'll never forget when we resourced the money for Malawi to get the school built there—Mercy High School. Sister Harriet told me about when she first went there, before the high school was built, and then seeing the school built during a later trip. She said, "If you went there when nothing was there, you wouldn't have thought of anything being there coming back a year later." Now you see a high school, with 150 young men and women no longer having to walk two hours to school but going in their own community. The fact that there's a waiting list now broke her down. Giving should have that type of impact on you.

I'm not saying there's no reciprocating treasure. I'm not saying you don't build for yourself treasures that are imperishable. Matthew 6:20 implies that there is a reward. However, that's not the only reason we give. We don't just give because we believe, "If I give this, then God's going to start my business. If I give God this, then God's going to enhance my bank account." No, sometimes it's just for you to be in on what God already wants to do. That's enough. It's enough just to be in on it and to be able to say, "Man, I can't believe that God allowed me to be a part of what he was sovereignly planning before the foundations of the earth, that I'd get a chance to resource that thing." My desire for us as believers is that we would be ministries of generational impact, and that if Christ isn't coming back for another thousand years, there would be a residual effect on the block, in the city, and in the world from the fact that we passed through here.

Most HBCUs started in the basements of churches. After slavery was abolished, only 5 percent of freed slaves were literate. The church began to take on the charge of literacy for a hundred-year period; while sharing the gospel, they were starting schools and literacy programs. The literacy level of Black people went from 5 percent to 70 percent. The Black church has done much for the Black community and other ethnic groups. The church in the city has always been committed to this mission, and we need to grab hold of the legacy of the orthodoxy and orthopraxy of the church.

We like to talk about the five solas. We also like to talk about inerrancy and infallibility, which are of stupendous importance. We insist on the centrality of the Word of God, the centrality of the glory of God. Now we need to port-wine reduce ourselves into the reality of being able to see some of that hit the block.

Jesus Sets the Tone for Generosity
2 CORINTHIANS 8:9

Paul writes, "For you know the grace of our Lord Jesus Christ: Though he was rich, for your sake he became poor, so that by his poverty you might become rich." When you don't agree with Paul, he goes to Jesus. Paul extracts *Christus exemplar*, Christ our example, from looking at *Christus victor*, Christ our victory, and points us to the penal substitutionary atonement of Jesus Christ. Paul helps us understand *Christus exemplar* by rooting it in Christ's incarnation, passion, death, resurrection, and ascension.

Jesus left stuff. He became poor, says this verse. That's a good translation. Additionally, John's reference in John 12:37-41 points to the fact that the man in Isaiah 6 to whom the angels were saying, "Holy, Holy, Holy"—the one who was sitting on the throne and his train filled the temple—was Jesus. He's sitting on his throne in all majesty and glory, and the Bible says he left that. In our come-up culture, we're not trying to come down. Jesus put himself in a position that expresses, "I'm going to become absent from heaven where angels wait on me hand and foot, even though I don't need anyone to wait on me, and where people call my name with the heavenly host of heaven for eternity." Jesus had all that. Jesus was next to the right hand of God the Father in the joy of the triune Godhead forever. He left that for you and me, and he became poor (Phil 2:5-8). How amazing!

We try to be hood rich and act as if we have money when we don't. If we do have money, we want to show it off with our material possessions. But Jesus didn't want to come here in his eternal bling. As a matter of fact, it would have been dangerous if he had come here in his eternal blingage. He would have wiped us out. So he cloaked himself, came down here secretly. He became poor because he wanted to settle down for thirty years and live a normal life to empathize with our existence on planet Earth. He wanted to experience our struggles, temptations, frustrations, and hurts. He allowed himself to take on an additional nature along with his eternal nature; he became human to come down and save us.

So he became poor. His parents, when he was a toddler and it was the time for the census, offered turtle doves and pigeons. That tells you how poor they were because that was a lower socioeconomic sacrifice that God allowed under the law. So based on a theocratic rule, he was born needing public assistance. Yet he owned everything. I don't know how you can be humble, knowing you own everything, and not grab hold of it.

But why did he do it? "He became poor so that by his poverty you might become rich" (v. 9). Amazing! In what ways did he make us rich? Ephesians 1:3 says he gave us every spiritual blessing in the high places. Romans says all things in the Father are ours. We're rich in truth, based on John 14–17; we're rich in relationship with God in John 17:3; we're rich in unlimited intimacy potential with God according to Ephesians 1:17; through the rest of that chapter, we will be able to be eternally conscious, truly waking up. We have the ability to stay woke based on Christ shining on us according to Ephesians 5:14. We are rich in the ability to address life issues with the gospel in Ephesians 5:16. And we are rich in another way with good works in Ephesians 2:10 and the whole book of Titus. That's the way we're wealthy.

Generosity Counts on Follow-Through
2 CORINTHIANS 8:10-12

Paul says, "And in this matter I am giving advice because it is profitable for you, who began last year not only to do something but also to want to do it" (v. 10). In this passage, he communicates, "You said you were going to give to this opportunity." Even for the unbelieving, the Spirit has stirred them to jump on board with this opportunity to serve. He is challenging and engaging God's people to make sure they keep their commitments. He's not saying, "Don't make commitments so you won't have to keep them." He's saying, "Make commitments, and keep those commitments." Paul is saying that to us as well.

In verse 11 he states, "Now also finish the task, so that just as there was an eager desire, there may also be a completion, according to what you have." Notice that he's not asking us to make unwise decisions. We're not going to pass a credit card machine down the row for you to pay on your credit card and put it on credit. He's saying to be generous out of what you actually have. So this involves thought. This is not an ecstatic stupidity. We're talking about thinking, measuring, praying, and then offering resources for God's kingdom to be built. He says that if the readiness is there, it is acceptable according to what a person has, not according to what a person does not have. The Bible teaches sacrificial giving; it doesn't teach impressive giving. He's not trying to get you to impress anyone.

My family tells me a story about a pastor of the church they were in before I was born. He was trying to do a building project. He saw these rich people coming in and enjoying themselves. So he looked at the giving records. He saw the giving was low even though the people dressed fancy and had material possessions. So he did something crazy: he took everyone's giving records and published them. Then when everyone gave, he would post their giving on the bulletin board. It built in the church a culture of people wanting their name on the bulletin board based on what they gained. So it got the effect he wanted for giving, but he didn't realize the negative effect on the souls of the people in the ministry.

So we're not condoning manipulation. The Bible says, "Don't let your left hand know what your right hand is doing" (Matt 6:3). We're not trying to impress one another with what we give; we're trying to honor the Lord and see his ministry go forward.

Generosity Has a Reciprocal Effect
2 CORINTHIANS 8:13-15

We don't emphasize up front the reciprocating effect of giving. However, giving does have a reciprocal effect. And God allows it to be a motivation for our giving at certain points. Store up for yourself treasures that are imperishable, not ones that are perishable where moth can eat up or thief can steal or rust can destroy. That's what Jesus says in the Sermon on the Mount, the most famous sermon of all time (Matt 6:19-20; see also 1 Cor 9:25).

Paul declares, "It is not that there should be relief for others" (v. 13). In other words, giving to the church shouldn't be the work of a few. It should be the work of each of us, with whatever finances we have, making a commitment to be a regular giver to what God is doing. Then when the opportunity for sacrificial giving comes, you sacrifice to give. So it shouldn't be a burden of a few. It should be the role of all. He says, "At the present time your surplus is available for their need" (v. 14). That is, "You don't know how your pocket is going to look later. So don't let God bless you with resources, and then you become arrogant and decide not to use the resource for someone else." Every good and perfect gift comes from the Lord, says Scripture (see Jas 1:17). Hence, consider your surplus at the present time.

God doesn't have to keep money in your account. He can sneeze and everything goes bankrupt. God gave you your resources, Paul says, "so that their abundance may in turn meet your need" (v. 14). In other words, don't let resources make you think you don't need anything from the Lord because sometimes having all you want in the natural doesn't mean you have all you need in the spiritual.

What he's saying is that giving is so spiritual that something does happen in the Spirit. When you sacrificially give, God, in his goodness, graciously provides for you too. His provision begins to work on you; it nurtures, challenges, pulls, and stretches you so that you can remember who it comes from and why he gave it to you.

Paul says, "There may be equality" (v. 14). In other words, "This is fair that you give for the resources of needy people to be blessed first in the body, first in the household of faith, then others." He is saying, "Don't think because you have some resources and they don't have any that you are better. Don't think your giving is only a one-way street. It is a mutual partnership between the ones who need and the ones who have."

Abundance applying to need (v. 14) alludes to the situation in the wilderness: "The person who had much did not have too much, and the person who had little did not have too little" (v. 15; see Exod 16:18). God is showing that he provides for both. He's saying that your giving your little money isn't going to make you poor. And they're not going to overrun you because God is supplying their need too. So it is like the manna God gave—some gathered a lot of manna and a lot of quail, or a little bit of manna and a little bit of quail. All were full equally, perhaps because the people who had more were able to share with the older people who could not get out and gather as much, and everyone had what they needed. In other words, what God provides for you is overflow for someone else.

One of the most legendary churches on the Eastern Seaboard is Concord Baptist Church of Christ in the Bedford-Stuyvesant section of Brooklyn. It has been guided by several well-known pastors, but the most well-known was the late Reverend Doctor Gardner C. Taylor, really the prince of preachers for his generation. He was the last of a dying breed of narrative preachers. He was the one who could tell a story and take you through the texts on a tour de force. His sermonizing is so legendary that all of his sermons are archived in the Robert C. Woodruff collection at Atlanta University Center as a part of American history.

Some people would look at Gardner and just see his massive collection of sermons. But he also invested his time at Concord Baptist Church of Christ in the Bed-Stuy neighborhood where African Americans faced economic turmoil after the depression and during segregation. When they couldn't get loans for housing, the church started a credit union. They started it as an implication of gospel mission. While preaching the most ecstatic and glorious sermons that are worthy to be archived as church history and American history, he and his church had feeding on the block.

Likewise, we must take the whole gospel forward wherever we live. We should consider opportunities in our immediate neighborhood. We cannot merely be focused on a space where we sit once a week. Let us help the people in our neighborhood, city, and church to be a part of what God wants to do to proclaim and practice the gospel in the urban context.

Reflect and Discuss

1. Have you had any negative experiences involving money and the church?
2. Why should giving not be done under pressure?
3. What's the proper motivation for giving?
4. How do Jesus and the gospel shape your view and commitment toward giving?
5. What should our giving go toward?
6. What are some of the reciprocal effects of giving?
7. Are you currently giving what God has called you to give to the local church?

Why Giving Is So Important

2 CORINTHIANS 8:16–9:5

Main Idea: We as the church must be dedicated to giving so gospel ministry can go forth.

I. The Church Must Turn Offerings into Ministry (8:16).
II. A Generous Church Starts with Trustworthy People and Trustworthy Systems (8:17-24).
III. God's People Must Be Dedicated to Giving (9:1-5).

A news report in 2016 about New Era Detroit presented a caricature of how people view the church. Most people I know in the ministry have a different disposition than was represented in the news report—the pastors owning Rolls Royces and living in million-dollar homes. Because of that portrayal, many people have an aversion toward the local church and a hardened disposition toward the idea of giving and generosity.

These people aren't just taking churches to task, as the reporter said, but any urban, inner-city entity that is benefiting from ethnic minorities' resources without replanting to strengthen the community economically. So they protest them. It is sad that the world has to be a prophet to God's people. The report further showed fighting in the community. Such a portrait nurtures distrust not only toward the local church but also toward the global church, as if that kind of behavior is representative of Christians everywhere.

When we look at the Scriptures and the calling of the church to love the Lord God, we recognize as believers that's not the character the church should have. Instead, what if God used our churches to change this caricature so that our communities would begin to look at the church as a viable change agent?

However, the challenge when we come to a text like this on finances and money is that we begin to wonder, "Okay, what am I about to get myself into?" Yet we know that everything in our lives as believers must be under the lordship of Jesus Christ.

If you know Jesus Christ as your Lord and Savior, everything is supposed to be under his lordship. So when something discussed in the Bible is perverted by people who claim to preach the Bible, you and I don't stop communicating what the Bible says. We just need to excommunicate the perversion. We need to deal with the perversion and get back to biblical principles. Once that is accomplished, then every area of your thinking, every area of your life is aligned with God's way of thinking and God's way of doing things.

The Church Must Turn Offerings into Ministry
2 CORINTHIANS 8:16

This vibrant text is filled with nuggets. It mentions Titus. Paul is writing to the Corinthian church, the church that has the money. He wrote about the Macedonian church already, but let's consider Titus.

Titus was one of Paul's "sons" in the ministry. Titus was in Antioch. He was probably from Antioch, which is in the southern part of modern-day Turkey, right on the edge of the Mediterranean Sea. This olive-complexioned young man became a ferocious believer in, what is to me, the top church in the New Testament. The reason I consider it the top church is that it was a gospel-preaching church—that's number one. Number two, all types of people came to that church from different ethnic backgrounds and were unified under the banner of the gospel. And three, that church lived with an open hand. If it wasn't for the Antioch church, there would be no New Testament.

Those different ethnic minorities of different colorings—half were North Africans in that church—were probably dark-skin, Black people. Niger was one of the leaders in the church. Don't let the traditional paintings and images fool you. Antioch birthed many ministers of the gospel, one of whom getting commissioned at his home church was Paul, along with Barnabas. Titus was a part of that church. Paul snatched him up on his missionary team and began to disciple him so that he could be used. Later, Titus would become the bishop over the churches in Crete, an island south of Greece, where he would appoint elders and plant churches. He would then oversee and nurture their commitment to the gospel.

So now we come to this passage in Corinthians. Titus is still in the training regimen, but he has submitted properly in his process to the point where Paul trusts him to supervise offerings. Now, why is this so important? Because look at what Paul says about Titus: "Thanks be to

God, who put the same concern for you into the heart of Titus" (v. 16). Earlier Paul had expressed his care for the Corinthians; now he says that Titus feels the same.

What is the care Paul has for them? In 2 Corinthians 3:1-3 he says they were his letter. He has invested so much discipleship into the church that he cares greatly about their souls. In fact, he cares more about their souls than what they could sow. You should know the church cares for you before it asks you to give.

The "concern" that Paul and Titus have for God's people is an *earnest* love. Now you have to understand, to have an earnest love for the Corinthians meant something because they were horrible Christians. They were hypocritical—in 1 Corinthians 6 you can read the list of sins they were walking in. Nevertheless, Paul and Titus love them even though they saw their mess. In other words, their mess didn't get in the way of their leaders' commitment to seeing Christ formed in them.

The concern that motivated Paul and Titus to love the Corinthians came from their experiences of God's love for them. When you're experiencing God's love for you, you can give away that love. But if you're not experiencing the love of God, you can't give away what you don't have. So when Titus begins this outpouring of this same commitment of wanting to visit, and travailing over the hearts and souls of God's people, it flows into Paul being able to trust Titus with God's people. It wasn't until Paul knew that Titus loved God's people that he could trust him with God's people.

Let me repeat that. The only reason Paul could send Titus to talk to the Corinthians about an offering was because he knew about Titus's love for them. He knew that his love for them was greater than what they had. You can't trust just anyone to a rich church. You know they had a little bit of money, but Paul knew their riches wouldn't get in the way and make Titus compromise, to go around what needed to be communicated. Titus could help them hear what they needed so they would grow. So Paul writes about this same earnest love that he and Titus share for them.

A Generous Church Starts with Trustworthy People and Trustworthy Systems
2 CORINTHIANS 8:17-24

Trustworthy people and trustworthy systems always can grow in this area. Verse 17 says, "For he welcomed our appeal and, being very diligent, went out to you by his own choice." Nobody had to make Titus serve. Now consider that he didn't have access to wire transfers or Western Union or some phone app to move money into an account. Literally, Titus had to go to the church to get it. Moreover, he wasn't transporting dollar bills; he was gathering heavy coins. Whatever the offering was, the church had to put it in a bag. Titus had to carry some heavy coins.

Second, public transportation didn't exist, so you either walked or dealt with a donkey. So you're walking with a lot of money on you. What does that let you know? That you're caper ready. Back in my day, if someone "ran on a caper," he was going on the block to do some dirt. There were a lot of dirt doers on Paul's block because they always knew that people were traveling with money. So when everyone was traveling, they would pounce on them and snatch their money. So Titus is investing himself when he says, "I'll carry the money." He is putting his life at risk. Leadership that takes no risk isn't leadership. Leadership that wants you to take risks but won't take risks is not leadership.

Titus was going to go with only two other men. I don't know what type of swords they had for the road—they didn't have guns back then. I don't know what they were going to do to protect the offering. I don't know if it was prayer or some angels. So the first trustworthy thing in ministry is that you have to have trustworthy leadership in place to steward the resources God has given.

Look at what Paul writes in verse 18: "We have sent with him the brother who is praised among all the churches for his gospel ministry." (Verse 22 will mention a second travel companion.) At first reading, this brother would seem to be out of place. Why would you send a famous person who preached the gospel?

Now, "praised" or famous doesn't mean celebrity preachers. Famous in the Bible is different from famous in our eyes. Biblical famous means low; human famous means high. Only what God accomplishes in someone's life would make them famous in the eyes of mature believers. So maturity decides stature, not eyes that are full of stars.

Why is the "gospel ministry" part important? Because ministry determines the culture of the church. I'm telling you right now, the pulpit is the most important central platform in the church—not because of the person who stands behind it but because of what sits on it and who is proclaimed from it. This thing is so important because it demands and it distributes, and doctrine sets the disposition of everything that it goes out to.

What does it go out to? Women's ministry. Men's ministry. Small groups. Church planting. All other programs find their theological and formational root in doctrinal, expositional, consistent preaching. It should line up with God's Word. The proclaiming eldership's communication within helps with accountability and the doctrine setting in the church.

The kind of ministry that hurts the church is *man-centered* preaching. That's what hurts the church. *Cause-oriented* preaching—your sermon is built around what happens. I know you need an in-season word, but sometimes you need a word beyond your season. You don't want the word when you get to where you're supposed to go, but you need a word that prepares you for where God's going to take you. And if you only get an in-season word, you'll stay in that season. You need a preparatory word. You need some word sometimes that makes you mad and makes you want to walk out and to toss some areas of your life.

You know someone doesn't care about your money when they tell you about your sin, tell you about how trifling you are, but then tell you about the God from heaven who came down and hung himself on a cross to bring you out of that mess. *Feel-good* preaching is to get to your pocketbook, but Bible preaching is to get to everything in your life. In *money-oriented* preaching, everything is a hermeneutic of money. "Hermeneutically, I see money everywhere like a sixth sense. 'I see dead people.' I see money, money, money, money, money." Run from that man or woman. If you hear anyone who preaches money-centered preaching, you need to run for your life.

Finally, ministry that hurts churches and doesn't set the tone for the church is *pastor-driven* preaching. If the pastor is bigger than Jesus, run for your life, and if everything in the gathering is pastor this and pastor that, run. If the only picture on the website is the pastor on every page, run.

Whatever is the center of the pulpit, that is what the center of the church is and what the center of the finances is. Take my word for it and take God's Word for it. But it's not low-honor culture. It's not the other side where the low honor is disrespectful because you're church hurting, then you act the fool and think you can act any kind of way. Why was this ministry important, and why did they send a preacher with them? Because preaching strengthens the church. How does it strengthen the church? It's *Christ centered*. In other words, the preachers and everyone should be so hidden behind the cross that you walk away with the cross and not the people who were proclaiming it.

The ministry needs to be *Word driven*. This is not where you read a verse and then go off on some stories but where you let the Bible explain what the Bible says. If the best thing about the sermon was the meme that attracted you on social media to come see it, and the graphics were beautiful, the website development was beautiful, and they developed T-shirts with the sermon series and banners, but then you come and sit under the preacher and it's not a verse in the Bible—all I'm trying to say is someone ought to have a word from the Lord.

It should be *historically informed*; it's not anyone's own private interpretation. It should be what's been said by believers for centuries. There's nothing new under the sun. I'm here to give you a fresh word, but there's a difference between a *new* and a *fresh* word. A new word is some made-up prophet babble. Instead, I'm supposed to continue to say what the church father said, what the apostle said, what Jesus said, what the prophet said but in a fresh way for today. I'm supposed to just keep saying that over and over again.

It should be *God glorifying*. Because of the preaching of the Word, your expansive mental, spiritual bandwidth should widen. When you hear about God and who he is, when you hear about his omniscience and his omnipresence, you should have an expansive reservoir of the glorious mysteries of God because of the preaching of the Word.

In verse 19 Paul writes, "And not only that, but he was also appointed by the churches to accompany us with this gracious gift that we are administering." The powerful phrase "gracious gift" points ultimately to the word for God's loyal love, which is the Hebrew word *hesed*. In the New Testament, "grace" and "mercy" were split into two words because *hesed* was too much of a potent word. It took two Greek words to communicate the untranslatable excellences of how God feels about us. Grace is God's unmerited favor toward us. In other words, this gracious gift points to the fact that we didn't save ourselves. Moreover, it should encourage us to view our resources through the lens of God's favor. All that we have is a gracious gift of God. When God provides for us, we don't complain about what he's provided.

Speaking plainly, many of us have been without a job—but when we get a job, we hate the job and complain about it. We forget how difficult it was not to have a job, and we don't remember that what we don't like about what we don't make could be nothing, but the Lord provided what we have. What God has called us to do is have a grace disposition toward our resources. We may have worked for it, but God didn't have to give us anything. So everything we have is from the grace of God. That means you and I need to see the overarching hand of God over our finances. And when we look at a gracious gift, the gracious gift is saying, "Man, my money just hit the account; this is the grace of God that I even got a job. God, I just want to thank you that this money got to me. Something could have messed up. I just want to thank you for it. All this is yours, but a portion of it is specifically yours. God, I want to get my mind wrapped around how to respond to the great grace that you've given to me by giving to your kingdom mission." So your gracious gift is knowing that you've experienced grace and not that you're tipping God to say, "Thank you for grace."

It's a gracious gift because it's not to pay God for something that some fool promised you. You don't pay for divine healing! Where's that in the Bible? These hooligans asking you for an offering for a healing: "If you want a healing, give this much." That's not in the Bible because it's a gracious gift when you give. You don't have to pay for God's promises because Christ already paid for them. He's called the key of David because he unlocks all the promises of God.

The Bible communicates with such insight. Notice that Paul writes about this gracious gift being administered, not given. This gift is a service. He says it's "for the glory of the Lord himself and to show our eagerness to help" (v. 19).

In verse 20 he adds, "We are taking this precaution so that no one will criticize us about this large sum that we are administering." He wants to put every effort behind, making sure that what was given in the offering is transmitted and transitioned into ministry because it's a reflection of God's generosity toward us.

Verse 22 says, "We have also sent with them our brother. We have often tested him." Now we don't know what the brother's background is, but we know that he has been tested. We don't know if anyone else was tested, but of this person, everyone else was saying, "We like him." Good, you can help. But this person was tested, and look at what the Bible says: "We have often tested him in many circumstances and found him to be diligent" (v. 22). It's good when God grows you and your growth crosses out and erases your former testimony because of the beauty of the transformational power of the gospel in your life. This brother has been diligent, "and now even more diligent because of his great confidence in you" (v. 22). Their faith was encouraging to that brother. Paul always shows great gratitude for faithful team members who take their call and commitment to God and the body extremely seriously (v. 23). Paul doesn't want to be embarrassed by the Corinthians' response to loving missionary ministers in good standing (v. 24).

God's People Must Be Dedicated to Giving
2 CORINTHIANS 9:1-5

Here in 2 Corinthians 9:1 the text reads, "Now concerning the ministry to the saints, it is unnecessary for me to write to you." Even though this is about the ministry or the relief of the saints, it still gives principles for receiving resources and how they are used. Verse 2 says, "For I know your eagerness, and I boast about you to the Macedonians, 'Achaia has been ready since last year,' and your zeal has stirred up most of them." Generosity sparks generosity.

Paul continues, "But I am sending the brothers so that our boasting about you in this matter would not prove empty, and so that you would be ready just as I said" (v. 3). In other words, don't make me look like a fool—like your mom used to say when someone was coming over to the house who hadn't been there before and didn't really know how you were yet. So Paul, because he knew the immaturity of the Corinthians, sent a delegation before him to get things ready so that when he got there the Macedonians wouldn't be mad.

Why would the Macedonians be mad? Because the Macedonians were a poor church, yet their offering was generous. This poor church gave a whole lot of money, and they sent some people from Macedonia who were going to come with Paul, after Paul's earlier delegation had already gone to get things set up. The Macedonians were eager to get there and see the beauty of the Corinthians' generosity. Why? Because the Corinthians had promised that they were going to give and give generously, and out of their commitment to give, the Macedonians also decided to give as a motivation to the Corinthians. But now the Macedonian generosity is upping the game of the people who really had the resources to be generous.

Let me address "generosity sparks generosity." I remember when first planting our church we had to raise money. Most of the time churches just get a mic and bank and start preaching for church planting or start-ups. But there's a more strategic way to start in which you get trained and developed. As you're trained and developed, you have to develop resources, which is to raise money. Before you even start ministering to the people, you raise resources so that you can be fully dedicated to the work, making sure finances don't get in the way of your ability to be committed to serving people. So my wife and I had to start raising money. We had people committed to giving $5, $10, and $100, to sow into the ministry. Then we ended up going to some influential people who believed in our vision and presentation and wanted to know who was on board. We told them we had twenty people from all over the United States. Of course, they wanted to know how much. We showed them our $20 givers and our $100 givers. They then introduced us to someone else. So my wife and I arrived in Philadelphia, and we were told that God had told the church leaders to sow $100,000 into the ministry. So as we were raising money and were asked what had been committed, now we could say, "A hundred grand." Then more money started coming in because generous giving generates generous giving. This is not a gimmick. Giving is supposed to cause and strengthen others to want to give.

This is grace giving, and we should consider these questions: Are you giving at or near your giving potential? Do you lay your resources before the Lord and think about the church that you get fed from and that you serve and that you're in community with? Is giving a priority in your spiritual life? This is a part of the gamut of being a believer. I'm not proclaiming Malachi 3 and talking about you're being cursed with a curse; that's not a motivation to give. Jesus Christ, according to Galatians, became a curse on the cross to wipe out the curse that should have come on us based on the law. Therefore, I'm not saying, "If you don't give and if you don't sow, your car is going to break down." But because God's been good to me, let me submit and think through how everything belongs to him, and then let me give as if everything belongs to him.

Giving should be a priority in your spiritual life. And why is this important? God in eternity past said that Jesus Christ was slain and names were written in the book of life before the foundations of the earth (Rev 13:8). Before Jesus Christ came and before we ever existed, God committed himself to being generous to us. He gave the best of heaven before we needed heaven. And before we were created, he wrote Genesis to Malachi to proclaim his pinning his promise to send Jesus. So he put on paper his covenant to say, "I'm going to save you. I said it in eternity past, but you weren't there, so I'm going to put it on paper for you so that you can see my level of commitment." Jesus Christ came on the scene as the eternal God-man, and all he kept talking about was what God said about him from Genesis to Malachi, to verbalize God's covenantal commitment of what he said in eternity past that he was going to do.

Now Jesus was here, then he died on the cross, and guess what he kept doing on the cross? Quoting Scripture and fulfilling Scripture to let you know that the signal of the cell tower of earth is reconnecting us with the eternal provider in heaven. Why is that important? Because God's the best giver. He's the generous giver. Therefore, we should give as a response to his gracious giving, which canceled the debt between God and man by Christ's death on the cross and resurrection. That's our motivation to give.

Reflect and Discuss

1. Why is it important to know that Africans and people of color played a significant role in the early church? How does this refute the popular claim that Christianity is the "white man's religion"?
2. Do you have church leaders who are committed to loving you and the flock despite hardships? If you're a pastor or church leader, are you committed to loving the flock despite hardships?
3. Why is giving important for conducting gospel ministry?
4. What does it mean to be a trustworthy and dependable person?
5. Why should giving start with this kind of people?
6. What are some kinds of preaching that hurt the church?
7. Why is it important to be a part of a local church with healthy, biblical preaching?
8. In what ways are you dedicated to giving? In what ways do you want to grow in that dedication?

110 Percent Kingdom Investment

2 CORINTHIANS 9:6-15

Main Idea: God wants to increase your giving capacity and bless your giving.

I. **God Blesses Generous Giving (9:6-7).**
II. **God Longs to Increase Your Giving Capacity (9:8-15).**

A young man started growing and going to church. He had gotten saved, he'd gotten baptized, and he started to grow. He finished college, he started his own business, and he had multiple streams of income, a multifaceted portfolio. He began to allow himself to be discipled. He was spoken well of by the community, and at a certain point, the young single ladies in the church took notice of him. He wasn't just spiritually fit; he was physically fine. And his fineness went on steroids because of his spiritual growth and his submission. He reached the point where he got deacon status. He was serving and willing to do so many things. One of the young ladies in his life group caught his eye. And when this young lady caught his eye and he thought she was fine on all levels, spiritually and everything, he was happy, and he started to try to pursue her. But she said no.

The ladies around her said, "Girl, you dumb if you don't marry him." He tried to protest too, but she still said no. He talked to the other brothers to find out if he was doing something wrong. He's trying to get all the counsel he can and trying to be a godly guy. She was attracted to him, but she kept saying that she didn't like him like that. And some of her friends said, "I think I know your problem: you've had so many bad experiences with men that it's hard for you to see a good one."

Sometimes it's like that with the church. We have so many bad experiences that when God presents to us an opportunity to have a healthy experience, not in a perfect community but in a growing community, it's hard to even see it. An opportunity that many of us want to resist is in the area of giving. We've seen giving mishandled and misinterpreted.

Most of us have seen unhealthy ways of giving. Yet as we come to this text on giving, I want us to frame our minds around *investment*.

We don't *invest* in giving and talk about giving enough in a healthy way. Not talking about giving, or talking about it and almost apologizing for even talking about giving, is not in accord with Scripture. Rather, God asked people for stuff in the Bible, as did the prophets, the apostles, and Jesus. So you should never have to apologize for asking people to honor God with their resources.

God Blesses Generous Giving
2 CORINTHIANS 9:6-7

In 110 percent kingdom investment, God blesses generous giving. I know that's simple, but I think it's important for us to internalize that. Look at what the Word says in verse 6: "The point is this." Paul is saying, "Let me stop beating around the bush, and let me say what I really want to say." He writes, "The point is this: The person who sows sparingly will also reap sparingly, and the person who sows generously will also reap generously."

Paul uses agricultural analogies of sowing and reaping to show how believers' lives are affected when they are financially giving and resource giving to the kingdom. He conveys simply, "If you don't give anything or you give very little, you can expect to get not much in return." The point of the text is that there is a return.

Concerning that return, I want to be careful that we don't make giving a triumphalist parade; in other words, you shouldn't just be giving in a way that's only about what you will receive. The spirit of this text is not only the reaping that God will do in your own resources but also the reaping of the original reason behind why you sowed the resource. If you don't give much, guess what? You don't receive much of what we would call harvest. I do believe that God provides financial harvest for people when they give. There is, based on this text, a harvest that comes.

My wife used to have a little pot where she planted cucumbers and basil. And then she had cucumbers and she had basil. I used to make this smoked Gouda, basil, and tomato omelet. When I went outside and snatched a little basil off, the aroma would catch me and then be on my fingers all day. But my wife did the work of putting the proper soil in, getting the proper seeds, and making sure she was caring for and watering them. And then we got to experience the benefit of what was sown. The same principle applies in giving.

In fact, Jesus says in Matthew 13:44-46 that the kingdom of heaven is like a treasure buried in a field that a person found and hid. Because of joy, he went and sold all that he had and bought that field. Then Jesus says, again, the kingdom of heaven is like a merchant searching for fine pearls. When he found a pearl of great value, he went out and sold everything he had and bought it. What is Jesus talking about? He says, the kingdom is so valuable that when you come across the kingdom, it's worth everything you have.

The kingdom is God's comprehensive rule over all creation. The way God develops the kingdom is he saves people, gives them kingdom resources, and nurtures their hearts based on spiritual growth. With that spiritual growth and with those resources, God changes their hearts' disposition. How much they value the kingdom causes them to say, "I want to participate." There are things God won't do until God's people release resources. There are things God just will not do because we are the mechanism through which his sovereignty moves in order for us to respond to the call of ministry or whatever we're called to do.

This is like when our church partnered to build schools in Malawi to keep the girls from being raped and accosted on their two-hour walk to schools outside their villages. They needed a school in their village, and this would be a great opportunity not only for them to go to school but also to provide a harvest of ministry to the girls and their villages.

The goal of sowing is thinking about the return that comes to the kingdom through your giving. However, God set it all up. So not only does the kingdom opportunity get blessed, but you, as a part of being a kingdom representative, get blessed. Now God could have just left it like this: "Just give, and that's it." He could have just said, "Just give, and the blessing is in just giving." But God boomerangs our giving; our sowing brings reaping.

Then Paul tethers our giving to our hearts. In verse 7 he writes, "Each person should do as he has decided in his heart—not reluctantly or out of compulsion, since God loves a cheerful giver." This word *reluctantly* means "sadly," or "from grief." The feeling of it would be, "All right, man, okay, I'll give."

My wife and I had our youngest two children ten months apart, which is a blessing and a challenge at times. When one of them was playing with something, the other one could have a great blessing in their hands at that particular time, and I don't know what it is about when the one gets it in their hand, but the other one thinks they want it. Or one of them might have something for a really long time, and we've already told both of them to share. I'll say, "Ephraim, share." He'll groan, and I'll say, "Son, you had it for an hour; give it to your sister." When he finally gives it to his sister, he goes, "Hmph." He gave it, but he didn't want to give it. The text says we are to avoid that spirit. The reluctant spirit is being a bratty child who gives because he has to, not because he wants to. Conversely, Paul commends the Macedonian church, who didn't have much to give but gave bountifully because they wanted to participate in kingdom giving. They saw the opportunity as bigger than what they had in their wallets. It's difficult to give if you don't have the maturity to see the opportunity. You must have the maturity to see good soil, and then when you see good soil, sow into it. If you believe the church where you are is good soil, you need to sow into it.

When my wife and I lived in the South (we're from the mid-Atlantic), we were amazed by the resource ministry. Not just the amount of resources available but the liberal delivery of wanting to share these resources was something that, to be honest, we had never experienced in our life. I can remember when my wife had one bout with cancer, and these white folk we had just met—brothers and sisters in Christ; all we know is we have the same blood type—let us use their car. I'm thinking, they don't know us, and they don't know if we're coming back; we can just keep on going. It was crazy: they gave us the keys to their car! Who does that? If you saw their heart for ministry, all they saw was us being called to Philadelphia. And they said, "We want to participate in saying before the throne of God that we sowed that way." They just had that disposition of giving. As this church got planted, people were saying, "I want to sow because I hear about what God is starting."

I hear about what God is starting, and it's the opportunity for God to do something. Paul communicates this is what giving is about. Giving is saying, "God, I want to participate in the opportunity to get some stuff done for the kingdom."

Let me just put something out here, a disclaimer for you. Don't complain about gospel ministry and the church if you don't give. Don't say that the church is full of hypocrites unless you are investing in making the hypocrisy quotient decrease. We need to be a community that participates deeply in the call of God and the beauty of what he's called us to do.

Paul says, not "out of compulsion" (v. 7). That means troubled in giving, nothing but obligation, this is what I have to do. But he says, "God loves a cheerful giver" (v. 7).

One of my favorite shows is the *Martin* show. I love *Martin.* I'm sorry. Forgive me. One of my favorite episodes is when he finally proposes to Gina. I won't use the last word he said, but he asked, "Gina, will you marry me ___?" And she replies, "This is what I've been waiting for all my life, for the man of my dreams to propose to me, and you couldn't come up with something better than that?" I'm speaking of this same disposition in giving under compulsion—giving because you feel like you have to, not because you want to.

You may have seen this extraordinary video of this man who proposes to his girlfriend. He calls her girlfriends to this restaurant and surprises her but then he says, "But this is not it." He puts them in a car to get her hair done with all her girls in a hotel room, and she puts on this dress. Boom! They go downtown, and all her family is there. She starts praising God. His proposal took thought; it took an investment because he valued her enough to go to such lengths so that she knew he was serious about marrying her.

In the text, giving is showing God how serious you are about him. "This is how serious I am. Lord, I'm so serious about it that I'm going to pause when I get my check and I'm going to say thank you." He could stop a check or two or pitch the bank account of the company you work at so that nothing shows up. So don't think God isn't in control of every cent that comes into your sphere.

God Longs to Increase Your Giving Capacity
2 CORINTHIANS 9:8-15

Increasing your giving capacity is what the reaping is about. Verse 8 begins, "And God is able." *Able* is the word for power. Power is focused on the verbal aspect of God's might and able-ness to do stuff. And it points to the fact that God is able "to make every grace overflow to you."

God loves and is passionate about flagrantly throwing unmerited favor your way. God loves to bless you. You can't continually dwell in a total depravity mindset: "I'm so dirty and I'm nothing." You're saved so you wouldn't be that anymore. Most of us believe God just loves to save us, but he does not want to do anything with the salvation that he's given us. No, God is saying, "I want to harness my saving grace on your life and flagrantly throw favor on you." Paul says to make it "overflow" to you (v. 8). Some translations read, "superabound," or "go above and beyond," to overflow with more than you need. The Lord loves to overflow his favor upon his children.

Why does God do this? "So that in every way, always having everything you need, you may excel in every good work" (v. 8). God loves to provide for his people. God loves not only to make sure your bills are paid but also to provide superabundantly for you. He richly gives you resources so that the overflow of those resources can give you a heart for his kingdom.

That means you don't wait until you receive money to give. All of us have received money before, but most of us don't think we have money until we have money. You know the difference. You know how when you're feeling lean you walk a certain way. You know how you walk a little differently after you paid the bills, and you have a little left; you can breathe and you can feel real good. But the test is when you don't have much, yet in your heart you have this longing to participate, and you're saying, "In this longing I have to participate, I'm going to now, where I am financially, make some sacrifices financially and watch the Lord provide."

I'll never forget my first ministry job. I was working at a marketing firm, I was working in south Dallas, and I was working at a church. I think it was just two jobs at that point. I just remember I had a whole bunch of jobs in a short period of time because I needed some resources to take care of my wife. We needed a miracle because we were in a situation where I was saying, "God, I'll just get a full-time job like this and a part-time job and work like that." And God made sure that none of that worked out. I was going to be a social worker and work us through seminary.

God said, "I'm not going to do it that way."

I was asking, "Can you make me feel more comfortable?" To be honest, I did not want to be in the start-up phase for a decade. I started this job making sixty in the mid-nineties, so I was thinking, "God, we could knock out this undergrad debt; we can do this and get that." I was planning out everything.

God responded, "Nope, you're going to work these two jobs, you're not going to have enough, you're going to have to give sacrificially, and I'll take care of the rest."

I said, "That is not the plan I'm looking for." My wife ended up getting sick and couldn't work anymore. Still, I decided, "You know what, we're going to keep giving. You have been good to us." I still don't understand the five fishes and loaves thing that God worked out, but we ate. People were spontaneous about bringing us groceries, and we could go to this place and pick out whatever clothes we wanted. In other words, God would meet us in our sowing in mysterious ways.

It wasn't really the money he was working on. If you think God was working on the money, you've missed it. He's working on your heart. He's working on your mind. He's working on your faith because then when you actually receive some money, you've been trained. You've been trained to be generous. And don't think because you have more, you are being generous. Generosity starts with not having much. What makes it generosity is the willingness to see the sacrifice that it takes to give it, even though you don't have it.

That's why Paul says, "As it is written: He distributed freely; he gave to the poor; his righteousness endures forever" (v. 9). He is not suggesting that giving causes you to be righteous. Rather, when you invest in kingdom opportunities, God will cause that kingdom opportunity to show off the glory of the righteousness in Christ that you already have.

Psalm 37 says, "Do not be agitated by evildoers. . . . Trust in the LORD and do what is good; dwell in the land and live securely" (vv. 1,3). Then David says, "Commit your way to the LORD; trust in him, and he will act, making your righteousness shine like the dawn, your justice like the noonday" (v. 5). What does that mean? What you've been waiting for God to do, he's going to show it off for everyone to see, and they will honor the fact that he's been with you through the process. What God is saying here—the harvest of righteousness that endures forever—points to 1 Corinthians 3:12-15. We build with "gold, silver, and costly stones." We give, develop, and receive heavenly rewards that we ultimately will throw at the Lord's feet, and the gift will endure as a reward for eternity. When you give, you maximize your opportunity to have eternal harvest to give to the Lord. You receive more to throw at his feet and more to see at his feet for eternity. Can you imagine watching your kingdom investment at Christ's feet for eternity?

Lastly, Paul says, "You will be enriched in every way for all generosity" (v. 11). As you are generous, he'll enrich you to be generous in every way, "which produces thanksgiving to God through us" (v. 11). Paul says, "For the ministry of this service is not only supplying the needs of the saints but is also overflowing in many expressions of thanks to God" (v. 12). Our giving not only goes to what we give to specifically, but ultimately it's an offering to the Lord. We must remember that reality: our generosity is an offering to the Lord. Giving says "thank you" to God. If you don't give, you are thankless. That's the point of the passage. If you don't give, you are thankless. Paul says, "Because of the proof provided by this ministry, they will glorify God for your obedient confession of the gospel of Christ" (v. 13). In sum, verses 12-15 cover Paul casting a vision for the funding that he was asking Corinth to provide. It must be stated that we need to redeem biblical asks from the body for money for mission. It wasn't taboo to do so in the Bible. Philippians is a support letter in and of itself. This section of Corinthians is as well.

Reflect and Discuss

1. What is the principle of sowing and reaping?
2. How does knowing God will bless your generous giving encourage you to keep giving?
3. How can the sowing and reaping principle be abused?
4. How do we guard ourselves from twisting this principle into a way to try to manipulate God with our giving?
5. In what ways has God lavished his grace on you and blessed you?
6. In what ways is God seeking to increase your giving capacity?
7. Have you ever had to give during hard seasons?
8. How did God continue to sustain you during those hard times?

Fighting the Right Battles

2 CORINTHIANS 10:1-6

Main Idea: Fighting the right battles involves using divinely empowered weapons. Paul tells us how to fight the right battles.

How to Fight the Right Battles

I. You Must Know What Irritates You (10:1-2).

II. You Must Use Divinely Empowered Weapons (10:3-6).

My wife and I have endured one of the most difficult seasons in a long time, when everything seems to be going haywire. In such seasons, we have to be careful not to fight each other. When all hell is breaking loose in your life, your tendency is to do stupid stuff. Now I know I'm the only human being who's trying to press toward the mark, so I'll just talk to me. I'll do stupid stuff and argue about stupid stuff, forgetting that we're on the same team. When difficulty happens to me and I don't have a divine perspective, I start doing stupid stuff and making not little mistakes but mishaps and major errors. I'm not allowing my mind to be calibrated by who God is, and I'm not allowing him to give me clarity in my life in relationship to what's going on. So my wife and I have to get in alignment with one another to identify what's going on, and then in identifying what's going on we decide to put our war clothes on. We don't put our war clothes on to fight each other. We put our war clothes on to fight the enemy together. The biggest enemy is not the enemy out there but the enemy that's within.

It doesn't matter what the enemy does to you. The question is, What is your response to what happens to you? Because your response reflects whether you'll give him room to stay or to flee. Sometimes the biggest rebuke you can give the devil is to ignore him. The Bible says, "Resist the devil" (Jas 4:7). Sometimes resistance is like "Do you hear something? I don't hear anything." And then he'll flee because he only stays where he can do work. But if you have some things in your life that germinate and build an environment for his influence, he will make himself at home. As a matter of fact, he may just hire the

Property Brothers from HGTV, and he'll renovate your mind to set up shop there today.

In this passage Paul wants to help the believers in Corinth face their spiritual immaturity by knowing how to fight the right battles. Have you ever entered a trial, and you just began to think stupid stuff, acting a fool? You're not calibrated yet to the fact that you're actually in a trial and that you want to let God do what he wants to do in you and apply it. God's work will not work in you until you calibrate the fact that God is at work and doing something within you. You must recognize that, no matter what season of life you're in, no matter what you're going through, no matter what challenges you face, God through Christ is at work within you. You must not become absent-minded. You can't allow the situation to create things in you that make you more bitter toward God instead of better in God.

If you're going to fight the right battles, the main point is this: fighting the right battle involves using divinely empowered weapons. Paul is challenging the people in the Corinthian church who are filled with spiritual immaturity and who don't want to function the way he wants them to function and the way God wants them to function. Paul is defending his apostleship, and he's finding that their disposition toward him as a leader, who has helped and influenced them, is based on faulty thinking that goes deeper than arguing with them. If he only argues about the issues between them, they will miss out on the deeper things they need to work on to grow and be conformed to the image of Christ. Likewise, sometimes you must not take things personally when you're having issues with someone. You need to see what's behind what's in front of you. If you don't learn how to see what's behind what's in front of you, you're in trouble.

You Must Know What Irritates You
2 CORINTHIANS 10:1-2

In verse 1 Paul is upfront about what irritates him: "Now I, Paul, myself, appeal to you by the meekness and gentleness of Christ." He is alluding to principles from the invitation of Jesus in Matthew 11:28-30, where Jesus says,

Come to me, all of you who are weary and burdened, and I will give
you rest. Take up my yoke and learn from me, because I am lowly and
humble in heart, and you will find rest for your souls.

Jesus is "lowly and humble" and invites all to come to him for rest, even
people who have a wrong disposition toward him.

Have you ever done something for someone, and no matter what
you did for him, he had no appreciation for it? The Corinthians began
talking behind Paul's back. Usually, Paul wouldn't answer critics having
issues with him, but because the issue they have with him is connected
to their growth and spiritual maturity, and because he's an apostle, he
engages it. If they reject him, they're rejecting the stream of blessing,
influence, and gospel strengths God brings through building the foundation of the church through the apostles and prophets. Therefore,
Paul gets in there and engages them. And he's a little mad with them
because they think he's a sucker. So he kind of throws the Bible at them,
in a godly way.

He says, "I who am humble among you in person but bold toward
you when absent" (v. 1). He heard through the grapevine that the
Corinthians said, "Paul, you know, he gets all up in your face when he's
there, and he's talking about the little stripes on his back. He's always
getting beat up through trials and stuff. So he's not really a muscular
dude, you know. But all of a sudden, these letters come, and in the
letters, he's spitting game we ain't never heard! Like, where's all this
weight coming from? It's like he's got a chip on his shoulder toward us.
But that dude, when that punk comes around, man, Paul ain't like this."
They're talking smack.

So someone snitched; someone said, "Paul, they're ragging on you,
saying you're a punk when present, but you're a beast when gone. I
think you might want to handle that. You know what I'm saying?" But
instead of arguing with them, he argues with the ideology—the fact
that they don't understand that humility and meekness point to Christ.
Instead, he suggests they admire people who assert themselves versus
those who submit themselves to the glory of Christ. He's going to challenge them about their faulty disposition toward him, which leads to a
deeper root of challenges with their spiritual life and with their soul.

So Paul says, "I beg you that when I am present I will not need to
be bold" (v. 2). In other words, "Don't separate my putting you on blast

from meekness and gentleness because it's not separate from that." He doesn't want to have to "be bold with the confidence by which I plan to challenge certain people who think we are living according to the flesh" (v. 2). Have you ever ministered to someone, loved on someone, and did it for years; then one person comes to her, gets in her ear, and it changes everything you did? That's what happened here. Paul invested in them; then the Judaizers came around and said one little thing, and they suddenly said, "Oh man, that's what's up. You know, I knew something was wrong with Paul. You know, I felt something, you know what I'm saying? I didn't really know, but you know how you get that feeling?" So they start putting Paul on blast and denouncing him.

You Must Use Divinely Empowered Weapons
2 CORINTHIANS 10:3-6

Paul essentially responds, "You're not understanding how the kingdom works. And because you don't understand how the kingdom works, you're letting foolishness influence you because there's something deeply sinister behind that." He says, "For although we live in the flesh, we do not wage war according to the flesh" (v. 3). Paul is being charged with using his spiritual authority in a faulty way. He should have a better track record with them. They believe what they want to believe on account of their own faulty thinking. So he has to explain to them that we walk in the flesh in the sense of being human beings because we have a body, but we don't wage war according to the flesh.

Notice he uses war language here. He wants God's people to think about what he's about to engage them with as his being in a war, and they need to recognize that they're in a war.

What's the "flesh"? The flesh isn't your body. The flesh is the mindset that is open to an influence by the world, the flesh, and the devil. It's the negative and demonic influence that comes in relation to the fall of Adam and Eve. The enemy uses that influence to access people. Galatians 5:19-21 says,

> Now the works of the flesh are obvious: sexual immorality, moral impurity, promiscuity, idolatry, sorcery, hatreds, strife, jealousy, outbursts of anger, selfish ambitions, dissensions, factions, envy, drunkenness, carousing, and anything similar.

Paul doesn't give an exhaustive list. Rather, he conveys, "It's stuff like this. I could keep going." You know, an immature believer or nonbeliever may not know the difference, but a person who understands and knows God should know the difference between what it means to walk in the flesh and to walk in the Spirit.

So waging war according to the flesh means the deeds of the flesh would flow out of unredeemed motives. If you use these fleshly mechanisms to fight, you reap based on the sphere of where you fight. What do I mean by that? The Bible says,

> *Don't be deceived: God is not mocked. For whatever a person sows he will also reap, because the one who sows to his flesh will reap destruction from the flesh, but the one who sows to the Spirit will reap eternal life from the Spirit.* (Gal 6:7-8)

Paul is helping God's people build a foundation of knowing where the fight actually takes place. An understanding of the foundation and ideology of where the fight takes place equips you to use God's weaponry properly. Otherwise, you could use a godly weapon for ungodly means.

One time I was preaching—this is a good while ago—and in the message I veered off to speak about homosexuality in an inappropriate way. A lesbian young woman was sitting in the congregation, and you should have seen the look on her face. After the sermon, she makes a beeline toward me, gets in my face, and begins letting me have it. So I said that we disagree on ideology, but I do think that what I did was wrong. And I said, "The way I handled that and brought that up out of nowhere was wounding to you. So can you forgive me?" Waging war according to the Spirit means properly using God's weapons for God's means that minister, not hurt, or that hurt for the right reasons, not the wrong reasons.

Let me clarify some more. At Thanksgiving, everyone has their own group of family members who come late to Thanksgiving, and they always have a van or a pickup truck outside. There's always something in there that they don't bring in the house because big mama and big daddy don't allow them to bring that mess in the house. So what they do is they go to the back of the pickup truck around there in the alley, they do a little "fuh fuh" and a little "cack cack," and then they come back in real nice acting a fool. You get up in the midst of that because you're the righteous Christian, godly person, and you go off in the midst of the family and show the fact that you're a Christian, show the fact that you go to church, show the fact that you know your Bible, and show the fact that you're better. You do more belligerent blistering than blessing.

So it's not just fleshly warfare itself that we want to avoid; it's even using godly mechanisms in ungodly and hurtful ways. Notice that Paul says, "The weapons of our warfare are not of the flesh, but are powerful through God for the demolition of strongholds" (v. 4). Our weapons are not Smith & Wesson or Remington. The mechanisms of our warfare are not of the flesh, but they have divine power. This idea of divine power is connected to 2 Peter 1:3: "His divine power has given us everything required for life and godliness through the knowledge of him who called us by his own glory and goodness."

Therefore, the connection of divine power by being regenerated through Christ gives us the ability by God's strength to use his weapons. God's weapons and divine power reveal his omnipotence; God offers us these resources to fight battles that he has called us to fight. Moreover, those divinely empowered weapons are specific to destroying strongholds. What is a stronghold?

When a city was built in biblical times, the inhabitants would construct walls high around it to make it difficult to scale them. You would have to go to strong war against it because such a fortified city could hold up against an attack. However, the thing Paul is calling a stronghold here isn't something positive. He's calling it something negative. And this stronghold is not fortified things on the outside of you but fortified things that are walled in on the inside of you. Paul refers to "arguments and every proud thing" (v. 4). A stronghold isn't a sin that we do on the outside of us. So viewing pornography is a sin, but it's not a stronghold. Alcoholism or drug use isn't a stronghold. Those are only sins that are expressions of the stronghold. My definition of a stronghold is this: *a mindset, value system, or thought process that hinders your growth.*

Every one of us has strongholds. I don't care how young you are, how old you are—you have foolish, dumb, stupid, ignorant ways of thinking in your life. Now, I'm not trying to beat you up. You need to admit that you have some stupid things that you think, that have been embedded in your heart and mind, that are a part of the matrix of your life's value system. If you do not admit that, you will not get to the place to develop and grow in the areas where God wants you to grow.

A stronghold is those stubborn things in your mind, those fortified ways of thinking. I like the way Tony Evans says it: "A stronghold is a mindset that accepts a situation as unchangeable" (*The Battle*, 293). A stronghold takes root, and it's what I call an unbelieving belief system. The enemy loves to use situations as arrows to plant these thoughts in your mind so that the stronghold exalts itself against the knowledge of Christ. That's what the Bible says: it makes itself bigger than Jesus in your life.

You have to find out what your stronghold is. Consider some little sins. Let's start with greed. The Bible calls it greed; we call it "being a boss" or "being on our grind." See, we have ways of coloring it. You know you have fits of anger, but "I'm a passionate person." You can't keep your eyes off the opposite sex: "I just appreciate how God has created people." This is the issue: you can have a stronghold and have the right theology.

You have the definition of a stronghold in your mind, and you know in the Bible that thing is wrong. But what makes the stronghold a challenge is that you exalt the stronghold above what you know about it, of what it says in the Bible that makes it wrong, and therefore you make room for it. You've created a renovated facility in your heart and mind for that mindset. You know it's a stronghold because it's there and it's a sin, but when someone bumps up against it, you get angry. You get irritated because you don't want God to challenge you in that particular area of your life.

Paul is helping God's people recognize that these strongholds exist and that God's people need to make war on them and deal with them. He says, "We demolish." He is teaching God's people how to treat those strongholds. He asserts, "We demolish arguments and every proud thing that is raised up against the knowledge of God" (vv. 4-5). In different areas of our lives, including my own, we'll be fighting until Jesus comes back to make him the biggest thing in our minds. Let me say that again. For you and me, in different areas of our lives, Jesus isn't a big deal in that area. The reason he's not a big deal is because we've made room for something else to be a big deal.

We need to talk to ourselves. Your most important conversations aren't the ones you have with anyone else. Your greatest and most challenging conversations are the ones you have with you. If you don't learn how to tell your thoughts what they need to be told, you're in trouble.

Paul says, "We take every thought captive" (v. 5). That's how you know you're in a war. But you can't take something captive until you fight off what defends it. When you go to war, you don't just go in and take captives. You must fight until something or someone surrenders.

And when he surrenders, you must capture him and bring him in. The problem with some of us is that we fought some wars and saw some victories, but we didn't take the thought captive. See, you can fight, but then if you leave the thought there, it says, "Really? I can stay?" That's why God would have his people wipe out some folk because once they grow up, knowing what happened, they're going to come and raise themselves up and build themselves up to come fight again. Your thoughts are the same way. You have to commit genocide on your thoughts. And that means you must see your thoughts as an enemy.

It's the way you need to think about sexuality. Some of you are in a season of your life where you wish you were married, and you're blaming this and that, and there's a chip on your shoulder. You're bitter with God. The stronghold isn't, "I'm mad because I want to be married." The stronghold believes, "God sees me suffering, and he doesn't care about me." Some of you have gone through something difficult, and you said, "Why did God let that happen to me?" In the back of your mind and heart you think, "Maybe God really isn't good." Then all these things begin sprouting up that become fruit of that stronghold's root. As you do all these different things, you've confessed the sin over and over again, and you're wondering, "Why in the world can't I get free?" Because an ideology has taken root below your thoughts, and it has made the environment fruitful for that struggle to be a struggle. You have to go to the root of those things.

Some of you need to take your mind to some deeper thoughts and ask the Spirit of God to work in you and to challenge you and to get to those deep places in your heart, in your mind, in your soul, in your spirit, so that you can be free. See, some of you have covenant eyes, some of you have accountability, and it still doesn't work. The reason is that there's something under there that says, "Man, the devil's got better honeys and dudes and sexual desires than God, even though God created sexuality."

Hold on! How in the world does the devil, who comes to steal, kill, and destroy, have something better than the manufacturer of the universe? It just doesn't make sense. But see, that's how stupid our fallen flesh can be. We all allow demonic ideologies to take root. That's why the Bible calls what the devil shoots at you "flaming arrows" (Eph 6:16). A flaming arrow, when it comes, doesn't just penetrate; it's on fire! So the tactic is not just to hit that one spot; it wants to spread. The enemy, when he hits you and penetrates you, his arrow is flaming. Notice that it didn't say "arrow," singular. It said "arrows," plural. The devil wants to permeate every single area of your life with his demonic ideologies. That's why you and I need to quit playing around and being lazy, and we've got to put on our war clothes. We have to stop being apathetic. When you're being apathetic, the devil isn't. The Bible says he walks around all the time. He never sits there. Remember his conversation with God in the book of Job. God asks, "What have you been doing?" (Job 1:7 GNT).

Satan answers, "Oh, I've been walking around." He's always thinking like this: "Let me see. They're not in community anymore. Oh, he's off by himself. She doesn't go to life group. He doesn't go to Sunday morning service; I'm gonna watch him for a while. Oh, she didn't read the Word this morning. Man, it's been twenty-four hours, thirty-six hours, forty-eight hours, seventy-two hours. He hasn't prayed yet. Got me one."

Satan is a master schemer; he watches you, and he wants you. He wants to destroy you. He has an arsenal of techniques from millennia of dealing with believers who refuse to fight. So what do we do? How do we take the thought captive? How do we use these divinely empowered weapons? What are the weapons? You're going to be surprised. The number one weapon is the verse I quoted earlier: "His divine power has given us everything required for life and godliness" (2 Pet 1:3). Why does that matter? Because trusting Jesus Christ as Savior gives us new life and connects us to everything God has made available to us. God isn't sending anything else from heaven, other than Christ returning for you. Okay? Stop asking God for self-control. Stop asking God for patience. He already gave that to you. The issue is never, "Does God give it?" The question is, "Do you access it?" How do you do that?

Number one, prayer. And I know that seems simple. But there's not power in prayer. There's power that meets you in prayer. Don't let the clichés fool you. Your praying doesn't do anything; the one who meets you there does.

Consider Jehoshaphat. He was a warrior king, and in 2 Chronicles 20, his enemies come against him. He drops down, puts on sackcloth and ashes, and goes before God, pouring out his heart in prayer. Why in the world, if someone is coming to kill you, would you pray? Instead, if someone's coming your way, you just go get your gun and go to work. Jehoshaphat does something different. He recognizes that without God, he will lose. He cries out to God, and guess how God answers? "You can stop praying. I've already heard you. Jehoshaphat, this battle is not yours; it is the Lord's."

Now Jesus is in prayer in the garden of Gethsemane. "Father, I don't want to go to the cross." That's what "let this cup pass" means (Matt 26:39). In other words, "I don't want to experience the mystical separation in my humanity from you. I know how brutal this is going to be because I've seen it in eternity, how I was going to die, because you slew me before the foundation of the earth." He has all that in his mind. And in the midst of prayer, he says, "You know what, though? Not my will but yours be done."

The weapons of your warfare are not carnal. You can cuss; you can fuss. You can get in the comments section on social media. You can tweet, and you can put articles out there, but at the end of the day, you better learn how to get on your knees and pray.

Number two: Get in the Bible. Half of professing Christians, even 80 percent, don't read the Word on a regular basis. You know that I'm telling the truth. Jesus, in Matthew 4, didn't say, "Devil, I served notice to you, and I come against you." He didn't say anything like that. This is the God of the universe. He didn't say one word that's outside the Bible when he was talking to the devil. He said, "Man must not live on bread alone but on every word that comes from the mouth of God" (Matt 4:4). That's straight from Deuteronomy. Therefore, you and I have to learn how to fight in the Word.

Recently, I experienced a discouraging week, not just because my wife has cancer but because of many other things going on. I've been in the Word, but I've just not been able to get my mind right. Why am I not focused? Sermon prep was tough, and then I'm reacting to every little thing with frustration because I just didn't feel like I was connected to God's Word. So I got on the phone with my spiritual father, and he asked me to tell him everything that is going on. Then he gave me some advice and prayed. When he prayed, this is what he prayed: "We don't want you to be unaware, brothers and sisters, of our affliction that took place in Asia. We were completely overwhelmed—beyond our strength—so that we even despaired of life itself" (2 Cor 1:8). That's how I felt for the last two, three weeks; I despaired of living. He said, "Beyond our strength." He said, "Indeed, we felt that we had received the sentence of death, so that we would not trust in ourselves but in God who raises the dead" (v. 9). And let me tell you something: I don't know what happened, but when I heard that, my spirit stood up and said, "Hmm, I feel him now," because God said to me, "Everything you're going through—I'm going to raise you and your wife up from the dead." All I needed was one word from God, and the stronghold in my mind was destoyed at that moment. You must get in God's Word for yourself! Put on your war clothes, the full armor of God—Ephesians 6; 2 Corinthians 6—because what the enemy will do is he'll shoot arrows that say, "Just give up; take your own life; divorce your spouse; quit your job; give up on that person." And then he'll allow statements to get into your mind that demean your value, so you don't value yourself. You have to get there. But as I was feeling that, my wife and I were on the way to a date, and I put on some music. I needed to worship. Usually, I put on some sexy music. Usually, I put on some Earth, Wind, and Fire or Commodores or Isley Brothers. Every now and then you need to shift the atmosphere. Before I could put that on, I had to put on some worship music. The Holy Spirit began speaking to me, and I got so overwhelmed. My wife was saying, "You need to pull over." As I began to lift up my hands and worship God, guess what happened? I took off the spirit of heaviness, and I exchanged it for the garment of praise.

This may be a problem for you. See, you may be standoffish or snobbish and don't understand that *worship and praise are weapons.* You don't get it yet. You may say, "It's because I'm wired this way. I'm melancholy, and I'm like that." Praise is a weapon. Let me prove it to you. The Bible says that Paul and Silas, when they were in prison, were way down in a repulsive pit. While they were there—frustrated and beaten up—my Bible says they began to pray and sing praises to God. Now, you would think that a person under those circumstances would just sulk and be frustrated and exchange war stories of frustration, but in the midst of their difficulty, and in the midst of the stench, they began to open up their mouths and give God the fruit of their lips. As they did, my Bible says that the foundations began to give up praise to God because if you don't praise him, the rocks will cry out. And the Bible says that because the foundation was shaken, the prison doors that were locked, the prison doors that were shut, the prison doors that were guarded by the enemies had to open up.

There are some things in your life that God isn't going to open up until you open up your mouth and give him some praise. There are some things in your life that God wants to do. Maybe you are still too aloof. You haven't been there yet. Maybe you haven't gone through anything bad enough, but I know the God I serve, that when you exchange the spirit of heaviness for the garment of praise, he'll do something.

I have one more story, this one about the children of Israel in the book of Joshua. Praise makes you look stupid. Can you imagine the Jericho army and the warriors with spears, bows, and arrows on the top of the wall listening to the children of Israel, with no physical weapons in their hands, carrying around trumpets and a box with sticks extending out of it? And they're marching, they're quiet, walking around. They're marching around, and they don't say anything. They do this for seven days. So the Jericho army is saying, "What are they trying to do?" On the last day, the Israelites stopped marching. And when they stopped, the Bible says that God commanded them to blow the trumpet. When they blew the trumpet, the Bible says, God told them to shout. They didn't use a battering ram. They didn't have those catapult things. They didn't have anything but a praise on their lips. And because they gave God the praise, because they gave God the glory, the wall began to respond to worship. The wall began to shake. And as the old song says, "The walls came tumbling down."

There's some stuff in your life that's standing up in place, and it's fortified, and it's strong, but if you would open your mouth and give him the praise, there's some stuff that will come tumbling down. Maybe you need to be in your shower and just sing "Praise the Name of Jesus." You need to sing "Victory Is Mine."

There are some things in your life that you don't need to wait for someone on the praise and worship team to address. You need to be the praise and worship team at home. You need to remove from your mind the faulty theology that "praise doesn't do anything." That's a stronghold. "Praise and worship are emotionalism." That's a stronghold. "Praise and worship are for those who don't believe the Bible." That's a stronghold. You and I need to learn how to use the divinely empowered mechanisms God has given us so that we can walk in the truth that we overwhelmingly conquer because of him who loves us. I'm telling you, when you praise, as Fred Hammond said, there will be "a fire in your heart." And guess what you'll find? As Jesus starts getting higher in stuff in your life, all the other stuff in your life will begin to plummet.

Reflect and Discuss

1. What are some things that irritate you that you need to be honest about?
2. How do you ensure that you don't let everything that irritates you lead you to fight over it?
3. What are divinely empowered weapons?
4. What are they given to us for? What do we use them for?
5. What's a stronghold?
6. How do we tear down strongholds?
7. What are some strongholds in your life that you need to overcome?

Stay in Your Lane

2 CORINTHIANS 10:7-18

Main Idea: The gospel brings clarity to you and empowers you to clarify things with others.

I. **Sometimes You Have to Clarify Things with Some People (10:7-12).**
II. **Sometimes You Have to Clear Some Stuff Up within Yourself (10:13-18).**
 A. Be comfortable with where God has placed you (10:13-14).
 B. Stay focused (10:15-18).

A person may spend four years in college, two years in graduate school, and another four years for a doctoral degree, only to realize when she steps into her craft that she doesn't enjoy it. Another person is thirty-five years old and working at a marketing firm as a telemarketer while starting other businesses. He lives in a rooming house and is unable to get his businesses going because he is all over the place. Such stories reveal a lack of self-awareness, particularly in this generation.

When there is a lack of self-awareness, you try to ascribe identity to yourself. Many of us have been so educated by memes that we haven't spent time with the means. We have an idea of what we want to be based on the visual matrix and artistry of online beauty, but we don't realize that our calling isn't based on the external; it's based on the internal.

In fact, God has given every believer assignments. When God calls you to a specific assignment and place, you must nurture and rest in his calling. If you're not satisfied with where you are and what God is nurturing you in, your dissatisfaction is not with your assignment; rather, your dissatisfaction is with the Lord. Until you get things right with him, you're not going to be satisfied wherever he puts you. Where you are geographically doesn't bring satisfaction. If you don't realize that the Lord and the Lord alone is the one who brings satisfaction, you're going to be in trouble. I've learned in this life: I've seen some ups and I've seen some downs, but if I've allowed the season I was in to get me off task for what God has called me to do, and if I find my identity in the task versus the Master, I get in trouble.

We come to a text where Paul is defending his apostleship. The Corinthians are part of his assignment and commitment to the Lord as an apostle—to go forth into Gentile lands and to proclaim the gospel where no one else was going to do it. In other words, he was called to be a gospel pioneer. And many times, when you're pioneering and in a new field with few measures or examples to guide you, it's easy to doubt. So you must remind yourself repeatedly of your calling or you'll get in trouble. If you don't recognize that God is using you as an imprint and a blueprint for something to come behind you because he has already gone ahead of you, you're going to get in trouble.

So Paul actually double preaches. He preaches to himself while he's preaching to the people. Sometimes Paul is speaking only to them. But sometimes it seems as he's trying to minister to others, he is also telling himself something in return. Have you ever been unsure, but as you began to tell it, and as you began to communicate it, the Holy Spirit began to rise up in you, and you began to feel a whole lot better? Likewise, in this passage, Paul is telling himself to stay in his lane.

I remember when my dad was teaching me how to drive. And I remember I was beeping at people, and my dad would say, "What are you beeping at?"

I said, "They're coming into my lane."

He replied, "Let me ask you this: Are you looking in front of you, or are you looking at them?"

I said, "What do you mean?"

He said, "If you look at the car beside you, it will look like they are drifting into your lane, but in all actuality, because you don't have your eyes in your lane, you're actually drifting into their lane." So God wants you to stay in your lane.

Sometimes You Have to Clarify Things with Some People
2 CORINTHIANS 10:7-12

You have to clarify things with some people every now and then under the unction of the Holy Spirit. Now remember: I said the Holy Spirit. God gives you the freedom to clear some stuff up. That means you must make sure God is speaking and not you. You must make sure it's God and not your guts. You must make sure it's the Messiah and not your mind. You must make sure of it.

In verse 7 Paul says, "Look." The exegetical term is not just referring to appearances: notice this is blue; that's orange; it's cloudy outside; the ceiling fans are moving. Those statements relate to sight. But Paul is using this term to call them to grow up. He is speaking of sight beyond eyesight.

When you become a believer, your eyesight changes. When you were not saved, you had a veil over your eyes. The cause of that veil, based on 2 Corinthians 4:3-4 (cf. Eph 2:1-3), is Satan ("the god of this age"), who has put a veil over your eyes to keep you from seeing the glory of the gospel. When you trust Jesus Christ as Savior, you no longer see through the veil because the Holy Spirit removes it. Nonetheless, in a fallen world, you still have the residue of the remembrance of what you saw when the veil was on. So in order for you to see differently, the Holy Spirit had to give you new eyes, blow a new spirit into you, and give you faith, so that when you see the gospel, you can appraise it and recognize it for what it is. The Spirit's renewing work not only applies to your justification but also to your sanctification.

In other words, it applies in believing the gospel for you to begin to see that God is offering you sight beyond sight. So here in this passage, Paul is calling the Corinthian church to look at things in a spiritual way versus a carnal way. Viewing things in a spiritual way versus the carnal way, particularly your assignment from God, involves sight beyond sight. God seldom does anything that people would normally view as something a person should do; he usually does things backwards from normal, so that you can know that when it's getting done, it must be done by faith. So Paul says, "Look at what's before your eyes—your spiritual eyes."

He says, "If anyone is confident that he belongs to Christ, let him remind himself of this: Just as he belongs to Christ, so do we" (v. 7). What is Paul doing? He's being careful to root his identity in his assignment under Jesus. The Corinthians have had Judaizers or false apostles coming in, trying to tread on the foundation that Paul has already developed in engaging the Corinthian church. And the members have been so hoodwinked by those who have been in their ear that they have almost begun to talk about the idea that not only is Paul not an apostle, not only is he not authentically who he says he is, but he also might not even be saved.

So you have to be careful when you're moving on your assignment that you don't listen to the foolishness of others. Paul has to root himself in the fact, once again, that he knows Jesus Christ as his Savior. People and things will come along your path, too, that will make you wonder whether you're on the right track.

A prophetess and her husband once came to my office. I affirmed them: "Don't despise prophecies, but test all things. Hold on to what is good" (1 Thess 5:20-21). Right. "Pursue love and desire spiritual gifts, and especially that you may prophesy" (1 Cor 14:1). I'm not against prophecy. But she replied, "Amen, pastor. I just want to let you know, I *sense* that your elders, some of them . . ." Then she, along with her husband, began talking about some of the church leaders here. So I'm thinking, first off, you haven't met anyone; you haven't even been to the church service, but you just saw an elder, a chill went down your spine, and you have something to say to me. Right? So I responded, "You know, I hear you, sis. Praise God, because I believe based on 1 Corinthians 11 that either men or women could prophesy, and you could give me a word. But tell me where in the Bible that, in principle, what you're saying is correct."

"Well, man of God . . ."

"Man of God nothing! Where is it in here?"

And they began to root their prophetic utterances in their feeling versus the verses. And I said, "Well, let the spirit of the prophets be subject to the prophets" (1 Cor 14:32). Then the meeting was over. You have to be careful what you allow to be an entrance to you while you're walking in divine purpose. You have to be careful of people who say they have a word but who haven't really heard anything. You have to be extremely careful.

Paul challenges this reality with them. He is encouraging the Corinthians in several areas. He says, "For if I boast a little too much about our authority, which the Lord gave for building you up and not for tearing you down, I will not be put to shame" (v. 8).

Paul writes to the Corinthians about the fact that God has him on assignment to build them up and not to destroy them. The word for "building up" here is a construction word, which means to bring something to completion. Now, within the framework of your assignment, as a believer, God has called you as a construction worker under his general contract, if you will, to bring something to completion. In the natural world, if we were building, we would have electricians; we would have drywallers and various people who have different departmental expertise. And what they're supposed to do, based on their particular area, is to bring that particular thing to completion. But then the building is dependent on others who have their assignments to bring their parts to completion. If everyone is walking in divine purpose and assignment, working in concert and staying in their lane, they will maximize their effectiveness.

Paul says that he didn't come to tear them down. Many times in your purpose, when people speak against what you're doing, they have misinterpreted. Why? In the last section we talked about strongholds and about destroying every argument that lifted itself against the knowledge of Christ. Whenever you're on assignment, you're going to come up against strongholds. Remember, a stronghold is a mindset, a value system, or a thought process that hinders your growth. But often we don't realize what we're attached to.

Our calling is to come up against the thing that exalts itself against the knowledge of Christ, but we're attached to it. You see, strongholds aren't attached to you and me. We're attached to the strongholds. The only reason a stronghold exists in your life is that you are attached to it and are letting it be bigger than Jesus.

However, when you're walking in assignment and are walking in the will of God, you will be a tear-down mechanism for the stronghold. But others may not understand because they are bound; they can't see that you're trying to strengthen them and help them and build them up. They see you as an enemy and as a threat to something they're attached to.

So the Corinthians misinterpreted Paul's assignment to challenge them in some areas as destroying them. Why would they say "destroy"? Because they were so attached to it, they didn't realize it was a part of their identity. So Paul is deep on assignment and trying to help them in this area. He declares, "I don't want to seem as though I am trying to terrify you with my letters."

He adds, "For it is said" (v. 10). Every now and then you have to let people know that you know what they said about you.

To be a Christian isn't to be scared. To be a Christian is to invest in confronting stuff. The cross is God's commitment to confront our sin. If you're going to take up your cross, that same seed is used. The cross needs to be used for confrontation. So Paul says, "Let's discuss this. Let's get into it. I'm on assignment." The Bible speaks of confrontational realities that are done in love, not some abrasive thuggery.

You may be saying, "I knew I needed to tell that person to back off!" No, that's not the disposition or spirit of what Paul is communicating. Rather, he conveys, "I'm going to quote you." You see, sometimes you need to bring a notepad to your confrontations.

Paul repeats their remarks: "For it is said, 'His letters are weighty and powerful, but his physical presence is weak and his public speaking amounts to nothing'" (v. 10). Paul is saying, "All right, I hear you. But let me tell you something." He replies (I think he raises his voice in this part), "Let such a person consider this: What we are in our letters, when we are absent, we will also be in our actions when we are present" (v. 11). In other words, "What we wrote from a distance, we'll say right in your grill." Paul is letting them know, "Don't be trying to act as if I'm not going to get at you now. You know I love you, so I can talk crazy to you, knowing that you know I love you."

He writes, "For we don't dare classify or compare ourselves with some who commend themselves" (v. 12). In other words, "We're not glorifying ourselves, and I'm not comparing myself to other people." He says, "But in measuring themselves by themselves and comparing themselves to themselves, they lack understanding" (v. 12). In other words, if you compare yourself to other people, you can always measure yourself greater. The standard is supposed to be Jesus, not me or them. So don't magnify yourself in that realm. He communicates, "We can do the measuring and comparison game, but that's not how we live because our standard and commitment is to the Lord Jesus Christ."

Sometimes You Have to Clear Some Stuff Up within Yourself

2 CORINTHIANS 10:13-18

Paul writes, "We, however, will not boast beyond measure but according to the measure of the area of ministry that God has assigned to us, which reaches even to you" (v. 13). Paul is saying, "Listen, you know you're walking in purpose when you don't go beyond what God has called you to do."

Be Comfortable with Where God Has Placed You (10:13-14)

Many of us want to be bosses. Yet we want to be Christian, you know? We want to be Christian Puffys (Sean "Diddy" Combs) and Christian Jay Zs (Shawn Carter). We want entrepreneurialism, having multiple streams of income. We've got this persona of what we want to be. We want to be a jack of all trades and a master of none. So the Bible says, "We don't boast beyond our limits" (see v. 13). This helps you understand being comfortable with where the Lord has placed you. You can get a natural promotion in man's eyes but go through a spiritual demotion in God's eyes. What's happening is you're basing "promotion" on the flesh, not on the spirit. That's why Paul says he doesn't boast beyond his limits. Instead, he glorifies God and stays where God has given him a sphere to work.

That means you have humility enough to live in the realm of divine expertise God has given you. For instance, my wife was at this appointment at the hospital, and a young doctor suggested a course of treatment. My wife said, "No, it's not that."

He pronounced, "You need to do this."

She insisted, "It's not that." Then she said, "Okay, thank you." The doctor left, and my wife called in the nurse practitioner.

The nurse said, "We'll get the head doctor."

The head doctor came and asked, "Who told you that?" We told him. He said, "That's not even his area as a doctor." He said, "In the medical profession, we never give advice outside of our medical expertise because that lacks humility."

Just because you studied medicine doesn't mean you practice in that particular area. You have to be careful about giving people advice outside your medical assignment because it could cause someone great detriment. Be comfortable with where God has placed you; be excited and thankful for the assignment and the season God has placed you in. "Assignment" is a beautiful gift because it means that which was apportioned to you—what God has given you to do. "Area of ministry" (v. 13) means a delimited area, a clearly defined and delegated territory.

Every believer has a spiritual gift that's part of his territory as well as natural talents that are part of his territory. Now this is the key: some of us have one, some have two, some have five talents. Don't ruminate because you don't have as many as someone else. Sometimes you can get just as much fruit as the person with five if you just maximize your one. Do not go beyond the limits of what God has called you to do. In staying there, you maximize well. I remember when I started ministry, I didn't know what area of ministry I was going into. But I knew this: I wanted to be a youth pastor for the rest of my life. And I wanted to sing, make some records, and bless people through worship. If you talk to people who knew me, they probably thought I was going to be in music. And I wanted to be a youth pastor, and I said, "I'll do that. That's pretty much it. That's all I want to do."

Then I'm in the choir at my church, and all of a sudden people are asking, "Do you have some time for counseling?"

I respond, "For what? What are you talking about?" Next thing I know, people are asking for counseling, and I'm doing premarital counseling. I'm thinking, "I'm a choir member. Why am I doing counseling?"

Then, before choir practice, they said, "Eric, do devotions."

And I'm wondering, "Why am I doing devotions? I'm not anyone's pastor here." You have to know, I never wanted to be a senior pastor. I don't know what's going on, but anyway, I just do it. Then God just kept doing stuff with it.

Then one day my pastor said, "I need a five-year plan for the youth ministry."

So I was on it: "Boom!" I started writing up the plan for youth ministry, started walking through how we're going to go through all four Gospels expositionally. I had small groups developed, and we're going to go on mission trips. And I presented it: "Bam!"

The pastor asked, "Man, what is this?"

I said, "The youth ministry plan!"

He said, "Man, this isn't a youth ministry. This is a church!"

When you are called to do something for the Lord, it's going to come out of you no matter what. I just had to come to terms with my assignment. Let me help you come to terms with your assignment. It's so important. Don't daydream about anyone else's assignment.

I was talking to one of my mentors recently, and he said, "Now, Eric, let me just tell you something. The grass may be greener over there, but it was manure there at one point in time." He said, "You may have some manure right now." He started speaking to my spirit. He said, "What began as manure grows up to thick, rich, fruitful grass." I don't know who is reading this, but your assignment may seem like a mess, and it may stink, but God is up to something. The mess you're going through is only fertilizer for your future. That's really all it is. God is fertilizing. That's why it stinks so bad: God is fertilizing the ground of your soul for what he's doing, where he's taking you, where he's blessing you, where he's making you, where he's transforming you, but you have to go through where you are.

Verse 14 says, "For we are not overextending ourselves." Paul's saying, "We're not going beyond what God wanted us to do." Then he adds, "As if we had not reached you, since we have come to you with the gospel of Christ." He's encouraging himself in his pioneering work in the gospel.

Stay Focused (10:15-18)

Look what he asserts next: "We are not boasting beyond measure about other people's labors. On the contrary, we have the hope that as your faith increases, our area of ministry will be greatly enlarged" (v. 15). As you walk in your purpose, the whole idea is that you will have broader areas of low-hanging fruit in the place God has sent you.

Don't waste your time if God said no. There's going to be hardship in your assignment. Paul preaches to himself because when he got his calling, he didn't walk right into it (Acts 9). He was willing to wait through the development season. Remember, he saw the resurrected Christ with his eyes. So he could have just gone right in, announcing, "I've seen Jesus; I'm going in!" But no, he had the humility to know that just because he had a calling from God, it didn't mean there wasn't a preparation season before his ministry and his assignment would be birthed. He sat down under people he was smarter than and more gifted than, and he made them his commissioning agency in Acts 13. And it wasn't until the Holy Spirit moved, and there was affirmation from those who were leading him, that he saw it was time to do it.

When times were difficult in his assignment, he didn't see it as God saying no to his calling but as an affirmation of his calling. What did Paul hear from the Lord on that day? God affirmed it through Ananias. Every time God says something to you, he will say it to somebody else so that it can be affirmed. If he only says it to you, you could be lying. The Lord said to Ananias, "I will show him how much he must suffer for my name" (Acts 9:16). Several chapters later, a prophet named Agabus got up, took off his belt, and tied himself up. He said, "In this way the Jews in Jerusalem will bind the man who owns this belt and deliver him over to the Gentiles" (Acts 21:11). Some young daughters, some real prophetesses, were also there. The Bible says, "The local people pleaded with him not to go up to Jerusalem" (v. 12). But he didn't see suffering as a reason to run from his calling. The Bible said he was willing to suffer and even die in Jerusalem for the name of the Lord Jesus.

You may think hardship means no. When you're going through a hard time, you think hardship can stop what God is doing. God does his best work when you're going through it. He does his best work when you're broke; he does his best work when you're dealing with sicknesses; he does his best work when you're out of a job; he does his best work when you don't know where to go.

It might be that if you had everything, you wouldn't listen to the Lord. Maybe if you had everything, you wouldn't pray anymore. Maybe if you had everything, you wouldn't get into the Bible because that would eclipse where you're supposed to be. But a hardship makes you pray. Hardship makes you get into the Word. Hardship makes you go to church. Hardship makes you say, "Even if he kills me, I will hope in him" (Job 13:15).

In verse 16 Paul writes, "So that we may preach the gospel to the regions beyond you." In other words, he wants to do pioneer stuff. He is saying, "I want to go to places where man would not boldly go, but because God has called me, and because God has assigned me, I'm going to go."

I remember when we were going to plant in North Philadelphia, and people were suggesting, "Go to Northeast; go to University City. Why in the world would you go to North Philly?"

And I replied, "Well, say, it seems like God does not send people to where they're comfortable." See, to go where no one went means that there's no cushion and there's no guide to what you're going to deal with. So Paul said that he didn't want to tread on another one's ministry.

Realizing that everything you're asked to do is necessary to what you should be doing, what should you be focusing on? Number one: What are your *core commitments?* First off, be a disciple. Many of us want purpose, but we don't want discipleship. Many of us want to be in that place where we are shining and we're able to make some posts to get some likes. That's not your purpose. Your purpose starts with being a follower, committed. Many people come to church, but a bunch of them aren't committed. A bunch of them are committed to premarital sex. Some of them are committed to a serial monogamy. Some of them are committed to blowing up, and they're not a disciple, and they don't want anything God offers. They just like to be around the church to check off their commitment, but they're really not walking with Jesus. And many of them are not committed, and their life is filled with turmoil and a lack of commitment because they are determined to do what they want to do. They look down on what it means to be a real believer. I'm telling you right now, God loves you enough to not let you run away from him. He loves you.

This is how I do mine. Let me give you some of my core commitments. As I said, first off, I'm a disciple. Second, I'm a husband. If you're not a husband, you're a single person who is a disciple in the community with single people. Third, I'm a father. Fourth, I'm a pastor.

And then, I'm stewarding my competencies. That is, I had to ask myself, behind my core commitments, what are my *core competencies?* Because if you don't know what your core competencies are, you'll just be doing a whole bunch of stuff. You need to let the track record of what people say you're good at and that you bear fruit in be what you continue to focus on and build on. I had to ask myself, "What should I be doing?" The elders are always helping me with this because I can be zigzag minded. So I have elders who are around me, or people who are around me and my wife, who will say, "No, you need the zoom lens here, Pastor. Do what only you can do." So, preacher, teacher, leader, writer— that's all I do. If it isn't that, I don't do it.

Your list of core competencies shouldn't be long. You may be *able* to do a lot of things, but you can't be *fruitful* at all those things. Let me give you one question that centers me all the time: What has God asked me to do? Not, what did people ask me to do? Some people who have walked with Jesus for a while know what I'm talking about. What has God asked me to do? If he hasn't asked me to do it, I don't do it.

That means you and I must look to Jesus, who was clear about his purpose. The God of the universe, who spoke everything into existence (except for man—he *shaped* him), came to die. There was a lot he could've done, but what did he say? "I did not come to judge the world but to save the world" (John 12:47). He could have judged because he had the authority to judge, but he knew that in hypostasis, in his incarnation, that wasn't what he came to do at that time; he was on a particular assignment. He would say stuff like, "I was sent only to the lost sheep of the house of Israel" (Matt 15:24). If Jesus needed to be focused, how much more do I? Then he tells them, "It is necessary that the Son of Man suffer many things, . . . be killed, and be raised the third day" (Luke 9:22). Jesus was focused.

Christians are all over the map, and Jesus is saying, "I didn't ask you to do that. I don't want you to do that. You're all over the place. You're trying to impress this person. You're trying to impress people who don't even care about you. They don't want anything for you. Stop trying to impress everyone, and instead walk in what I required you to do." You see, family of God, some of you need to stop playing with your spiritual life and seek God, seek his face. Some of us have thrown up prayers, "What do you want me to do?" And then you go on and do what you want to do. You may need to set aside some time and pull out a journal and pull out your Bible. You may need to miss some meals and pray and travail with God and hang with God. Then look for signs, like David said: "I call on you, God, because you will answer me" (Ps 17:6). The thing you're seeking, that you're deep into now—have you sought God about it? I'm just asking you questions. Has it been comprehensively affirmed by his Word, by a sense in your soul, and by others who have watched you and affirm that that's what you should be doing? Have opportunities to execute and do that thing been open for you? If those four things are not happening, cross it out and go on to the next thing.

The example given by the Lord Jesus Christ (*Christus exemplar*)—his death, burial, and resurrection from the grave—was the most focused event in human history. The power that comes from his life lets you be a disciple, to be able to walk in that type of focus.

Reflect and Discuss

1. Why is it important to tune out the foolish lies of people and listen to the truth of God's Word?
2. How can you tell when people are attached to their strongholds?
3. What people or things do you need to confront in your life?
4. How does the cross of Christ empower you to confront those things?
5. Where has God assigned you in this season, and what has he assigned you to do?
6. How can you grow in being content in your calling, purpose, and assignment?
7. In what ways do you need to grow in commitment to being a disciple of Jesus?

Christians: Do Not Be Deceived

2 CORINTHIANS 11:1-15

Main Idea: Do not be deceived by Satan or anything that would lead you away from Jesus.

I. **God's People Reject Anything That Devours Their Commitment to Jesus (11:1-6).**
II. **Godly Leaders Are Willing to Make Significant Sacrifices to Promote the Gospel (11:7-9).**
III. **Satan Always Makes Deception Look, Feel, and Seem Convincing (11:10-15).**

The Bible says, "In later times some will depart from the faith, paying attention to deceitful spirits and the teachings of demons, through the hypocrisy of liars whose consciences are seared" as if with a branding iron (1 Tim 4:1-2). Jesus told his followers,

> *Many will come in my name, saying, "I am the Messiah," and they will deceive many. . . .*
> *If anyone tells you then, "See, here is the Messiah!" or, "Over here!" do not believe it. For false messiahs and false prophets will arise and perform great signs and wonders to lead astray, if possible, even the elect. Take note: I have told you in advance. So if they tell you, "See, he's in the wilderness!" don't go out; or, "See, he's in the storerooms!" do not believe it.* (Matt 24:5,23-26)

I believe the prophecies of old in these passages are coming to pass like napalm. If you pay any attention to what's going on in the world, or if you have any type of social media feed, these times have been filled with people communicating their denouncement of Christianity. A young woman gives her spiel on why she was walking away from Christianity or the church. A man who claims to be a pastor or a Christian artist announces that he left the Christian faith.

I'm always interested to know about someone who *claims* (and I emphasize *claims*) to have had been a Christian: what was so powerful that he found out that he is no longer a Christian? So I'm looking at the television screen and waiting to find out because obviously something new happened that I don't know about and a whole lot of other people don't know about to give us reasoning behind why a pastor who says he's a pastor has left the faith. Then he says one of the reasons he left the faith was because the Bible was created by oppressors. I'm thinking to myself, "When?"

He says, "AD 325, at the council of Nicea."

OK, you mean to tell me, you don't know that the Bible was written over a fifteen-hundred-year period by about forty authors, and their books connect with one another? But you're saying that the Bible was written in one year—in the year AD 325 they created Christianity and the Scriptures—even though the church fathers in North Africa were quoting the Scriptures from the time of Christ all the way up to AD 325 and beyond. But the Bible was created in AD 325 by oppressors. Athanasius, who's called the black dwarf from North Africa, was one of the leading spokesmen for giving us the understanding of the hypostatic union, based on Philippians 2:1-11, from which he declared the two natures of Christ. Athanasius was from North Africa, and he was a short, stubby little guy with a round nose and dark skin. You say it's the white man's religion, but I'm confused because whiteness didn't come up until about the late 1500s in North America. And if you're saying the southern Europeans were whites, the whiteness of Europe was created by Britain later on, so they didn't even consider them a part of the same nationality. So now you're saying there's a unified Europe that created a white man's religion, and they were at Nicea in AD 325, even though the British didn't get Christianity until AD 1000. So I'm kind of confused.

I'm going through that rant because there is this trend, particularly among Black millennials, to say you're woke, but you do not know that you're going to sleep. The more I hear the foolishness of those who say they were Christian, I would say you were never a Christian because to become a Christian isn't to make a decision to be in the church. To be a Christian is to be redeemed, by which you have faith in Jesus Christ, who was not a white man with blonde hair and blue eyes, if that's your hang-up. And even if he was, who cares?—but he wasn't. So let's debunk that. He was probably olive- to dark-skin complected, and he probably had wooly or curly wavy Indian type hair, like people buy out of the stores down the street. The recessive gene of blue eyes wouldn't have hit

Semitic peoples. It's just simple stuff. *But he died on the cross for our sins and got up from the grave on the third day!*

My concern is that we have such a shallow Christianity in our day. So many people are concerned about foolishness, and anyone can bring up a false history. I am not dumb enough to believe everyone reading this believes the gospel. Some of you reading this book are on the borderline of belief. Some of you are in the faith, and some of you believe you believe, and you're in the church, but redemption and restoration and regeneration haven't made it into you. So let's not confuse a person who attended church with being the church.

This stuff isn't new; the devil has always been at work. The white man is not the devil. Some horrific things have been led by those who are white in history, but white people are not crafty enough to be the devil. Let me just debunk that.

Now let me help my white people feel good. The target isn't on you. We love you because we're blood-bought together as believers in Jesus Christ.

If you're Black, don't let your anger toward the atrocities in white history make you forget that, if they confess Jesus as Lord and are really redeemed, they become your brothers, even more than those according to the flesh who don't know Jesus.

That's not how some define *woke* out there. For some, in order to be woke in our world, you have to hate all white people, even if they're Christian. But that's not the Bible, and I will not try to relate to woke, fallen, Pan-Africanists by cursing white people who know Jesus. I'll talk to my white brothers and sisters about privilege and race, but I'm not going to deny their salvation if they know Jesus Christ.

Okay, we got that out of the way. So Paul is really challenging the church in a powerful way about deception. Deception is not merely intellectual; it's also spiritual. If you don't treat deception as a spiritual issue, you're going to be vulnerable.

God's People Reject Anything That Devours Their Commitment to Jesus
2 CORINTHIANS 11:1-6

Look what Paul says in verse 1: "I wish you would put up with a little foolishness from me. Yes, do put up with me!" Paul is about to amp up a little bit. This is the biblical, exegetical language of the turnup. If you want to tick one of the apostles off, just act like you don't want to serve Jesus but still call yourself a Christian. They're going to turn up; they're going to go from zero to sixty in two seconds—faster than a Bugatti. Paul is saying, "Do I really have to defend my spiritual authority?"

There are two types of defense: self-centered defense and God-centered defense. Self-centered defense means, "Listen to whatever I say, and don't check anything because I am the covering of the house." None of you have heard that before, right? "Don't go to any other churches or ask my permission to go to another church. If you go to this church, you must call me every time you're going to be somewhere." A God-centered defense rests on the transparent teaching and preaching of the Word and dares you to seek God on it and stands in the truth of it.

So Paul says, "I'm about to talk some foolishness." That is, he's about to defend his apostolic authority. Look where he roots his authority of what he calls "foolishness." In other words, "Do I really have to talk to you about being centered on Jesus?"

So here's where he goes in verse 2. He says, "For I am jealous for you with a godly jealousy, because I have promised you in marriage to one husband—to present a pure virgin to Christ." This is one of my favorite verses in the Bible. Whenever my affections for Jesus wane, there are two verses I go to. One is, "As a deer longs for flowing streams, so I long for you, God" (Ps 42:1). And then I like this one in 2 Corinthians because it points me to the fact that the lowest common denominator of the Christian faith is devotion to Jesus. Paul expresses that he has divine jealousy for the Corinthians.

You must understand, jealousy can be a good word in the Bible. In the Ten Commandments, God talks about worshiping him and him alone. When he says that, he says, because "I . . . am a jealous God" (Exod 20:5). The reason God can be jealous is *jealous* here isn't a negative term. This is not like the "Martin Lawrence and Gina" jealousy, where Martin's just acting a fool. We are not talking about George Jefferson jealousy, right? Some of you don't know what I'm talking about. It's okay. My forty-and-ups got it. They know who George Jefferson is. It's not Archie Bunker, for my white folks. Or *Seinfeld*, or *Friends*—we have to be diverse. But I digress.

Jealousy in the Bible is the ability to feel a certain way about what's authentically yours. A husband or wife who sees their spouse peeking at something else and trying to get at something else outside God's design through covenant has the right to be jealous because what's supposed to be theirs is being given to someone else. Biblical jealousy involves something God has given to you but someone gives to someone else. You have the right to jealousy for it. Why? Because it's been authentically ordained as yours. That's why the commandment says, "Do not covet your neighbor's wife" (Exod 20:17). Why? Because covetousness means a dissatisfaction with the blessings God has given you.

Jealousy in the Bible is God saying, "The glory and devotion that are rightly mine should be given to me and not anyone else." That means God has the right to continue to challenge you when you put your family above him. He has the right to challenge you when you work so hard that you don't have the energy to spend time with him. God has the right to reprimand you about anything that obstructs the depth of intimacy he has called you to because what's rightfully his is being given to someone or something else.

That's why Paul says, "I am jealous for you with a godly jealousy" (v. 2). He offers a cultural and spiritual analogy: "Because I have promised you in marriage to one husband—to present a pure virgin to Christ" (v. 2). He's using rabbinic history, the way the Hebrew culture did marriage. You couldn't just walk up on a little honey that you liked. Fathers were big in their daughters' lives. A father would always have to know where his daughter was. He oversaw her sexuality and fought for her to remain a virgin because her lack of virginity could bring shame to the family. He could get less money through the betrothal, which points to her worth.

So a man would talk to his father and say, "Pops, I want to marry this young woman."

Then his father would go to her father and say, "What's up, man?"

Pops be like, "What you need?" He's like Will Smith and Martin at the door, you know, in *Bad Boys*. "What you want, dog?"

"My son likes your daughter."

"So, what's his name? What does he do?" He'll put out an APB about that man's son. A man can't just come in another man's house and take his daughter. So before he even talks to her, Daddy gets talked to. When they work through this, the couple is ready to be married. Then the betrothal takes place, and they agree on the bride price. The bridegroom gets ready and the bride gets ready, but the issue is, he had to be able to get the bride price. If he didn't have the bride price, he had to go get a job. He wasn't always trying to start a business that never brought any money into the house because he was living in his mama's basement.

So what would happen is—this is awkward—the whole family and the whole city would be there. Pops would hand a bedsheet to the son. They would consummate the union. After they finished—this is weird, isn't it? I just couldn't imagine—he hands the sheet out the window. His father looks at it with the elders of the city. If there's no blood on it, they pay less for the girl. Her value is lower because there was a deficiency, an impurity.

Paul is saying here, "I betrothed you to one husband as a pure virgin in Christ." We're in the betrothal period right now. And you've got to understand, betrothal was not like our engagement. In their day it meant an actual marriage. It was legally binding. Paul is challenging them, and he's challenging us, that we shouldn't be letting anyone sway us because we're already promised to Jesus Christ. That means you shouldn't be easily talked to. You may—I don't want to be vulgar—you may spiritually give it up too easily. The text is saying, even if someone works hard for it, whatever it is spiritually in your life, you shouldn't give it away because it's only for Jesus Christ. Paul says that you are supposed to be pure, but you're made pure by Jesus, not yourself. But what you do is you walk in the purity that Christ has given you through belief in his death, burial, and resurrection. In other words, remain in the faith.

In verse 3 he observes, "But I fear that, as the serpent deceived Eve by his cunning, your minds may be seduced from a sincere and pure devotion to Christ." This is profound. He's saying the church is the new Eve because Jesus is the new Adam. Now that Jesus is the better Adam, the church is supposed to be the better Eve. Jesus doesn't sit around while the devil talks to his bride, like Adam did. Adam was standing there. The Bible says, "She also gave some to her husband, *who was with her*" (Gen 3:6; emphasis added). This punk dude, he's standing there: "Talk to my wife if you want to, homey."

But now Paul says, "You know what? Devil start talking to you, bat him off." But what does that come from? Devotion to Christ. He asserts, "Deceived . . . by his cunning." The devil is a crafty dude. He comes up with all types of stuff—stuff you're not expecting. The devil isn't going to come with a pitchfork—he doesn't look like that—and some horns and red skin. The devil is going to come smooth, in a tailored suit, nice shoes, bespoke jacket. But you'll know him by its character family.

Paul doesn't want us to be led astray from sincerity. Some translate it "simplicity." Now simplicity doesn't mean simplistic. Rather, it means having things uncluttered, so that you can clearly see and experience Jesus Christ. In your walk with Christ, there must be a level of sincerity and commitment, purity and devotion to him. So we don't follow the advances of the enemy; we submit to the glory of the one who saved us by his mercy and grace and gave us the strength to follow him.

Verse 4 says, "For if a person comes and preaches another Jesus, whom we did not preach, or you receive a different spirit, which you had not received, or a different gospel, which you had not accepted, you put up with it splendidly!" The Corinthians were spiritually immature. They were entertaining things that had nothing to do with the core of what it means to be a believer. In our day we look at the Corinthians as if they were crazy, but some of us entertain foolishness. What are the new Jesuses of our day that people try to get us to believe in? Horus and Osiris? It's like they never existed. Now Jesus is a sociological hippie, the blond-haired, blue-eyed Jesus. But then it goes to a different spirit: "I'm sitting with the ancestors." Now, if an ancestor answers, run.

Speaking plainly, I have a family member who lost his wife and struggled greatly. It was difficult. They'd been together for years and years. And he called me, and he said, "Eric, she visited me."

I said, "Who?"

He said, "My wife visited me. She came into the room, and I smelled her presence was there. And she just laid back in the bed with me and told me everything's going to be all right."

I said, "Nah, that wasn't her."

He said, "What do you mean?"

I said, "Well, in Deuteronomy 18 it's something called sorcery or inquiring of the dead. When a loved one passes, a demon attempts to comfort you through taking on the identity of that person, to draw you away from devotion to Jesus Christ. And then your life is preoccupied with the death of that person versus the death of Jesus."

You need to be careful what you allow in the sphere of your existence as a believer. The Jesus of the Bible that we worship is not any of those things. All those realities of the Jesus we know predated the world. He even appeared as theophanies. He's worshiped by angels and humans, and he's given the highest name in the universe. He appeared in history over and over again.

In verses 5-6 Paul refuses to get sidetracked by the "super-apostles." The Greek calls them "hyperapostles." He says, "Even if I am untrained in public speaking"—even if you don't like my rhetoric—"I am certainly not untrained in knowledge" (v. 6). He's saying, "I'm a beast. I know my information. I know this sounds crazy, but I do know the Bible and the gospel." He states, "Indeed, we have in every way made that clear to you in everything" (v. 6). He doesn't hold back anything they need to know about the Word. They should know this.

Godly Leaders Are Willing to Make Significant Sacrifices to Promote the Gospel
2 CORINTHIANS 11:7-9

Paul is trying to debunk false leaders who call themselves hyperapostles: "Or did I commit a sin by humbling myself so that you might be exalted, because I preached the gospel of God to you free of charge? I robbed other churches by taking pay from them to minister to you" (vv. 7-8). Now, when it says he robbed churches, that doesn't mean he went over there and took some bad offerings. Some of you are thinking, "See, that's what I'm talking about. The church is always on some offerings. You're always robbing someone of something. That's why I don't fool with Christians." But he's not using the word *robbing* in that way. He's communicating, "You should have been supporting me financially, but because of where you were spiritually, I didn't take what I could have taken. Instead, I raised support from other congregations to minister to you, so that nothing got in the way of me ministering to you."

If you have leaders that don't ever sacrifice, or people who are never willing to make a sacrifice so that the gospel's hearable to you, but they're always emphasizing what you must give to them, you're under false leadership. Paul said, "I rob other churches to bring you the gospel."

Satan Always Makes Deception Look, Feel, and Seem Convincing
2 CORINTHIANS 11:10-15

In verse 12 Paul declares, "But I will continue to do what I am doing, in order to deny an opportunity to those who want to be regarded as our equals in what they boast about." I don't have a problem saying that.

Because a falsity is happening in the church and among these people who call themselves the church that aren't really authentic churches. Paul calls them several things; he calls a spade a spade. First, he calls them "false apostles" (v. 13). The Greek is *pseudapostoloi.* "Apostles" means those who were sent forth. So *pseudo* or "false" before it suggests that they were falsely saying they were sent by the Lord. In our day we have people saying they're apostles, but they're not. A real apostle had to see the resurrected Jesus or his ministry.

He also calls them "deceitful workers." They act as if they're doing ministry, but they're just trying to get stuff from you. For example, when I listen to people who say they left the church, I ask, "Give me some good information about why you left." So I'm listening to it.

"They were about money." Okay. "Everything was built around the pastor and his wife." Okay. "They only did this. They didn't do any outreach. They didn't do _____."

And I'm thinking, "That doesn't sound like the church to me. You may have left something, but you didn't leave the church."

"Man, they were really preaching the gospel. I didn't agree with that. They were spending time in biblical community with one another. It seemed a little cultic, but they loved one another. And they spent time, when someone had a need, they took care of the need. As a matter of fact, they did clothing drives for people, and that was confusing to me. They planted churches in Africa; that was confusing to me. They built schools. They planted churches in different poor neighborhoods, and I think it's just to get money. But why would you plant a church in a poor neighborhood to get money? I mean, I'm so confused by that." If that's what you left, then let's talk.

So when Paul engages in this, not only do we know we have the truth, but we get to proclaim and show that we're not deceived, because we have the real Jesus. In fact, Jesus is used to being ridiculed. His birth was called a bastard birth by the Pharisees in John 8. So even his birth, they had issues with. His ministry, they had issues with. They said Jesus was a drunkard and spent time with sinners talking to them about the kingdom while drinking wine. He was accused of unfaithfulness to the Word, accused of being demon possessed. He was accused of being a blasphemer. He died a sinner's death, was placed in an expensive grave, and was raised from the grave on the third day. He was accused of being a ghost, accused of being not a historical person or of being a white European, a myth, and a creation of the oppressors. Now, I don't know about that Jesus because that person doesn't exist. Whenever they post a picture of that guy online saying, "This is who you worship," I don't know who that is. But I will tell you exactly who I worship and why I worship him. I worship him because I'm grateful that I will never have to worry about deception. I'm glad that God has made a way for me out of no way, but I know that that's not enough. I know him as the bright and morning star. I know him as the most holy one. I know him as a Nazarene. I know him as the only begotten of the Father, the only wise God. He's the only blessed Potentate. He's the precious Cornerstone. He's the Prince of life. He's my ransom. He's my Redeemer. He's the resurrection and the life. He's the ruler of Israel. He's my salvation. He's my sanctification. He's my Scepter. He is my second Adam.

Let me see if I can call the roll. He's Adam's Redeemer. He's Abel's vindicator. He's Abraham's sacrifice. He's Noah's ark. He's Moses's bush on fire. He's Joshua's captain. He's Gideon's fleece. He's Samson's power. He's David's music. He's Solomon's wisdom. He's Jeremiah's balm in Gilead. He's Ezekiel's wheel in the middle of the wheel. He's Daniel's son of man. He's Matthew's King. He's Mark's Suffering Servant. He's Luke's Great Physician. He's John's Word made flesh. He's the coming of the Holy Spirit in Acts. He's my Waymaker. He's my lawyer in a courtroom. He's my doctor in the hospital. He's my clothes when I'm naked. He's my food when I'm hungry.

I was sinking deep in sin, . . .
Sinking to rise no more;
But the Master of the sea
Heard my despairing cry,
From the waters lifted me—
Now safe am I. (James Rowe, "Love Lifted Me")

I know he's all right. He's God of all gods. He's the Prince of the universe. He's the Superstar of eternity. He's the heart fixer. He's a mind regulator. He's my soldier. He's my warrior. He's my captain.

I'm so glad that one Friday, they hung him high and they stretched him wide and he died. He dropped his head in the locks of his shoulders. It was quiet all night Friday; it was quiet all night Saturday; but early Sunday morning, he got up with all power in his hands, and he's coming back for a pure church. He's coming back for a holy church.

He's coming back for a beautiful church. He's coming back for a sanctified church. He's coming back. Are you ready? I'm so glad we're not under deception, but we're under the truth of the one who is un-debunkable. And I pray that you continue in the Lord with strength and with encouragement.

Reflect and Discuss

1. What are ways you see people being deceived into rejecting Christianity?
2. What is godly jealousy?
3. In what ways is God seeking to make sure you're completely devoted to him?
4. What are some foolish, unbiblical things you've been entertaining that you need to let go of?
5. Do you have pastors and/or leaders who are willing to make sacrifices for the gospel? If you're a pastor or leader, are you willing to do that?
6. How does Satan make deception look and feel convincing?
7. How do the gospel and truth of God's Word help you overcome deception?

How to Break the Illusion of Self-Strength

2 CORINTHIANS 11:16-33

Main Idea: To break the illusion of self-strength, we must boast in our weaknesses, not our strengths.

I. **Paul Uses Boasting as a Subversive Tactic (11:16-21).**
II. **Paul Boasts according to His Flesh (11:22-29).**
III. **Paul Prefers to Boast in His Weaknesses to Break Self-Strength (11:30-33).**

One of my favorite TV shows of all time is *Good Times*, which I mentioned watching with my children earlier. They called it *Good Times*, but they had a lot of bad times. I'll never forget when James Evans Sr. died. After they came from the repast, everybody left the house, and all the children—J J, Michael, and Thelma—were bewildered by the fact that Florida Evans didn't seem to be grieving. You can tell—I mean, Esther Rolle is just a great actress—she was pushing off the reality that her husband had died. She was trying to be strong for everyone else, but her children were concerned: "Mom needs to deal with this. She needs to grieve this; she needs to work through this. We're working through it, and she needs to work through it." And then everyone was in the other room, and you may remember the scene: a bowl was thrown to the ground, and she uttered those four-letter words, which will ever be our hashtag whether there's Internet or not. She yelled it three times; they gathered around her, and in a departure from the regular *Good Times* way, it concluded with no music. That's how you know it was a serious episode.

All that to say, we learned a beautiful lesson in the natural that is so true in the spiritual. It's only so long that you can go trying to be strong in yourself. Human strength is limited. Because human strength is limited and life is so hectic, it's almost as if even despite the fall, God has created us to be able to run to him over and over again. I don't know if you've ever been in a situation where you were trying to be strong, but when you got home, you were crumbling. I don't know if you have been in a situation where you put on your game face—I mean, your "A" game, your poker face; everyone thinks everything is good with you—but then you got in the shower, and you didn't know the difference between the water coming out of the shower and the water coming out of your eyes.

Human strength is a joke, but I know a God who's mighty in power, who's mighty in strength, whose strength is from the utmost to the utmost. No matter what you're going through, no matter what you're dealing with, God has strength, not just to match but to overtake the pain you're dealing with. This section of chapter 11 examines God's strength in our weakness. Paul addresses this topic with the Corinthians because they haven't become theologically Christian.

That is, they became Christian by regeneration but not by growing in their understanding of a biblical worldview. So they admire people who assert themselves; they esteem people who are pushy and demand attention. They love the individualistic disposition of a narcissistic culture that causes you to look at you and you alone. And that errant view upended their spiritual lives. You see, when you believe that you are the center of the universe and all strength comes from you, there will be a breaking point. But Paul and the leaders in the Bible are trying to save you a trial. Trials shouldn't be created by you. Trials should just be stuff because you're walking with Jesus. Paul's trying to save the Corinthians from it.

Sometimes that's how you are when you're a parent raising your children. You're thinking, "I'm trying to save you from something now. If you won't listen, I'll meet you on the other side when you've come to your senses." That's what Paul's trying to do: save God's people from some stupidity.

Some leaders and people have come in who are trying to create and recreate the church at Corinth into an unhealthy church. They want to focus on those who are leading the church versus keeping the focus on the Christ of the church. Whenever you have a church where you say, "Everything comes through leadership to me in order for my life to be a blessing, and I have to do good to them in order that I may be blessed," you have actually created another mediator.

In other words, if it's leader centered—if I want to be blessed, I give to the leader because all my blessings from God come through leadership, not God's lordship—you're in trouble in that church. So we come to this passage, and Paul is challenging the Corinthians about "What's the difference?" What are "strong" and "strength" in God's eyes?

Which brings me to my one and only point. **If we are going to know
how to break the illusion of self-strength, we must boast in our weaknesses, not our strengths.**

Paul Uses Boasting as a Subversive Tactic
2 CORINTHIANS 11:16-21

Paul states, "I repeat: Let no one consider me a fool" (v. 16). Paul's
going to play on words so beautifully. It's like good '90s hip-hop
wordplay—like hip-hoppers of the day don't know what wordplay is
because that's how the music is sometimes. Paul says, don't think me
foolish, but then he declares, "But if you do, at least accept me as a fool"
(v. 16). Paul, you said not to consider you a fool but to accept you as a
fool. And he says, "So that I can also boast a little" (v. 16). This text is
humble swag!

What makes it humble swag is the way he's going to turn it because,
in their day, the way a speaker would come in was not to have someone
else read their résumé ahead of time. You'd come up and give your
résumé while you're communicating, which would be unthinkable. You
know, imagine a preacher coming to the church. "Hello, everyone. How
you doing? I have three doctorates."

Or someone says, "I have a master's degree. I preach around the
world."

You'd be thinking, "Wow." Or maybe you would walk out at that
point, but in their day, a self-referencing introduction was acceptable.
But Paul is bewildered because they don't understand how the kingdom
works. They don't recognize the nature of what makes a godly leader
and what makes an ungodly leader. So Paul adds, "What I am saying in
this matter of boasting, I don't speak as the Lord would, but as it were,
foolishly" (v. 17). So he's playing on words here and communicating,
"God doesn't usually want people to operate like this, but he's going to
give me some freedom. This is not the norm, but I'm under the inspiration of the Holy Spirit. So he's going to give me some freedom to flip
what boasting really looks like when it comes from heaven versus when
it comes from earth. When boasting comes from earth, it exalts the person talking; when boasting comes from heaven, it exalts the one who's
being talked about." Paul is trying to let them know that this is not his
normal modus operandi. But, "I'm going to play with you because of

the way your culture works and what you appreciate." He writes, "Since many boast according to the flesh, I will also boast" (v. 18).

Now, the way he wants to boast is not according to the flesh because that's what he's saying they're boasting like. He says he's going to boast, but notice he didn't say, "I will also boast *in the flesh.*" He hides what he's going to boast about so he can see whether they can tell the difference between a fleshly boast and a spiritual boast. Notice the way he begins: "For you, being so wise, gladly put up with fools!" (v. 19). In other words, you say you can spot a con man, but you put up with stupidity a whole lot.

When I was little, I'd be outside in Washington, DC, hanging out on the porch. Back then we didn't have strong AC. You know those old windows with the lead paint just chipping off. You may know nothing about that. We raised the window, and the dirty screen would be right there. My dad would want the breeze to come in while he's listening to one of the TVs that sit on the floor. It was called a "console." It had a turntable in it that you open up. It had the eight-track player right beside it. He had some Al Green or the Commodores playing.

I'm outside and I'm with some folk and, in DC, we call it jonin', right? With kids talking about you real bad. So kids are out there just dogging me, and my dad calls me and says, "Hey, boy, come here." So I come into the house, and he sits me down. He says, "Son, never want to be somebody's friend so bad that you put up with their foolishness. Now go back outside."

My dad was trying to shepherd me in what foolishness is so that I could recognize it and not put up with it. That's what Paul is doing here. Paul is saying, "Listen, don't put up with foolishness." Listen, church, don't put up with foolishness. Visitors, don't put up with foolishness. Local assembly people, don't put up with foolishness. Look what he says: "You, being so wise" (v. 19). Then he expresses, "In fact, you put up with it if someone enslaves you, if someone exploits you, if someone takes advantage of you, if someone is arrogant toward you, if someone slaps you in the face" (v. 20). It was as if they were hazing in the church.

I have a few examples of being enslaved: lacking the real sense and understanding of the gospel, legalism, easy believism. So many things can enslave people. Telling people, "If you don't give, you will be cursed with a curse," even though Christ paid and became a curse so that he can be the cure. Or controlling tactics to cause you to be a believer based on controlling your life for outcomes only God can bring. Paul's trying to help them walk in what it means to be free in Christ.

Freedom in Christ doesn't mean irresponsibility. Don't think that. What he's saying is, "They're enslaving you to their philosophy versus chaining you to the Lord." If you're chained to the Lord, that obligation flows out of the gospel, meaning it's motivated by what Christ has done for you.

Enslavement is motivated by what you do for Christ that you think makes you righteous. But the reverse is true when you're truly enslaved to the Lord. Every time you look at him on the cross, you'll say, "I'm just going to go ahead and do the right thing." Every time you look at his pierced side, you'll say, "I'm going to just go ahead and do it." When you look at the holes in his feet, you're saying, "Man, he did all that. I might as well go ahead and do it." When you look at the piercings in his wrist, you say, "I'm just going to do it." You're motivated by what Christ has done for you, knowing that what you do for him doesn't mean anything if it's not flowing from him. Enslavement by man is to be in true bondage; enslavement to Christ is to be free.

Paul wants them to understand what freedom looks like. He'll give some examples that Christians aren't going to like because we don't like these kinds of passages. We like the passages, "I have been remarkably and wondrously made" (Ps 139:14). "The LORD will make you the head and not the tail" (Deut 28:13). "The LORD will protect your coming and going both now and forever" (Ps 121:8). We like those passages, right? We don't like the passages that lay out what biblical Christianity is because biblical Christianity is at its best when things aren't going right.

Paul makes fun of them in a facetious way. He exclaims, "I say this to our shame: We have been too weak for that!" (v. 21). In other words, if you find strength in enslavement, we're too weak to enslave you. You see the play on words here? "If you value people putting you in bondage, I'm weak in that particular area of my life because that's not my goal." As a matter of fact, Paul implies there are ways he could have manipulated them, like "I led you to Christ; we baptized. There's all kinds of ways you could've owed me some stuff." But remember in the last chapter, he said, "I robbed other churches. I didn't even ask for an offering." I know most of us wouldn't pass that up.

In verse 21 he adds, "But in whatever anyone dares to boast—I am talking foolishly—I also dare." He even feels it as he's writing. The dashes there are sort of like a parenthetical pause. He's saying, "Do they really want me to go there?" Have you ever had someone who was coming at you? You were thinking, "Do you really want me to go there?"

That's the spirit of the passage. He says he's speaking foolishly, and he dares to boast. In other words, "In speaking like a fool, I'm playing with you right now because I'm actually speaking like a wise person, so I'm really reverse bragging and you don't even see it."

Paul Boasts According to His Flesh
2 CORINTHIANS 11:22-29

In verse 22 he starts bragging, "Are they Hebrews?" He already knows they are. He says, "So am I. Are they Israelites? So am I. Are they the descendants of Abraham? So am I." They were saying, "Paul's from Tarsus. He's really not from Jerusalem. So we're more Jewish than he is because we were geographically raised in Jerusalem. He was raised in Gentile territory." So he's communicating, "Are they trying to pull that card out? They don't even understand how this works. I'm going to beat them at their own game."

In verse 23 he asks, "Are they servants of Christ?" He says, "I'm a better one." That's in the Bible. That's crazy. You ever heard someone say, "You can't serve the Lord like me. You can't lift him up like me"? Or, "You can't preach the gospel like me. You can't lead people to Christ like me." It's almost as if he's an emcee or a rapper right now. Why would he say he's a better Christian? Because they are not at all. He wouldn't compare himself as a way to say that he's a better server, but he's using their boasting technique as a way undergirded by the Spirit to show them who they are and who they're not. He admits, "I'm talking like a madman." Paul feels it as he's writing it. He keeps qualifying the statement. He's still being facetious.

And then he communicates, "All right, let's get to it. You don't want to do this. Don't try to pull out the spiritual bank account on me because I have a litany of stuff I've done for the Lord if we're bringing that out, like 'Far more labors.' I've gone places." How many churches have they planted? That's what he's saying.

He says, "Many more imprisonments" (v. 23). They're thinking, "Imprisonments? How's that good?" That's what he wants them to think. Are you getting this? They're thinking, "That isn't a good thing to put on your résumé, that you were in prison." But he's talking about imprisonment for the Lord. He says, in other words, "What makes me different from them is that they aren't willing to go to jail for this. You aren't ready. Listen, I've been to jail, and I know I'm sounding crazy right now."

Then he declares, "Far worse beatings" (v. 23). Who would admit that they got beat up a bunch of times? Usually, if you're promoting a fight, you want to show only the clips of the ones where you knock someone out. But he's saying, "I have a highlight reel footage of me getting beat up for Jesus."

Can I just say one little parenthetical thing? Christianity isn't the resort brochure some preachers present. Have you ever seen a beautiful brochure for some place, but when you get there, you think, "This isn't really what I expected"? Some people present Christianity as this resort, and then you become a Christian and you ask, "Where are the palm trees and the virgin piña coladas they were talking about?" Sometimes we present this Christian faith that doesn't exist. Now, I'm not trying to make the Christian faith gloomy either. But what I am trying to say is that you can go through different things like this and still have a gracious, glorious, joyful experience in the Christian life.

Paul asserts, "Far worse beatings." The Greek says, "They put hyper hits on me." In fact, he speaks of often being "near death." Then he says something even crazier. He says, "Five times I received the forty lashes minus one from the Jews" (v. 24). Five times? This is how he is showing he's qualified for ministry.

He's saying, qualification for ministry is not the things on your résumé that people like; it may be the things people don't like. In your life, some of you think your best Christianity is when you taught a lesson or when you said an "Amen" at a certain point in the sermon. However, your best Christianity is when you are allowing God to keep you through some mess. Your best Christianity is in the midst of your greatest brokenness because that's when the rubber really meets the road. For example, you lose a baby; you trust the Lord. You get sick; you trust the Lord. You lose your job; you trust the Lord. Everything in your life breaks down; you trust the Lord. You got a divorce and you're depressed about being divorced and wondering whether you can survive, and God kept you and you kept walking with him. You had a baby out of wedlock and you feel the shame of it, but you said, "I'm going to keep on going." Guess what? You're at your best because you're allowing the Lord to keep you. You're not at your best when you're at your best. You're not at your best when you think you're killing it. You're at your best when you're barely hanging on.

Then Paul acknowledges in verse 25, "Three times I was beaten with rods." He was beaten by two different groups of people. He was beaten regularly by the Jews. Then he was beaten by the Romans. So he's catching beatings by his own people, and then he was being beaten by people who were not his people.

Then he says he was stoned once. In Acts 14 Paul went to preach in the city of Lystra. They got mad at what he was saying. Can you imagine what they did to him? We're not talking about pebbles, like skipping-the-water pebbles; we're talking about bricks! Men with a brick ministry—Pow!—surrounded him. He was getting hit like some outrageous footage you'd see on your phone. He gets knocked clean out. And this is what's amazing about the text: the disciples gathered around him, and he got up, went back into the city, and started preaching again. Now see, that's the type of God we serve! You can get stoned, you can get jumped, you can get beat up. And even after that, when God's people get around you, they pick you up and help you to go back to doing exactly what you were doing. That's what it means to be a believer in Jesus Christ.

Paul continues, "Three times I was shipwrecked. I have spent a night and a day in the open sea" (v. 25). No coast guard existed back then. No distress beacons. No flare to shoot up in the air. Mayday, mayday! None of that. So when they became shipwrecked, they didn't know where they were. He had already been shipwrecked three times when he wrote this letter.

It happened to him again later; you can read it in Acts 27. So can you imagine? He's being taken into custody. They get shipwrecked. Not only is he arrested, but they don't know where they are, and all the food is gone. Paul says, "Do you know what I did during those times? I reached out to the Lord. 'Lord, I don't know where I am. I got shipwrecked in this place. I'm under chains. You brought me this far. I believe you can keep me. Please don't let me die like this. Help me to get to Caesar to preach the gospel. I want to get to Caesar to preach.'"

Have you ever been in something where your life felt shipwrecked? You had no navigational techniques or anything to rescue you from the desert island you were on. All you had was a God who sits high and looks low.

Paul adds, "In the open sea" (v. 25). Sophisticated sailboats didn't exist either, so you had to depend on the wind. They just put the sail up and tried to go in the right direction with the stars to navigate them.

Paul suggests, "There were times where the sail broke, and I'm on a ship going to preach the gospel, not knowing how I'm going to get there. And we're just at the whims of the sea." But little did the sailors know, Paul knew the master of the sea.

Have you ever been shipwrecked? Have you ever been caught out in the middle of the sea? Have you ever felt as if your life was just drifting? Let me say, if your life is drifting, that's where Paul can help. When strong Christians find themselves in weak situations, their neediness is exposed. When you are in a tough situation where you've done everything you could do to get spiritually from point A to point Z, and you're not moving, the God of heaven, even at that point, is there. He's allowing you to be in a situation of weakness to expose how strong you're not!

What he wants to do in your life is so powerful. He has a plan for you. When you grow in Christianity, when you grow as a believer, you begin to say, "You know what? This is probably the Lord trying to work on me." That's when you know you're growing. You don't just respond, "Man, I'm so sick of this. I did all this work to get to this point. Now I get to this point, and I can't even get a job. I can't even do this. I don't know how I'm going to pay rent next month."

You don't vent. Instead, you ask, "I wonder what the Lord is up to? I wonder what God is trying to show me; I don't wonder about my destiny." Your life is not about your destiny. Your life is about God making you look like Jesus. If all you want to do is to get to this place where you feel like you're something—because most of us, when we think of destiny, we think, *One day I'll feel like I'm valued when I get to the place where I'm dreaming to get*—the answer is no. That's not how the Christian life works. Your value doesn't come from your destination; it comes from the one who's designed you.

Paul continues, "On frequent journeys, I faced dangers from rivers, dangers from robbers, dangers from my own people, dangers from Gentiles" (v. 26). He's saying, I've just been through it. He goes on, "Dangers in the city, dangers in the wilderness." He's saying, "You thought the city was bad, the rural areas are bad too. The devil's everywhere." "Dangers at sea, and dangers among false brothers." He's just going down the line. "Toil and hardship, many sleepless nights, hunger and thirst, often without food, cold, and without clothing. Not to mention other things, there is the daily pressure on me: my concern for all the churches" (vv. 27-28). He expresses, "My greatest trial is wondering how the souls of the people I'm ministering to are doing, not the stuff I'm going through."

That's what a parent does. A parent worries more about their children than they do about themselves. Paul says it beautifully. He says, "Now you want to talk about being weak?" He asks, "Who is weak, and I am not weak? Who is made to stumble, and I do not burn with indignation?" (v. 29).

Paul Prefers to Boast in His Weaknesses to Break Self-Strength
2 CORINTHIANS 11:30-33

In verse 30 he writes, "Let me just tell you Corinthians: 'If boasting is necessary, I will boast about my weaknesses. The God and Father of the Lord Jesus, who is blessed forever, knows I am not lying.'" Then he mentions the governor and the believers in Acts 9. As soon as he started his ministry, he was dealing with persecution—he had to be let out of a window in a basket. This is the life of a person who's called.

Ironically, Paul's ministry had become disappointing to the Corinthians. Does that sound familiar? It sounds like Jesus. Jesus's ministry for many was disappointing because they wanted heaven to open up and for God to congratulate him and for Jesus to smite the earth fully and destroy Rome. The Jews wanted that type of ruler. They were thinking, "When the Messiah comes, he's going to knock all of you out and kill you. Watch!" Then the Messiah comes, born of a virgin, in some uncharted little Bethlehem. Then he grows up in a city that people say he's from there, and, wow, he's a carpenter. Splinters in his hands. Used to working hard, carrying stuff. God comes and becomes a blue-collar worker.

That's not how you want God to come to the planet. You want him to show off his deity and boast that he is God. But the Bible says he "did not consider equality with God as something to be exploited" (Phil 2:6). Jesus submitted by suspending himself from independent use of his attributes. That doesn't mean he didn't have them. He just didn't use them without permission. That's why he needed the Holy Spirit—because he wanted to show us submission to the Spirit, absent of applying the Spirit's power. Christ was omnipotent, and on occasion he'd give them a glimpse. He said, "If I wanted to, I could just shout, and God would send legions of angels down here to wreck shop. I don't even have to do anything." Christ was preaching, but no one believed in him. God not being believed! God being questioned! They said, "Prove to us that you are who you say you are." Blasphemy! He heads toward a cross, showing weakness, crying out, saying, "Pray for me!" But his friends don't pray for him. He gets flogged. His body exposed, he gets nailed to a cross and dies, but it's all God's paradoxical plan of weakness. On the third day he got up with all power in his hands. The way to strength is through weakness. I pray that we get that. Don't be afraid to be weak because that's where God meets you. "The LORD is near the brokenhearted; he saves those crushed in spirit" (Ps 34:18). So, if you're going through something where you feel empty, get ready for a breakthrough!

Reflect and Discuss

1. Why is human strength limited?
2. Why is it hard for us to admit our weaknesses?
3. What is true, biblical Christianity?
4. Why is it important for us to understand that hardships and suffering will come with following Jesus?
5. Why was Paul's ministry perceived as being disappointing?
6. How do the life and example of Jesus help us to be secure when people are disappointed in us?
7. How does the gospel free us up to be honest and transparent about our weaknesses?

Why Weakness Is Your Greatest Strength

2 CORINTHIANS 12:1-10

Main Idea: God does his best work when you are weak.

I.   It Is Better to Boast in Our Weaknesses (12:1-5).
II. Thorns in the Flesh Expose Our Weaknesses (12:6-8).
III. God's Grace Is Sufficient for Our Weaknesses (12:9-10).

As we've been trekking through 2 Corinthians, we've found that Paul doesn't tend to use the best tactics at communicating his résumé. For the most part, we would put our best foot forward to communicate how impressive and great we are so that people would view us in a particular way. But Paul uses the paradoxical principle that I believe is pertinent to our progress because, if you and I are going to recognize how the kingdom works, we must understand paradox. Over and again the Gospel narratives through Jesus Christ present to us beautiful paradoxes such as, "In order to gain your life, you have to lose it; in order to be exalted, you have to humble yourself, not assert yourself in pride. If you give up everything, I'll give you everything." It's the principle of the biblical paradox.

We find ourselves here in what many see as a difficult passage if you focus on the minutia of the passage. But I find beauty in this passage that exalts the paradox I think the church, particularly in America, needs to turn to. I believe the church in America thinks we're strong based on our alliances politically. We think our greatness is connected to where our financial alliances lie. We believe our connection to the powerful of Earth makes us powerful. But in the Bible, particularly in Jesus's life, he didn't align with the powerful. He aligned himself with the broken. He aligned himself with those who had challenges. If you imagine a school cafeteria, he wouldn't have been with the sports folks and the cool kids. He would have been with some nerdy kid sitting off to the left all by himself or herself with no friends, getting bullied all the time. Jesus would have felt at home with the worst of the worst. The problem with many of us is we want to align ourselves with where we want our identity to be in humanity rather than spiritually.

So we come to a somewhat familiar text, but if you dig deeper into this text, it will change the trajectory of how you view the Christian faith. This text is not quick-fix Christianity or "Come forward, and I lay hands on you, and you fall to the ground and get up and everything's okay." We prefer easy-street Christianity or Christianity as a microwave. Most of us think of Christianity as a microwave process of maturity, but it's more of a Crock-Pot. The best stuff is cooked slow.

One way to cook tough meat is to sear it and cook it quickly; it may smell good, but it's still going to be tough. But if you put it in a Crock-Pot and just turn it on and leave, low temperature and slow cooking will break down all the sinews and collagen that make it tough and uncuttable. And when it's done, the meat will melt in your mouth. Why? Not because it worked out fast but because it was low and slow. The way up is to be low and slow. The problem with us is we want to be high and quick, but in order to be high, you have to be low.

In this text Paul is telling the Corinthians that they're the fast-paced, money-having Christians. This was that mainline church, if you will, with pristine grass taken care of by some manicuring company that comes through with great machinery. You know, in some cities when you hire someone, the dude may just be walking up the street. The Corinthian church wouldn't hire some man walking up the street. They would call a special company to come fix everything up. They're used to a certain level of things. They're used to a caviar lifestyle, so anything that causes them lowness, it looks like a basement or a left field of the life they would want. So Paul challenges them on how they're relating to spiritual leadership and even their own lives. The problem with having that mindset is, when something difficult happens, you'll get confused, which brings me to my first and only point.

If you are going to recognize and understand why weakness is your greatest strength, I have one point: **God does his best work when you are weak**.

It Is Better to Boast in Our Weaknesses
2 CORINTHIANS 12:1-5

Paul states, "Boasting is necessary. It is not profitable, but I will move on to visions and revelations of the Lord" (v. 1). The Corinthians like boastful leaders, leaders who talk about themselves more than they talk about Jesus. So Paul took the format, the artistic and rhetorical format of boasting, and flipped it on its head. He abases boasting and, in doing so, exalts Christ above himself, even though he was boasting in the way they liked. At the end of the day, they probably weren't going to like what he was saying that much because it didn't center on him, which would make it center on them. When he says boasting is not profitable, he's speaking of boasting in general.

He makes a comparison to these leaders whom he called "super-apostles" because they prided themselves in ecstatic, spiritual experiences with God. The Bible wasn't the central theme of how they viewed everything in their life. In order to affirm the Bible, they said, you have to have a special experience, and that's what makes the Bible valuable. Now, I know people don't believe that today, but I'm just saying that's the sense of this passage right here; that was their disposition. So these super-apostles would say things like "I had a revelation the other night, and I felt God come into the room with me. I sensed Jesus's beard on my shoulder. And I slipped into a deep sleep, and he began to talk to me." However, Paul asserted previously in 1 Corinthians 4:6, "I have applied these things to myself and Apollos for your benefit, so that you may learn from us the meaning of the saying: 'Nothing beyond what is written.'" So Paul wants them to allow truth to inform their experience.

Then he speaks about "visions and revelations." He communicates, "I've had some myself, as a matter of fact. I don't really care to talk about many of my visions and revelations." Nonetheless, he's going to speak of visions that unveil what was previously concealed by God, and of revelations as well. These are vivid pictures of experiencing God through ecstatic, existential experience.

In verse 2 he speaks of himself in the third person. He says, "I know a man in Christ who was caught up to the third heaven fourteen years ago." The phrase "caught up" indicates that Paul didn't initiate God giving him a vision or revelation; it happened to him, he didn't happen to it. In other words, Paul wasn't sitting around looking for this type of experience. Whenever God does something supernatural like this, it's always an interruption of your life rather than you pushing forward to get it from God. So the idea of "caught up" suggests, "I was actually transported by God into this situation. It was out of my personal control to administer the information." If you are trying to get the information, you've given yourself the information; but if it was disclosed to you, God gave it to you.

Paul was "caught up to the third heaven" (v. 2) There are three heavens, and the one you look at right now is the first heaven. Second heaven is the universal realm where all the stars and planets are. The third heaven, biblically, is where the throne of God is, the dwelling presence of God. The heavenly places resemble the way we look at the outer court, the inner court, and the most holy place of the tabernacle. The dwelling presence of God in paradise or heaven is the most holy place, the holy of holies, and you can't just get in there; God has to let you in there.

As the Corinthians are reading this, they're saying, "Oh, snap! I've never even heard of the third heaven. Wow! Paul must be tripping. He's really showing off right now. So he received revelations and dreams and visions. He got caught up to the third." They're listening, but little do they know, he is not going to use it like they think because the way they would want him to use it is to further exalt himself. He's going to do the exact opposite.

He says, "Whether he was in the body or out of the body, I don't know; God knows" (v. 2). So Paul, even under the inspiration of the Holy Spirit, tries not to add anything to this experience. Some of us say, "If we'd been telling people a story and talking about being under the inspiration of the Holy Spirit, we would just come up with some stuff." We would just say, "I remember when . . ." Paul said, "I don't really know what happened." You see, under the inspiration of the Holy Spirit, he had the humility to say, "I don't really know how this works." Walking with Jesus is not knowing every nook and cranny of everything.

You don't have to settle your soul to remain stable in the faith by filling in gaps God didn't fill for you. Don't ever be scared of the gaps God doesn't fill. When you try to fill in gaps, you can fall into unbelief because that's not truth or information God has given. That's you trying to settle your soul about what you think should be there. If God did not say it, be careful not to add, "As the Lord told me."

I try to say, "I sense—I don't know if it was God, may have been, may have not—but this is what I sense is not against the character of what's in the Scriptures." When someone has the humility to qualify an experience, that's when you know you can listen to that person. But when someone says, "Thus says the Lord," he is lying.

Paul communicates, "God knows." He doesn't talk about his heavenly experience with great assertions but rather with great humility.

In verse 4 Paul speaks about "this man," but he's talking about himself: he "heard inexpressible words, which a human being is not allowed to speak." Maybe when Paul got up to the third heaven, the angels told him, "Don't even say anything; just look." Did your parents ever do you like that? He gets to heaven, and he's just dumbfounded by this experience that he had.

It seemed in the 1990s that everyone was having an out-of-body experience, and they knew everything that was going on. "I saw a light, and someone came in, and I was in heaven, and I saw . . ." Right. Conversely, Paul says, human beings are prohibited from even talking about such experiences. So if someone tells you she had an out-of-body experience and learned various details about heaven, she is probably lying.

In verse 5 he states, "I will boast about this person, but not about myself, except of my weaknesses." Now he's going to start his boast, but in exalting himself, he will abase himself and point to God's strength.

Thorns in the Flesh Expose Our Weaknesses
2 CORINTHIANS 12:6-8

Paul asserts, "For if I want to boast, I wouldn't be a fool, because I would be telling the truth. But I will spare you, so that no one can credit me with something beyond what he sees in me or hears from me" (v. 6). He conveys, "I'm not going to try to fill in gaps or use this as an opportunity to make you my audience. I'm going to let God do the work." Similarly, the Bible says, "On that day the LORD exalted Joshua in the sight of all Israel" (Josh 4:14). God is a better positioner than you. Some of you are in some situations where you think you deserve something. You're trying to finagle your little way into places where you're not yet authorized to be. God is going to press on you.

When God does it, you will know his confidence; when you do it, you don't know how long you're going to be there. Please refuse to be there. If you can, by your own strength, by your own might, by your own hand, get yourself there; then by your own hand, you must keep yourself there. But if God is the one who does it, and he works everything out and moves stuff out of the way for you, I guarantee you, it will last longer than your hand could ever hold it. So Paul communicates, "I don't want anyone to think of me more than what I am and what I'm telling you. I'm not telling you this to give myself a great position before you, but I'm telling you this for a greater and more in-depth reason."

So he says, "Therefore, so that I would not exalt myself"" (v. 7). Know why? Because Paul had pride issues. God does things in your life to keep you from something that he knows is a struggle for you. Don't ever get mad at God for knowing what your kryptonite is. Paul knows that it's easy to feel exalted, "especially because of the extraordinary revelations" (v. 7). Now if I go to heaven and am given freedom to talk, I am going to struggle with pride. "I've been to heaven. I've seen the throne of God. I've seen angels." I could just talk. That should bring some credibility, right? But God knows how to do certain things for our good to help us to remain character credible, so we don't blow it because of the experiences that he gives us.

Consider Paul's "extraordinary revelations." Paul could be thinking, "Enoch walked with God; then he was not there because God took him" (Gen 5:24). Enoch isn't coming back to talk about it. Elijah—fiery chariots came to get him. He didn't come back. Jesus saw Moses and Elijah on the Mount of Transfiguration, and Jesus shut the disciples down from talking about the experience until the proper time. So these ecstatic, heavenly experiences are few and far between in the Bible, yet there is a "shut mouth" disposition toward them. But I get to come back fully, possibly to talk about it.

Yet Paul discovers, "Because of the extraordinary revelations . . . a thorn in the flesh was given to me" (vv. 7-8). The famous thorn in the flesh. Who knows what it is? I would not waste my time trying to pontificate on whether it was a chronic illness, emotional challenges, or human enemies. I don't know what it was. It was a thorn. What does a thorn represent? Have you ever been stuck by a thorn? Have you ever had something sticking you, and it just held there, and there was nothing you could do about it? We had old wood floors back when we lived in a row house. I don't know if you ever were barefooted, and you slid across the floor—I felt it again just thinking about it. Lord help me!—and one of those splinters just anointed the bottom of your foot. You thought you were being tortured. A thorn is that type of feeling. Just imagine it being there without blood, without the injury doing any damage to you, but it just leaves the pain. That's what Paul is experiencing. Paul is experiencing unending pain appointed and anointed by God.

If you like the prosperity gospel, this isn't the text for you. This messes up the whole prosperity gospel, which purports that God always heals those with faith. Now, I believe God healed my wife, so I'm not suggesting God doesn't heal. I believe. I pray to that end. But look at what Paul says: the thorn was "in the flesh." The question is, is it in his fleshly mindset or in his literal body? We don't know. Did God do something to prick at the fleshly disposition he had toward pride and conceit? Whatever it was, it was enough so that, every time it pained him, it reminded him of his need to need God. You need to need God, but he knows you won't. So God puts you in a position to need him. Some of you are trying to pray yourself out of needing God. You don't know that's what it is, but some of the situations God has put you in are for your good, and you can't pray them away.

What's theologically stupendous about this passage is the Bible says "a messenger of Satan" was sent to "torment" him (v. 7). That's crazy. Because of the surpassing revelations, God is the one who did this, but God used the enemy as a messenger. The Greek word there is *angelos*: a demonic angel, a demon to torment him or to get on his nerves all the time. Can you imagine something getting on your nerves all the time?

Paul says it was "so that I would not exalt myself" (v. 7). It's almost like Pinocchio pain. Let me explain what I'm saying. See, Pinocchio, when he lied, kakow! His nose came out. Boom! When Paul was probably dealing with some conceit, that messenger from Satan was freed by God to harass him to humility. I won't attempt to deal with all the exegetical commentary issues here because it doesn't necessarily change the principal point: God is demanding that his people understand that the person he uses greatly, he always pains deeply.

Some of us have prayed, "God, use me." Prepare for pain! "God, take me and help me minister to this person." Prepare yourself for some pain. "God, put me on a platform in my job and in my position where I can help others in this particular way." He says, all right, but you know not what you're asking for. That's why grandma always used to tell you, "Watch what you pray for because you don't know what your prayer demands."

So don't look at people who are in pristine positions with discontent when you don't know what God had to take them through and is taking them through to be there. You don't know the story behind the victory. And you have to be careful about coveting what God has for someone else. You must learn how to be thankful for where God has placed you and what God is doing in your life and where God is developing you and what God is working out. The fact is, the true gospel says, if you're going to be used greatly, you're going to be tormented (see Mark 10:38). You're going to be harassed. I can go down a line.

I remember when I first got into a seminary, and I thought I blasphemed the Holy Spirit. Now, I know I can't lose my salvation because the Bible says, "Everyone the Father gives me will come to me, and the one who comes to me I will never cast out" (John 6:37). For two whole years I wrestled with this unmovable disposition of whether I lost my salvation or I still had my salvation. I read a commentary that helped me out. It said some Christians believe they have blasphemed the Holy Spirit, but one who believes he has blasphemed the Holy Spirit hasn't because, in order to blaspheme the Holy Spirit, you have to be extremely callous, and you wouldn't even believe that you did it.

Furthermore, every time God did something great in my life, he did something painful to me. I can remember, when I was about to graduate from school, I was really excited to get my seminary degree. I was about to go into the church and help some people. We lost our daughter, our oldest child, six months in. Lost. I can remember going and getting an assistant pastor position, and I'm all excited! I'm teaching at a Bible college in my mid-twenties. You know, I'm the young gun. I'm preaching. I'm leading praise and worship. I'm in the dream job, and all of a sudden, my wife's liver disease gets worse. I couldn't fully celebrate myself because of my need to need God.

When we were launching this church, and I was excited about the little bit of buzz we were getting around it, guess what happened? My wife went through her second bout of cancer while the church was launching. Then my book *Manhood Restored* came out, and *Unleashed* came out, and *Beat God to the Punch* came out—and I'm excited about winning some awards and accolades. I'm saying this because I'm about to "weakness" this thing. Indeed, suddenly, throughout all the process, something devastating would happen with my wife. It would push me into hearing God say, "Don't believe the press, and don't believe the hype about yourself, but drive yourself into me and see your need for me, beyond your need for self-exaltation."

For me, this text is not some theological argument. It is an imprinted reality on my soul. Every time God does something great in your life, he'll let you enjoy it; he'll let you have joy in him. But the moment he sees the disposition of your taking it beyond enjoyment for his glory, he will insert a thorn in your life to challenge you to remember it in view of him. You may be questioning me because you haven't really been through anything yet that would demand that, but keep on living and you'll see it! This thorn was given to him in his flesh, it was planted there, and God placed it there.

There are boundaries around your life. As a believer, there are hedges, and God at any time it is needed will allow entry points into those hedges for the enemy, like he did to Job. God even said to the devil, "Go on and do whatever you want in his life."

And the devil replied, "Look, every time I try to get in on Job, that thing you do—that favor, grace, protection, covenant relationship stuff—keeps me from getting him."

God says, "All right, I'm going to take ring one off of him. Now you can't touch him, but you can touch everything in his possession." Notice that God lovingly limits the devil's access. You may have been to a concert where you got an all-access pass. The devil never gets an all-access pass to you.

Then the devil says, "I took everything from him. I was hoping he would turn on you, but you were right. But I bet you, if you let me get at him—get at him and turn up on him—I bet you, he would curse you."

God said, "Do you know what? I'm going to take ring two off. You can't take his life, but you can do whatever you want to him." Guess what Job's struggle was. Pride! God used the process to help him be disabused of the ignorance and magnanimity of his pride.

So returning to Paul, he did what we would do in such desperation; he prayed, "God, in the name of Jesus, I don't know what this is." You have to understand, Paul has healed people, and he has seen people raised from the dead. He has been in prison, down at the bottom of a prison, singing hymns and singing praises to God while in chains. He sang and prayed, and suddenly the prison doors opened, and he was led out by angels. He has seen God accomplish wonders over and over.

So Paul concludes, "If I can pray and people are raised from the dead, then I will pray to God, and my thorn should be gone." Paul says, "Lord, in the name of Jesus Christ of Nazareth, remove this thorn from my flesh." No answer. "Lord in the name of Jesus Christ of Nazareth, I am in agony and in pain. I don't know what's going on. I rebuke this in the name of Jesus and beg you to loose me from this." No answer. Finally, "God, in the name of Jesus Christ, who sits at the right hand of power, the one who will come to judge the living and the dead, I come against this sickness or whatever it is on my life, this storm, and I ask that you would remove it." Paul confesses, "I pleaded with the Lord three times" (v. 8). Even the one who can heal others had to plead for himself.

God's Grace Is Sufficient for Our Weaknesses
2 CORINTHIANS 12:9-10

Then Paul received his answer: "My grace is sufficient for you, for my power is perfected in weakness" (v. 9). Oh my! That's the answer he received. God is saying, "I'm not going to take it away." God is saying, "My grace is enough for you. In order to deal with the pain, press into my grace."

In other words, "You're so under my unmerited favor that I can pain you, and I know you'll still trust me. I can discipline you, and you'll push into me. I put this as a safety mechanism for your character." I know it's hard to say "Amen" to pain, but how beautiful that God loved him enough not to let him get away.

Have you ever felt like everyone else gets away with something, but you don't get away with anything? Don't get mad at that. That is grace. Let me say it again. It's grace that God doesn't let you get away with being messed up. It's grace because there are some things and some places I would have been in my life if it had not been for God cutting me off, stopping me, and pulling me back.

God is saying, "My unmerited favor is enough. And my power is perfected in you when you're weak, not when you're strong." When my wife and I were buying a house, we looked it over with my father-in-law. We noticed several cracks, so I concluded that we weren't going to buy the house. My father-in-law was not concerned because he used to own a construction company. So I'm talking to him and pointing out cracks everywhere.

He replied, "Nah, those are good cracks, son." How in the world do you have a good crack? He said, "The cracks are just signals of something. See, when you build a house and you put it on the foundation, it has to settle, and everything above the foundation should settle and move with the foundation as the foundation is being settled into the soil. So this, son, this is an old crack. These aren't new cracks. When it settles, you'll see cracks and misalignments above the foundation, but it's a sign that the foundation is secure because these cracks, they look like weaknesses, but it's really to show you the strength of the foundation, which is now secure." Likewise, you may have some cracks, you may have some bumps, and you may have some bruises, but it is just God taking you through something so he can settle the foundation of Christ that's inside your life. You may be hurting, you may be in pain, you may even hear some spooky sounds in your life, like in an old house, but all that amounts to is the foundation getting settled and your being put in the place God has for you. Never worry about a crack because a crack may mean that you're being connected to the cornerstone.

Ultimately, we see the beauty of Jesus Christ in all this because in Jesus becoming human and setting himself up to experience being weak, God, who ran everything, became a baby and allowed his diaper to be changed. He allowed someone to wipe his tears. Christ, the Creator of all things, set himself up for weakness. But then he went to a rugged cross, allowing himself to be beaten—weakness; allowing himself to be spat on—weakness; allowing himself to be cussed out—weakness. Little did his accusers know that what took the greatest strength was to die for people who were hating on him. The fact that Jesus Christ could do that is the most powerful thing in the universe, for his name's sake.

It reminds me: I'm a Marvel buff, and I love watching cartoons with my children. In the comics the Hulk is different from what he is in various media. When the Hulk gets hurt, he actually gets stronger. The more you beat him up, the stronger the gamma radiation runs through him. And the stronger and larger he becomes, the more the villains must figure out how not to hit him, to prevent him from gaining more strength. Just as the Hulk gets hit and gets stronger, so has God set your soul up through Jesus Christ: the more they slay you, yet will you trust him (see Job 13:15).

I pray that we will be people who do not look for pain, but when God leaves us in something, we don't complain the whole time but ask God, "What are you up to in me? How do you want me to see you?" I've been going through this over and over again. That which lags is probably a thorn. When it lags, are you afraid? You may have had elders pray for you, pour oil on you, and nothing moves you. You may find yourself in the middle of a thorn. Instead of focusing on the difficulty of the thorn, use the experience to drive you more deeply and press into the Lord. That's what we've got to do; we must press into the Lord. God loves you enough to not let you get away with long seasons of intimacy-less-ness. So if you're going through something difficult that God hasn't taken away, God is trying to pull you into a deeper intimacy.

And as one of my professors said, "God doesn't have favorites, but he does have intimates."

Reflect and Discuss

1. Why do many Christians, especially in the West, tend to have a false sense of strength?
2. How does Paul boast in a way that's different from the Corinthians' form of boasting?
3. Why is it important for you to boast in your weaknesses?
4. What is a thorn in the flesh given by God?
5. In what ways has God put thorns in your life to teach you lessons and grow you in humility?
6. Why is conviction and confrontation of sin an act of God's grace?
7. In what ways did Jesus become weak and embrace weakness?
8. How does the example of Christ and the gospel encourage you to embrace your weaknesses?
9. How does God exchange our weaknesses for his strength?

Commitment of a Disciple Maker

2 CORINTHIANS 12:11-21

Main Idea: You must be willing to face the hardships that come with being committed to disciple making.

I.   Be Willing to Be Misunderstood (12:11-13).
II. Be Willing to Go the Extra Mile (12:14).
III. Be Willing to Make Exhausting Investment (12:15).
IV. Be Willing to Be Demonized (12:16-19).
V.   Be Willing to Be Broken (12:20-21).

How many of you have ever written a letter to someone? I know we're in a different age. I think it's impersonal, if you have a friendship with someone, and they send you an email. It just strikes me as odd, unless it's business related. But writing a letter—there's something about the pen, something about seeing the stroke of the hand, the lettering, and the intensity, particularly if you can understand people's handwriting. I have doctor's handwriting, my wife says, so only a pharmacist spiritually can understand my writing. Letters are sent to communicate some of the most personal, relational information. Indeed, when someone passes away, having their writing is different from having an email from them; you have what they penned to you and what they took the time to use their hands to communicate. Chuck Swindoll, the former president of Dallas Seminary, was famous for his short notes to people. I believe C. S. Lewis would answer everyone who wrote him because he felt if they took the time to write him, he was obligated to write something back. Of course, everyone has something to say on Twitter and Facebook, but letters are personal.

Often, the letters that are most challenging to write are from those of us who write better than we talk. Writing provides the way for your mind and heart to consider thoughtfully what you want someone to hear from you. That's the spirit, I believe, of what Paul is doing here with the Corinthian church. Although he's under the inspiration of the Holy Spirit, he's ending this letter on a hard note. Homiletically, you usually want to end on a different note. As a pastor or teacher, we want to end with hope. But as we look closely at this passage, we find hope because Paul has a sincere heart for the Corinthian church. His purpose in writing to them is to help heal the gaps in their relationship and invite reconciliation to restore their communal fellowship. Paul is ending this letter on something I believe every believer should one day be able to identify with—discipleship. Discipleship is the most rewarding, encouraging, and painful thing you could ever be involved in. I don't know if you've experienced it yet, but every believer should make a disciple. Making a disciple is joining someone on his journey while you yourself are on your journey to look more like Jesus. Discipleship isn't helping someone on a journey that you're not on. Discipleship is the willingness to expose the good, bad, and ugly of your life to show him the process by which God is malleably working in your life to make you look like Jesus. You may be just a few steps ahead of him, and you're saying, "Join me in this process, and maybe you'll get something out of it."

So here we see Paul mulling over those he had invested in. My prayer for us, as we dive into this text, is that, for those who don't relate to it, one day you will. One day, I want you to relate to disciple making. One day, I want you to relate to investing in someone else sacrificially. It's something different for the soul when you decide you're going to pull your life out and open your life up. When you open your life up, you make yourself vulnerable. That vulnerability is where discipleship happens.

One of my favorite passages in the Bible is where Jesus says, "Sit with me. I feel grieved. I need you to stay awake and pray" (Matt 26:36-41). He asked his disciples for help. How amazing that Jesus felt the need for prayer. If Jesus, in making disciples, asked his disciples for prayer, how much more do we need it?

If you look at Paul's other letters, such as Romans, he ends the letter excited: "Greet Phoebe; help her with whatever she needs. She's a beast for God. She's a deaconess in the church. She leads well; help her. Tell this one hi. Watch out for that man." Then in Galatians he ends with "From now on, let no one cause me trouble, because I bear on my body the marks of Jesus. Brothers and sisters, the grace of our Lord Jesus Christ be with your spirit" (Gal 6:17-18). Or Ephesians: "Peace to the brothers and sisters, and love with faith, from God the Father and the Lord Jesus Christ. Grace be with all who have undying love for our Lord Jesus Christ" (Eph 6:23-24). In Philippians Paul concludes with, "I am fully supplied" (Phil 4:18). And then he says, "And my God will supply all your needs according to his riches in glory in Christ Jesus" (Phil 4:19). Colossians and Thessalonians—it just goes on and on and on, these beautiful endings. When you come to this ending in 2 Corinthians, you're confused. Why in the world is he ending this letter broken and hurt? Because discipleship, when you're wrestling with disobedient disciples, is painful.

Be Willing to Be Misunderstood
2 CORINTHIANS 12:11-13

If you're going to be a committed disciple maker, you'll see that you must be willing to be misunderstood, even while God's hand is working through you. In verse 11 Paul writes, "I have been a fool; you forced it on me." He is saying, "You put me in a situation where I didn't want to go there like that with you." Have you ever had someone who took you there? I'm not speaking of cursing at them; I'm speaking of giving a sanctified knockout punch. He said, "You forced me to say stuff I didn't want to say to you because I was hoping you would repent before it got to this point."

Then he says, "You ought to have commended me" (v. 11). That is, "If anyone should be affirmed, it should have been me." When you invest in people, you discover that sometimes the people you give to the most don't appreciate you the most. The people you invest in the most appreciate you the least. And guess what: you're called to still invest.

Paul is hurt. He is saying, "I can't even believe we got to this point where I have to talk to you about what I am to you. I shouldn't have to pull out the Rolodex of my commitment to seeing Christ formed in you. Why would I even have to get to that point to where I have to even talk about that? You should be the one announcing and giving thanks for God's grace through me in your life." Can you feel the discomfort in a disciple-maker's voice when making such a claim? But Paul has to bring it up.

Then he says, "Since I am not in any way inferior to those 'super-apostles,' even though I am nothing" (v. 11). Oh, this is powerful here. When you invest in someone, he will sometimes listen to people who mean him no good before he listens to you who have spent money out of your pocket, burned midnight oil, broken up fights, and put clothes in the cleaners because he wept on your shoulder.

This is for the disciple makers. If you aren't a disciple maker, you aren't going to feel this right here. For disciple makers, you can feel it when someone can hear a lie and accept it, but when you give her the truth, it doesn't go the other direction. You're confused at why, and your heart is rent because you're thinking, "How in the world are you blind to the fact that they're taking from you, that they're pulling from you, that they're draining you, that they have no good for you?" Then you get with her—this is the text now—and she acts like you are the one who is against her. Discipleship is just like that. At times you will be betrayed in discipleship.

I'm just telling you, discipleship isn't for the faint of heart, but it's for those who are believers who are called to do it.

In verse 12 Paul goes back to what he likes to do. He says, "The signs of an apostle were performed with unfailing endurance among you." He's communicating that he did signs and wonders through his own hands, but then there was not a quick response to the message of the gospel. The signs and wonders were given to affirm the message. However, sometimes when God affirms you to a person, you must be careful as a disciple maker not to rush forward.

Being a disciple maker often means you want more for people than they want for themselves. That's your job. The challenge is to avoid getting impatient with how God grows them. You have to be careful not to get frustrated because only God can grow people; your teaching doesn't grow them. That is, teaching exposes them to what they need help in. But they have to take hold of it and internalize it; then God adds the growth. God adds growth; people don't grow themselves. That's why the Bible says, "Work out your own salvation with fear and trembling" (Phil 2:12). That means they take hold of what makes them look like Jesus. But the Bible says right after that, "For it is God who is working in you both to will and to work according to his good purpose" (Phil 2:13). God can't work his good purpose in disciples that you make until they take hold of what you give them. You have to be patient with their process.

You do need a place to vent, though, because you can't vent everything to the people you're mad at. It's not healthy. And if you did, you would cause a greater gap and a breach. So again, you must be patient. Sometimes you must step back from them after your season of ministry is up to allow time for God to work.

When your disciples don't like you anymore, you have to back up. It's just like raising kids: when they are older, you can't go to a twenty-six-year-old child's house and tell them what to do in their house. You just say, "Okay, you're out my house; you're out of my pocket too," right? All the grown parents said, "Amen! Don't come back here. Amen." When he mentions "signs and wonders and miracles" (v. 12), he is underscoring his affirmation of being an actual apostle. He wants them to understand his work and his commitment to them. He's trying to explain that the Corinthians had counterfeit people around them who didn't have their good in mind. They just wanted to use the Corinthians for their own agenda. So Paul is communicating, "They're not even real; they're not even Christians; they're not even believers. They're false people who are using you to get at your resources." Paul is making a last-ditch effort: "This is the last time I'm going to tell you this." Sometimes you have to have some of those "last time" talks with some folk where God hasn't provided peace in that relationship, but you have to say the last things to try to help them.

The Bible says, "As far as it depends on you, live at peace with everyone" (Rom 12:18). You must be careful about letting how you feel get in the way of pressing beyond their hatred for you.

In verse 13 Paul asserts, "So in what way are you worse off than the other churches, except that I personally did not burden you? Forgive me for this wrong!" Paul is saying, "What demand did I make on you different from the other churches? Do you have a subsidized gospel?" No such gospel exists, where some commit more and others can commit less. The Corinthians have the same commitment that every other church has to support the work of the gospel—no more and no less.

He adds, "Except one thing: you didn't pay me. They paid me to serve you." In the Corinthian culture, they liked to pay for wisdom. In other words, in their culture, they had street emcees. They had street battles rapping words. When they saw a street battle, the well-to-do people would pay them to come to their house and rap for them like the way you would pay for a violinist to play while you eat with your spouse. They would hire a person for artistic enjoyment without internalizing the message communicated.

So Paul says, "I'm not going to receive an offering from them. If I did, their disposition toward investing in the ministry would look more like their hiring me just to enjoy what I have to say rather than internalizing the gospel. So what I'm going to do is, I'm going to raise support from other churches." However, because the Corinthians didn't pay for it, they didn't value it. They didn't value Paul. But these false teachers came in asking for payment. The Corinthians valued them because they nurtured them in their fallenness. Paul is trying to take them beyond their fallenness, but they can't see the difference between being ministered to and being bribed.

In discipleship relationships, you're going to always wrestle with people misinterpreting you. You're going to have a lot of come-to-Jesus moments.

You may be on the other side of it, saying, "Amen." You're the disciple like the Corinthians. You need to submit yourself. We will come back to the disciple maker, but if you are a disciple, you need to learn how to hear some things. You need to learn how to hear a hard word so you can grow and look more like Christ. You need to hear some stuff. Don't complain about not getting invested in if you don't show up in the places where investment happens.

Be Willing to Go the Extra Mile
2 CORINTHIANS 12:14

This is what a disciple maker does: goes the extra mile to close relational breaches. Consider what Paul says in verse 14: "Look, I am ready to come to you this third time." Paul had been with them two times already. Have you ever gone where you knew you would encounter relational conflict and opposition, but you still went anyway? Paul is willing to go again a third time because he says, "I'm going to go one more time, and that's it. I'm going to try again for you to interpret my commitment to you a different way."

He says, "I will not burden you" (v. 14). He's not asking them for anything. He continues, "Since I am not seeking what is yours, but you." What heartfelt words: "I don't want your stuff; I want you." Discipleship happens when disciples know you want their good. That's what disciple makers want. I don't want your stuff. Don't give me a present. Don't give me a birthday gift. Don't give me a shout-out. All I want is you. If I walk away from this stripped but loved, that's enough. If we're reconciled, that's enough. Even if we never talk again, but you don't talk bad about me and I don't talk bad about you, that's enough.

He says, "For children ought not save up for their parents, but parents for their children" (v. 14). Children aren't necessarily obligated to take care of their parents financially. He expresses, "Because you're my spiritual children, I'll bite the bullet. I'll pay my way to come meet with you." This is just straight, real ministry right here. "As a matter of fact, I'll pay for the meal. How much it costs for you to get there—I'll pay for it." He wants to overcommunicate that he doesn't want anything from them.

I remember when I was reconciling with someone, and we had to have a mediator. I called for the meeting with two people, and I said, "I'll pay for your plane ticket—the whole nine yards." I didn't have the money, but I was going to find it. I told my wife, and we agreed. I wanted to go the extra mile. And I hated every minute of it. I'm about to pay for this, and I know I'm filled with the multifaceted Holy Spirit, and this is what God wants. I'm paying this guy to come and to halfway cuss me out, but I'm going to do this because the Bible says it, and that's it. My affections will come along one day.

Be Willing to Make Exhausting Investment
2 CORINTHIANS 12:15

"I will most gladly spend and be spent for you." Wow! How amazing. In other words, you disciple makers want to exhaust yourselves, even if you never are encouraged by hearing gratitude for doing it. Even though you have a full schedule of things to do, you're willing to meet later. This is what disciple makers do.

Be Willing to Be Demonized
2 CORINTHIANS 12:16-19

Starting at the end of verse 15, Paul says, "If I love you more, am I to be loved less? Now granted, I did not burden you; yet sly as I am, I took you in by deceit!" Paul is shrewd. He essentially uses language that's used of the devil. The devil is crafty and deceitful, which is what they called Paul. This happens in disciple-making relationships.

Now some disciples will flourish. They grow, and they multiply fruit a hundredfold. Those disciples—their growth just does your soul good. You just look at that picture to get encouragement. You just say, "Thank you, Jesus, for that one." I used to say, "I just need encouragement to engage this one because this one didn't go like that one. So I'm going to be encouraged by that one, so that when I go back to this one, I can have it in mind. I don't know if I'm going to feel about this person what I feel about that person, but I'm going to do it anyway because I'm being obedient to you. " Then you have to engage someone who totally misunderstands you, who demonizes you, who has talked about you and has railed about you like a dirty dog, but you have to be the godly one to take the high road and not return evil for evil.

They called Paul the devil. They said he's crafty. Hold on! Paul is saying, "I didn't take any money from you. How am I crafty?" Have you ever known someone who just has it out for you? You're wondering, "What is going through your mind? Where did you get this caricature, this evil avatar, of me?" Guess what: it's okay to be upset. You will be demonized.

Ask Jesus. Jesus was healing people, changing lives, and they said that he cast out demons by Beelzebub. Jesus responds, "What kind of sense would it make for the devil to be in me and me cast out a devil, when the devil wants to oppress and possess people; why would Satan cast out Satan? It doesn't make any kind of sense." But when people are warped about your investment into them, they make up stuff about you, and they can't see the illogical, irrational, reprobate philosophy that has killed their heart. So you have to be willing to work through all that.

In verse 17 Paul asks, "Did I take advantage of you by any of those I sent you?" And then he shouts out one of his disciples on the sly: "I urged Titus to go" to you (v. 18). That was one of his ace disciples, one of his hardworking spiritual sons, and he is saying, "Now I'm going to show you, without saying it, what disciples of me look like in the way they relate to how I discipled them." This is amazing. It's artistic. He says, "And I sent the brother with him" (v. 18). I don't know who this is, some other brother. I don't know if he didn't want to say his name to them because they were mad at him too. The Bible doesn't tell us, but it says here, "Titus didn't take advantage of you, did he?" (v. 18). Paul is communicating, "I didn't take advantage of you. And the way I invest in people, I train people to be the same way." You see what the process of discipleship is; it's not braggadocio. That's not what it is. Rather, "I do have a heart to invest in you, and the thing I usually come to you with is the same, nothing different. I paid Titus's way by raising his support." He says, "Didn't we walk in the same spirit and in the same footsteps?" (v. 18). Look how meticulously Paul lays this out. It's beautiful!

He continues, "Have you been thinking all along that we were defending ourselves to you? No, in the sight of God we are speaking in Christ, and everything, dear friends, is for building you up" (v. 19). The verb form "building up" means to properly construct something and bring it to full completion. Consider a general contractor. A general contractor may not do all the work, but he makes sure that all the work gets done well. Paul conveys, "That's my role in your life." The role of a disciple maker in a person's life is not to be everything to him but to make sure he gets connected to everything he needs to grow. That's important.

Thus, a disciple maker must see what's needed. A general contractor comes in and determines, "This is what needs to be done. Let me make sure I get electricity. Let me make sure I get people to drywall the studs and the demo, and make sure that happens." A disciple maker is meticulous about giving oversight to a person's discipleship without being their all-in-all.

You have to be careful of being people's all-in-all—of trying to be their Messiah or parent whom they still need. God cares about the disciples you disciple more than you do. That's the first lesson of disciple making: if you don't believe God cares more than you, you will try to save them yourself, and you will exhaust yourself with trying to save people whom Christ already died for. Your role is to *point* them to Jesus, not *be* Jesus. That's important. You have to know when a disciple is getting too needy, to the point that they think you're their all-in-all. And you have to let them know. You have to starve people of things they think they need from you so that they can need it from the Lord instead of you. This is gold. This doesn't come from just reading a book. You have to be willing to work yourself out of a job. That's what a disciple maker does. Disciples will never be complete when you're finished, so you have to have a beginning and an ending to your disciple making. They can have access to you, but they can't have the depth season they had with you.

Paul called them "dear friends" (v. 19). This wording is amazing. They were loved by God and by Paul. Even in the midst of this conflict, they're loved. Don't let opposition and hurt from a disciple make you treat them tragically. He still calls them dear friends.

Be Willing to Be Broken
2 CORINTHIANS 12:20-21

Paul writes, "For I fear that perhaps when I come I will not find you to be what I want" (v. 20). He's saying, "I would hate to get there, and we are still at that point." Then he says, "And you may not find me to be what you want" (v. 20), meaning, "I hope you create your expectations of me from the right perspective versus any false perspective." This is key.

He continues, "Perhaps there will be quarreling [between us], jealousy, angry outbursts, selfish ambitions, slander, gossip, arrogance, and disorder" (v. 20). He's saying, "That's not what I want to happen when we get with each other. I fear that this is what it's going to turn into. It's going to turn into just a stalemate—verbal war and character war. That's not what I want out of this." He ends it by saying, "I fear that when I come my God will again humiliate me in your presence, and I will grieve for many who sinned before" (v. 21). He's expressing, "It would be humbling to me if I come and you haven't spiritually grown from all my investment." The idea of "humiliate" here points to brokenness. A disciple maker wants the people they invest in to be better than they are—to flourish and mature.

Then he says, "And have not repented of the moral impurity, sexual immorality, and sensuality they practiced" (v. 21). It would be a tragedy if they have not turned and changed their minds. Paul ends on that note.

Jesus is familiar with this experience Paul was having. Jesus was denied by the people he created. He was doubted by his disciples. He had one of his aces, Peter, swear that he didn't know him—even after three years of hearing him speak, seeing him feed five thousand, watching him raise people from the dead, and having him give him more fish than he had ever caught before.

Jesus went through that. Jesus went through investing in people and seeing them turn on him. The difference between you and Jesus—he knew that they were going to do that because it was prophesied. Yet he still invested in them because he saw that there was another side to what God was going to do in their lives, even though there was a deep breach in their relationship.

One of the best scenes in the Bible is when someone was on the shore and Peter couldn't quite see him (John 21). And the man yelled out to Peter, "Hey, friend, did you catch anything?"

He says, "Nah."

"Cast your net on the other side of the boat."

He wants to come back, "Am I the fishermen or are you the fisherman?" The Bible says that Peter did it and caught 153 fish. That probably reminded Peter of the time he met Jesus (Luke 5:1-11). Here he didn't know who it was because he couldn't see him. He just knew that the catch reminded him of his Lord. The Bible says that he jumped into the water and swam to shore.

Jesus already had fish cooking for him, even though Peter had caught fish out there. The Bible says Jesus, the resurrected Christ, with his own hands made breakfast for the guy who betrayed him. Then he confronts him. "Do you love me?"

"Yes, Lord. I love you." Jesus asks him this three times. Peter thought, "Why are you putting me through this? This feels weird." But Jesus had disciple-making reasons.

Jesus had said, "After you've fallen, you're going to strengthen your brothers" (Luke 22:32). So on the day of Pentecost, the guy who previously swore that he didn't know Jesus preached, and over three thousand people met Jesus because Jesus remained committed to him, even in the midst of his betrayal.

What it means to be a disciple maker is not to give up on people, even when you want to. Not giving up on people doesn't mean you're always in their life directly; it just means you think rightly about them in wanting for them what God wants for them, even if you're not the one to give it to them.

Reflect and Discuss

1. Have you ever experienced being misunderstood? Elaborate.
2. Why is it so hard to go through being misunderstood by others?
3. How does knowing God's hand is on you help you overcome the difficulties of a misunderstanding?
4. What's a relational breach?
5. Are there any relational breaches in your life you need to close up? If so, what will it look like to do that?
6. How do the gospel and your identity in Christ help you overcome being demonized by others?
7. In what ways do you need to grow in seeing others as loved by God when you're in conflict with them?
8. Are you currently broken over the lack of progress in the lives of anyone you're discipling? How does God comfort you through that and help you have tough conversations with them?

Take a Good Look at Yourself

2 CORINTHIANS 13

Main Idea: Recognize that self-examination is a major part of the faith.

I. Paul's Final Challenge to the Corinthians (13:1-4)
II. Paul's Call to Self-Examination (13:5-10)
III. Paul's Final Exhortations (13:11-13)

We have come to the close of our work through the book of 2 Corinthians. I'm hoping you found something helpful for your soul—to help you develop, to help you grow, and to help you to know God more effectively. We've gone through so many contours. First Corinthians and 2 Corinthians are tightly bound together, although they have different angles to them. They are coherent and are tightly bound together by what they're trying to communicate to the Corinthian church. Paul has said a lot to the Corinthians. He's challenged them; he's encouraged them. He's always tried to promote God's redemptive work in their lives. I'm excited that being a believer doesn't mean you are under condemnation, but you get a chance for God to see an eagle-eyed view into your mess and then redemptively, by the power of the cross, deal with your stuff. That is a good moment to thank God for his mercy in your life—that you're no longer looking at judgment.

Paul's letters to the Corinthians display the patience of God with us. When you look at the type of sins that they were wrapped up in, that God would still write two letters to them and send apostles to them is marvelous! Imagine the many questions we would have answered if we had some apostles, some real ones anyway, that were sent to us. We would be able to ask them numerous questions because they had a great access. But carnality and sin can fog our eyes from what we have right in front of us. We need to be brought close to examining ourselves because sin and carnality can take over our commitment, crush our Christ-centeredness, and bring calamity to the work God has entrusted to us.

Examination is good; it means God has given you the grace to see. The blinders of Satan have been taken off your eyes. I'm so glad I no longer have Satan blinding me from seeing the glory of the gospel of peace.

Paul has spoken to the Corinthians about multiple concerns. He's talked to them about being in cliques. He's communicated that believers can go through a mess and that God comforts us and allows us to comfort others even while we're still going through difficulty. He's declared that he's qualified for ministry, not because of whether he lives in a penthouse or in a ranch but because of the sufferings God uses to qualify him and show him he's on the right track.

The message of Christianity is remarkable. Difficulty doesn't necessarily mean you're off course. Difficulty can mean you're absolutely, unadulteratedly right on course. Isn't it remarkable that you can be in the middle of a storm—the worst storm of your life—and God is right there with you? What a wonder that the power of the gospel and the voice of the Spirit can speak to us in the midst of our suffering. This is a confrontational letter, so it ends the same way—fairly confrontationally. Christianity is not a sucker religion. It's not a weak religion. It is a faith where you sometimes find God in your face, telling you about yourself, so that you can grow.

Paul's Final Challenge to the Corinthians
2 CORINTHIANS 13:1-4

Paul is telling them about themselves. Look at verse 1: "This is the third time I am coming to you." This declaration is both an act of grace and an act of finality. Sometimes when you're confronting someone, she must know that you're open to talking to her and listening to her. But she also must know there's going to be a limit to how many times you talk to her about this conflict.

For instance, have you ever spoken to someone numerous times, and finally you say, "I'm going to tell you one last time"? Paul's declaration has that spirit to it—not an expectation of a fistfight breaking out but rather that disposition of "Frankly, I'm sick of talking to people who should be growing and walking with the light. Why am I talking to you like this?" The first time Paul went to the Corinthians, they heard the gospel and made professions of faith. They became believers in response to his first visit. That's the key thing to say here.

I remember when I was with a well-known evangelist. This man, every time we preached, a thousand people came forward. It was the most amazing thing I've ever seen in my life. I asked him about it. He said, "I call these professions of faith." This text is going to help us to recognize biblically why, when someone confesses Christ, we call it a profession of faith.

The first time Paul visits there, he does an altar call or whatever he does to say, "Who wants to trust Jesus as Savior?" Boom! They made a profession of faith, saying they trusted Jesus as Savior. He disciples them for a little while, he and his team. Then Paul and his team go do other work under persecution, or whatever he's facing. Later, he gets word that the Corinthians are conflicted. They're saying they're saved, but they're acting in a way that doesn't look like that. So Paul decides he has to make a trip back to Corinth—the second trip. He gets there, and it's worse than he thinks. As a matter of fact, he even hears it before he gets there. A young man has started engaging in activities with his stepmother. So Paul asks them, "Has it gotten that bad where you people can be desensitized to this type of sin?"

As a matter of fact, the church wouldn't deal with it. They were letting people get away with stuff, and there was no community commitment to one another. So they would just let people come in and live how they wanted to, calling it the gospel, calling it biblical. "Oh, you're forgiven. Just keep doing you." I know we don't do that today, but they were saying, "Just do you."

But Paul says, "Listen, this type of stuff you're doing, it's not even seen among non-Christians. Unbelievers are looking at you and thinking, 'Wow, they want us to become that? So, Christ makes you worse than we already are?'"

The church was never supposed to be a picture of us saying, "I'm saved by grace but live like hell!" God doesn't make an investment to send his Son from heaven to earth to do all that he did—die on the cross for our sins—for us to live a life that doesn't submit. That doesn't mean we don't sin, but we don't focus on it as a lifestyle.

So Paul is coming this third time, and it's about to get interesting. He says, "Every matter must be established by the testimony of two or three witnesses" (v. 1). Uh-oh. Now when an apostle or someone in the Bible says that, you know it's countdown time. This is like "Houston, we have a problem," because this points back to Matthew 18 and Deuteronomy 19:15. This points to when believers have to be engaged. When you say you're a believer but live in unadulterated, unfathomable sin, you go through a process to lead you to church discipline. No one functionally in the Corinthian church is helping the church become more sanctified, to become a more effective example for the Lord, Jesus Christ. So

Paul has to make a trip there because no one is man or woman enough to deal with the sinners in the camp. He's essentially asking, "Am I going to have to bring church discipline against the entire church?"

This is why churches go out of existence in our day. Churches don't go out of existence because of money problems. All churches are going to have money problems. Churches go out of existence when churches refuse to be churches! So Paul is challenging them and giving them another opportunity for repentance. That's the beauty of God: he's patient.

In verse 2 Paul says, "I gave a warning when I was present the second time, and now I give a warning while I am absent to those who sinned before and to all the rest: If I come again, I will not be lenient." This is pointed. "I'm going off." That's what he's communicating. "I'm not mincing my words. I'm going through the roof." Why? Because he loves them. When you love someone, every now and then you can go through the roof when you talk to them because sometimes some people don't understand nice. Some people, you can't say, softly, "Now man, I just want to talk to you. Would you just consider not doing that anymore?" You have to shout, "Listen, I done talked to you fifteen times about the same thing!"

Now, don't use words that are outside the realm of eternality. Godly admonition. You can raise your voice but don't curse. That's not the gospel.

So Paul said he's not going to be lenient. He's not going to spare anyone. He had to deal with these issues because the sanctity of the mission of the gospel is connected to our willingness to be a community that wants to grow spiritually. He goes further. He says, "You seek proof of Christ speaking in me. He is not weak in dealing with you" (v. 3). Paul led them to Christ and walked with them, but then when he says something they don't agree with, now they're not saved; they don't believe. Paul says, "So now I'm not an apostle because I'm challenging you? I was an apostle when I was helping you—when I led you to Christ, when I baptized you, and you were excited." That's when you know you must check your heart. The truth doesn't change. You must be careful of trying to conform God to you.

The Corinthians are trying to conform the Lord to their own rubrics, and Paul is challenging that reality by saying, "Listen, don't try to make me wrong because I'm telling you truth now, right?"

They reply, "Well, Paul, the truth quota is up for the day, and you can keep going."

But he comes back that Christ is "powerful among you. 'For he was crucified in weakness, but he lives by the power of God'" (vv. 3-4). Paul is playing up against the same idea that the Corinthian church values: Christian weakness as true weakness and human strength as stronger than Christianity. You have to understand, these were the elite. These were the Tribeca Loft Christians, the Lower East Side, Upper East Side Christians. These were the Chestnut Hill Christians, the Park Avenue Christians. This is $50,000-a-year-for-private-school-children Christians.

They weren't hood rich; they were rich rich. See, hood rich get a dollar and put all their money around their necks. These rich rich Corinthians were more subtle; they didn't wear much bling.

However, they expected to come into church and be treated with worldly value in a heavenly place. Poor people would come in, and the rich rich would act like they're better than the poor. The Corinthians brought their worldly values into a Christian sphere. Paul is challenging them because they don't think they're bad. Their value in the world doesn't hit their character. So he has to keep chipping away at their view of strength to help them understand what weakness in Christ means. It's difficult to identify with a rich God who makes himself poor when you value riches. Why would God make himself poor? They're backing away from the gospel because the gospel devalues what they value. So Paul challenges them: "I'm really concerned about where your faith is going."

Paul's Call to Self-Examination
2 CORINTHIANS 13:5-10

Paul urges, "Test yourselves" (v. 5). The idea is to examine or put something to the test to ascertain its nature, particularly its character and authenticity. He tells them to examine or test themselves to see whether they are in the faith.

For many years I thought, "No, he can't be saying what I think he's saying." And some scholars believe this text means to test yourself to see if you're operating in the sphere of where Christianity takes place. So I said, "Oh, maybe that's what it means." No, no, no! When you don't like the Bible, don't pray, don't respond to sermons, never get convicted about your sin, and can sin freely with a profession of faith but never feel the conviction of the Holy Spirit, you must ask a tough question: "Am I really a Christian?" You might say, "Don't judge me. Only God can judge me." You don't want him to do that. I don't want God to judge me. Jesus says, "If you believe in me, you've passed out of judgment." So if you say, "Only God can judge me," that means you haven't passed out of judgment. That's why Paul is saying, "Test yourself to see if you're a Christian. Check yourself, examine yourself, to see if you're authentically saved."

Do you truly know Jesus as your Savior? In Matthew 13 Jesus tells the parable of the wheat and the tares or weeds. Some servants planted wheat, but they went back later, and weeds started to grow up next to the wheat. They told their leader, "Listen, your enemy has sown weeds among your wheat."

He went out and looked at it and said, "Yes, don't pull the weeds out because if you pull the weeds out too early, their roots are entangled with the wheat, and so you'll uproot it and destroy the wheat. So wait until it's harvest time; then you can harvest both, and separate the wheat from the weeds."

There's a day coming when Jesus is going to tell who's his and who's not. So many have this easy-believism view. "Did you say the prayer? Did he say the prayer? Just say the prayer. I confess with my mouth, Jesus, Jesus." They don't understand what happened. Many times, we have people say stuff, but they don't really understand the weight and gravity of salvation. They don't understand that they have to repent of their sin. That's why we've got to stop asking people, "Do you want to go to heaven?" The Bible never teaches that. The Bible never teaches us to preach heaven. Show me in the Bible where the Bible says, "If you want to go to heaven, trust Jesus." The Bible never says that.

Jesus says something different: "Today you will be with me in paradise" (Luke 23:43). The Bible says, "This is eternal life: that they may know you, the only true God, and the one you have sent—Jesus Christ" (John 17:3). So when you preach heaven, you actually preach another gospel. Going to heaven was never the goal of our salvation. As a matter of fact, we won't spend eternity in heaven. If you read Revelation 21, we'll be on earth. Want to go to heaven? Heaven's just a holding place for the redeemed, in the presence of God, until his tabernacle comes to earth.

I want to be where he is. That's what the Bible teaches: "Where I am [Gk *eimi ego*] you may be also" (John 14:3). Heaven is about Christ. Heaven is about access to God. Heaven is not about heaven. So if you focus people on heaven, you just have a hopeful sinner. Instead, we proclaim *him*. That's what Scripture says (see Col 1:28).

So when the Bible says, "Test yourself" (v. 5), in this self-examination process, can you sin and feel nothing? Can you just go your way? Can you just say, "We're good"? Can you just look at porn over and over again and feel nothing? Can you get drunk night after night—hangover, Tylenol, ibuprofen, water, coffee—and feel nothing? Can you be prideful and angry and greedy and not feel anything? See, that's how you know you're not saved. You know you're not saved if the Holy Spirit never convicts you of sin. Be afraid if you can do what you want to do and come to church. Be afraid that you can lift your hands and worship and cry to a God you care nothing about. "I cry and worship. I feel his presence." No, no, no! That's endorphins. That's not the Spirit. It's music therapy if you don't know God, yet you worship.

I'm telling my story because I grew up in the United Methodist church. I was an acolyte. I grew up in the hood. I wasn't smoking weed, like my boys; I wasn't wildin' out. I was a serial monogamist, so I thought I was better. I didn't sell crack, so I thought I was better. People told me I was better than everyone: "Eric, you're the good kid." And I believed I was the good kid. I believed I was better than my friends who were getting shot up, better than my friends who were getting pregnant out of wedlock. I believed I was better because people told me I was better.

And I was an acolyte. We wore waist-level robes. We lit the fire, and we walked down the aisle and sang, "We're marching to Zion, beautiful, beautiful Zion." I'm marching, and you know, I'm about seven. I light the fire, and I sit down. "Look at Eric."

From my youth, I used to sing in church. I sang "Kumbaya" at four years old, and people broke down crying. I went to youth choir practice. I would tell my boys on the block, "Yo, come with me to church today."

They said, "Any girls there?"

I said, "Yeah!"

They were like, "Bet, I'm there."

So the people said, "That's the biggest drug dealer on the block up in here. Eric brought him. Man, God's hand sho' is on Eric!" But all I did was tell him there were some girls at church. Dudes up in there with beepers on, coke in their pockets, and wads of cash. I'm thinking, "I'm better than this."

I went to college because of the hardness of my household, in the sense of my parents trying to raise me. I didn't like that. My friends had more freedom than I had. So I went to college, and I decided, "I'm going off. I'm finally going to lose all my mind." But I'm a serial monogamist. I'm not like them. I said, "All my friends are wildin', but I don't hurt girls and stuff like that."

Then one day I was liking this little honey, and she says, "I'm going to church."

I said, "I'm going too. I have to go with you to church." Shoot, go to church! I grew up in the church. I was an acolyte! I used to sing in church. Then I said, "Forever my lady." So I get in this church. I'm like, "Man, I'm gonna go here a few times, and it's going to be on with her." So I'm sitting down, and I'm scheming. Then someone stood up at the podium and preached vicarious substitutionary atonement. I thought, "What is that?" Something was drawing me to this death. I realized that I was a schemer. I was a liar. I was a fornicator. I was a greedy man. I was a whoremonger. I was prideful. And I threw myself on the mercy of the cross for the first time, not knowing that all those years I did not know God! I was a weed, a child of wrath, a son of Satan being manipulated, following his tactics. But one day, in one moment, all my pride, all my greed, all my fornication, all my hates—all of it was washed away by the blood of the Lamb.

Somebody reading this, you've been going to church because you like the fellowship. You go because you like the worship; it's deep words and cool music. The preacher wears jeans sometimes, everybody can use slang, and people can enjoy themselves. All that's great, but none of that saves you. You've got to repent and be washed in the blood by faith in the Lamb of God, Jesus Christ.

Paul's Final Exhortations
2 CORINTHIANS 13:11-13

Paul ends this letter driving home several simple exhortations to the Corinthians. He wants them to "become mature, be encouraged, be of the same mind, be at peace," and he invokes God's love and peace upon them (v. 11). He calls for not merely personal maturity but communal maturity. In other words, an overall church character where they would be viewed as a spiritually grown-up group of people. Every church should have an overall character that is marked by spiritual health and a deep and enduring commitment to Jesus Christ. May we all attain to the unity in the faith that the Lord Jesus died to create. We don't fight *for* unity but *from* unity. Our unity was secured on the cross and completed with the resurrection.

Reflect and Discuss

1. In light of God redeeming us in Christ, how does he expect us to live? Elaborate.
2. What is church discipline, and when should it be used?
3. When there are sin issues that don't require church discipline, why is it important that they still be repented of and dealt with?
4. In what ways does the gospel challenge your views and actions that have been shaped by the culture you live in?
5. What does it mean to test yourself?
6. Have you tested yourself to know that you're in Christ by faith? Why or why not?
7. How do we avoid negative, morbid introspection?
8. How does self-examination lead to greater assurance of salvation?

WORKS CITED

Arnold, C. E., ed. *Zondervan Illustrated Bible Backgrounds Commentary.* 4 vols. Grand Rapids, MI: Zondervan Academic, 2002.

Evans, Tony. *The Battle Is the Lord's: Waging Victorious Spiritual Warfare.* Chicago: Moody, 2008.

Fesko, J. V. "John Owen on Union with Christ and Justification." *Themelios* 37:1 (2012). https://www.thegospelcoalition.org/themelios/article/john-owen-on-union-with-christ-and-justification.

Guthrie, G. H. *2 Corinthians.* Baker Exegetical Commentary on the New Testament. Grand Rapids, MI: Baker Academic, 2015.

———. "2 Corinthians." Pages 1127–50 in *The Baker Illustrated Bible Background Commentary.* Ed. J. Scott Duvall and J. Daniel Hays. Grand Rapids, MI: Baker, 2020.

Hawthorne, G. F., R. P. Martin, and D. G. Reid, eds. *The Dictionary of Paul and His Letters.* IVP Bible Dictionary Series. Downers Grove, IL: IVP Academic, 1993.

Keener, C. S. *The IVP Bible Background Commentary: New Testament.* Downers Grove, IL: IVP Academic, 1994.

Krejcir, Richard J. "Statistics and Reasons for Church Decline." *Church Leadership.* Accessed October 12, 2021. http://www.churchleadership.org/apps/articles/default.asp?articleid=42346.

Mason, Eric, ed. *Urban Apologetics: Restoring Black Dignity with the Gospel.* Grand Rapids, MI: Zondervan, 2021.

Metaxas, Eric. *Bonhoeffer: Pastor, Martyr, Prophet, Spy.* Nashville: Thomas Nelson, 2010.

Watson, Thomas. *The Doctrine of Repentance.* Accessed May 21, 2021. Available online at http://www.desiringgodchurch.org/web/2021/04/09/the-doctrine-of-repentance-by-thomas-watson.

SCRIPTURE INDEX